JANE AUSTEN'S FAVOURITE BROTHER, HENRY

JANE AUSTEN'S FAVOURITE BROTHER, HENRY

CHRISTOPHER HERBERT

AN IMPRINT OF PEN & SWORD BOOKS LTD.
YORKSHIRE – PHILADELPHIA

First published in Great Britain in 2025 by
Pen & Sword History
An imprint of
Pen & Sword Books Ltd
Yorkshire - Philadelphia

Copyright © Christopher Herbert, 2025

ISBN 978 1 03613 316 0

The right of Christopher Herbert to be identified as the Author of this work has been asserted by him in accordance with the Copyright, Designs and Patents Act 1988.

A CIP catalogue record for this book is available from the British Library.

All rights reserved. No part of this book may be reproduced, transmitted, downloaded, decompiled or reverse engineered in any form or by any means, electronic or mechanical including photocopying, recording or by any information storage and retrieval system, without permission from the Publisher in writing. No part of this book may be used or reproduced in any manner for the purpose of training artificial intelligence technologies or systems.

Typeset in INDIA by IMPEC eSolutions
Printed and bound in England by CPI (UK) Ltd.

The Publisher's authorised representative in the EU for product safety is Authorised Rep Compliance Ltd., Ground Floor, 71 Lower Baggot Street, Dublin D02 P593, Ireland.
www.arccompliance.com

For a complete list of Pen & Sword titles please contact:
PEN & SWORD BOOKS LIMITED
George House, Units 12 & 13, Beevor Street, Off Pontefract Road, Barnsley, S71 1HN, UK
E-mail: enquiries@pen-and-sword.co.uk
Website: www.pen-and-sword.co.uk

or

PEN AND SWORD BOOKS
1950 Lawrence Road, Havertown, PA 19083, USA
E-mail: uspen-and-sword@casematepublishers.com
Website: www.penandswordbooks.com

For Emily, Sophie, Molly and Flora

Historians cannot close down debates for all time. Nor do they seek to do so. The subject thrives upon argument and assessment, because people in past eras as well as those writing later histories often have differing perspectives, rival interests and competing values. And it's right that multiple viewpoints be aired. Human experiences, being complex, demand complex evaluations.
>Penelope J. Corfield, *The Georgians* (Yale University Press)

Man is such an odd animal, such a mixed untidy bundle of follies and inconsistencies and incongruities, that it is impossible for a discerning observer to look at him for long without smiling.
>David Cecil, *A Portrait of Jane Austen* (Penguin, 1980)

Contents

Acknowledgements		xi
Timeline		xiii
Chapter 1	Enter Henry Austen, Jane's Favourite Brother	1
Chapter 2	Growing up in the Rectory	7
Chapter 3	The Political and Intellectual World of George Austen, Henry and Jane's Father	18
Chapter 4	Improvement, Enclosures and Livings	30
Chapter 5	Henry Austen: Oxford University and *The Loiterer*	42
Chapter 6	The Oxford Militia	54
Chapter 7	Henry's Promotion and Marriage	62
Chapter 8	The Lure of Finance	75
Chapter 9	Henry's Success and Luck	85
Chapter 10	More Banking Developments and Publications, 1807–1813	96
Chapter 11	Death, Taxes and New Opportunities	105
Chapter 12	Increasing Work and Anxiety, 1814–1816	119
Chapter 13	Henry's Illness and his Bank's Demise	128
Chapter 14	The Empty Future?	140
Chapter 15	Return to Chawton and Jane's Death	152
Chapter 16	Publishing Jane's Books, Chawton and Berlin	164

Chapter 17	What did Henry Believe?	172
Chapter 18	Henry's Life as a Clergyman in Farnham	181
Chapter 19	Bentley and Final Days	189
Chapter 20	Conclusion	201

Appendix	204
Chapter Notes	205
Bibliography	219
Index	225

Acknowledgements

It is not possible to write about the Austen family without rapidly becoming aware that many people have researched, studied and written extensively about Jane and her family, and some have also ventured to write about her brother, Henry.

This book is deeply indebted to the writings of several outstanding Jane Austen scholars, including David Cecil's *A Portrait of Jane Austen*; E.J. Clery's *Jane Austen, the Banker's Sister*; Li Ping Gen's facsimile edition of *The Loiterer*; Clive Caplan's papers in the journal *Persuasions*; Frank Willan's research on the Oxfordshire Militia; Claire Tomalin's wonderful biography, *Jane Austen: A Life*; John Avery Jones's absorbing and scholarly papers in *Persuasions* about Henry's banking career; Irene Collins's *Jane Austen and the Clergy*; the meticulous research work of Brenda S. Cox; and, of course, Deirdre le Faye's monumental research published as *Jane Austen's Letters*; plus J.R. Western's *The English Militia in the Eighteenth Century*. I have tried not to plagiarise any of them and have acknowledged my sources in the endnotes, but the fact is, without their groundbreaking work, I simply could not have written the book you have in front of you. The greatest tribute you can pay these scholars is to read their papers and books yourself...

Locally, in Surrey and Hampshire, I am indebted to Brigid Fice of Bentley, for her kind help in providing insights from Bentley's village history, to Sophie Reynolds of Jane Austen's House, Chawton, whose generous help has been invaluable, to David Rymill and his colleagues at the Hampshire Record Office, Winchester, and to Jane Lewis and colleagues at the Surrey History Centre, Woking. Also, I extend my thanks to Jan Wood and colleagues at Devon Archives, Exeter, and to Naomi Oakley and colleagues at the Wiltshire Archives, Chippenham.

I am most grateful to Laurence Carter for drawing my attention to the entry about Henry Austen in the Registers of St Andrew's Church, Farnham, and to Peter Duffy for suggestions concerning my understanding of early nineteenth-century banking. Of course, not being a banker, there is no guarantee that my understanding is still not incorrect …

I should also like to thank the staff at the British Embassy in Berlin for their courtesy in trying to track down details of Henry Austen's sojourn in that city.

I am truly indebted to Heather Williams, Commissioning Editor at Pen and Sword, and to the copy editor, Linne Matthews, for their superb and efficient help with the manuscript. It has been a privilege and a joy to work so closely with them.

But above all, my thanks are due to Jan, my wife, whose life has been, and remains, devoted to the study and teaching of English literature; from her I have learnt so much. She has inspired and encouraged me more than I can ever express.

Timeline

1764	26 April, marriage of George Austen and Cassandra Leigh
1765	13 February, James Austen born at Deane
1766	26 August, George Austen, junior, born at Deane
1767	7 October, Edward Austen born at Deane
1768	July/August, Austen family move to Steventon
1771	**8 June, Henry Austen born at Steventon**
1773	9 January, Cassandra Austen born at Steventon
1773	The Reverend George Austen becomes Rector of Deane
1774	23 April, Francis Austen born at Steventon
1775	16 December, Jane Austen born at Steventon
1779	23 June, Charles Austen born at Steventon
1805	21 January, death of the Reverend George Austen

Henry Austen

1788	Goes up to St John's College, Oxford
1789	January, first edition of *The Loiterer*
1792	Awarded a BA
1793	April, enlisted in the Oxford Militia
1794	Becomes Acting Paymaster
1796	January, awarded an MA
1797	31 December, marriage to Eliza de Feuillide
1798	Henry, Eliza and Hastings de Feuillide live in Upper Berkeley Street, London
1798	Adjutant in the Oxford Militia
1801	Sets up as army agent in Cleveland Court, London

1801	May, the Reverend George and Mrs Cassandra Austen, Jane and Cassandra move to Bath
1801	9 October, death of Hastings de Feuillide
1803	Henry Austen's agency moves to Canon Row, Westminster
1805	Henry Austen's agency moves to 1, The Courtyard, Albany
1805	Henry and Eliza live in Michael's Place, Brompton
1806?	Agency renamed: Austen, Maunde and Austen
1806	Jane, Cassandra and Mrs Austen leave Bath to live in Southampton
1807	Henry Austen's bank moves to Henrietta Street, London
1809	Henry and Eliza move to 64, Sloane Street, Chelsea
1811	30 October, *Sense and Sensibility* published
1813	28 January, *Pride and Prejudice* published
1813	25 April, death of Eliza de Feuillide/Austen
1813	May, Henry Austen moves to live at Henrietta Street
1813	Henry becomes Receiver General of Taxes for Oxfordshire
1814	Henry moves to Hans Place, Knightsbridge
1815	23 December, *Emma* published
1816	March, Austen, Maunde and Tilson Bank fails
1816	21 December, made deacon by the Bishop of Salisbury
1816–20	Curate of Chawton
1817	31 May, ordained priest by the Bishop of Salisbury
1817	18 July, Jane Austen died
1817	20 December, *Northanger Abbey* published
1817	20 December, *Persuasion* published, but frontispiece states '1818'
1820–2	Rector of Steventon
1822–30	Perpetual Curate of Farnham, including Bentley (1824–30)
1830–9	Perpetual Curate of Bentley
1839–42	Retired, Colchester
1842–50	Retired, Tunbridge Wells
1850	12 March, dies, Tunbridge Wells

Chapter 1

Enter Henry Austen, Jane's Favourite Brother

On Friday, 10 September 1824, a small group of people made their way along a footpath to St Andrew's, the ancient parish church of Farnham in Surrey. The party consisted of Robert Sampson,[1] a maltster, and his wife, Hannah Jennings, who was carrying in her arms their baby daughter, Joyce. Robert, Hannah and the friends accompanying them huddled close, one or two of them casting smiling glances at the baby.

They pushed open the oak door in the North Porch, glad to get out of the rain. That summer had been particularly wet and the puddles through which they had splashed had dampened their shoes and mud had stained the hems of their clothes.[2] Nevertheless, they were looking forward to a special occasion. They were going to church to have the baby christened.

Meeting them just inside the door was the 54-year-old perpetual curate,[3] the Reverend Henry Thomas Austen. Dressed in cassock,[4] white surplice, hood and scarf, and wearing preaching bands at his neck, he was a tall figure with receding grey-white hair and had a charming smile. He welcomed them. He had been in post for two years, having previously been, in 1817, Curate of Chawton, Hampshire, and had then followed in his father's footsteps, becoming Rector of Steventon in 1820. He had had to hand over the living three years later in favour of his nephew, William Knight, son of his wealthy brother, Edward. And now, in Farnham, Henry was in a financially reduced but demanding role as the Perpetual Curate of St Andrew's.

Having greeted the family, he took them towards the font and there, using the words from the 1662 *Book of Common Prayer*, he proceeded to baptise Joyce. It was a delightful but formal service. However, there was a snag. Henry Austen had discovered that Robert Sampson and Hannah Jennings had not been legally married. He wrote in the baptism register:

> Cohabiting as man and wife having been married by licence on 23rd December 1820 which marriage having been discovered to be illegally performed on the part of the Officiating Minister, they were married by licence this tenth day of September 1824 by me Henry Thos [*sic*] Austen, Curate. See Folio 135 in the Register of Marriage.

It would be interesting to know the background to this little story – but does the slightly officious tone adopted by Henry Austen reveal anything about his character?

Let us leave that question for the moment and ask a more pertinent one: Who was he?

The simple but partial answer is that he was the brother of Jane Austen, the novelist. And this is why he is so fascinating. As her favourite brother and having been responsible for getting her novels published, it is possible that knowing a little more of his life might shed some oblique light on her life and works.

In a letter to her sister Cassandra in April 1805, Jane wrote about Henry: 'I had a letter from him [Henry], in which he desired to hear from me very soon—His to me was most affectionate and kind, as well as entertaining;—but there is no merit in that, he cannot help being amusing.'

That one throwaway remark reveals how close the relationship was between Henry and Jane and how much they enjoyed each other's company.

But in fact, he was much more than simply Jane's affectionate and amusing brother. He himself had had an interesting and dramatically varied life in his own right, which, as we shall see, was marked by extremes of both triumph and tragedy. Through the exploration of his life, we shall not only get to know him as a confident and extravert character but also gain some interesting and unexpected insights into society, politics and belief in late eighteenth- and early nineteenth-century England. So, what was his background?

Henry Thomas Austen was born on 8 June 1771 at Steventon, Hampshire. As was then the custom, he was baptised privately on the same day and was received into the Church one month later, on 12 July. He was the fourth son of the Reverend George Austen (1731–1805) and his wife, Cassandra, née Leigh (1739–1827). Henry had three older brothers: James (1765–1819), George (1766–1838), and Edward (Knight) (1768–1852). His younger siblings were his sister Cassandra (1773–1845), his younger brother, Francis (1774–1865), his sister Jane (1775–1817), and the youngest brother, Charles (1779–1852).

Henry's father, George, was the Rector of Steventon from 1761 to 1805, and of Deane, a nearby village, from 1773 to 1805. He had been presented to the living of Steventon by Thomas Knight I, his second cousin, who was a wealthy landowner in Kent and Hampshire, and was presented to Deane by his uncle, Francis Austen, a rich lawyer. In fact, George Austen was still at Oxford in 1761 when he was gifted the living, and although he was technically the Rector, he did not move to the parish until 1764. Meanwhile, it was looked after by a curate, the Reverend Mr Bathurst.

Steventon was a tiny village consisting of about thirty families,[5] living in a few rows of cottages and other dispersed dwellings that stretched alongside a muddy lane in a shallow valley. Most of the village men would have been agricultural labourers, and their wives, in addition to bringing up their children, would have spent such leisure time as they had spinning wool or flax.[6] St Nicholas Church and the Manor House were about three-quarters of a mile from the main village and to get to the church required a gentle climb up a narrow lane lined with thick hedges, frothing white in summertime with Queen Anne's lace.[7] Opposite the Manor House, which had been in the hands of the Knight family since the early eighteenth century, was the simple thirteenth-century church of St Nicholas and its ancient churchyard. The setting, whilst beautiful in a soft, southern English, Hampshire way, was nevertheless quite remote.

The remoteness is captured in the account by James Edward Austen-Leigh of the time when the Austens moved from Deane to Steventon in 1771. He describes the lane along which they travelled as 'a mere cart track so cut up as to be impassable for a light carriage. Mrs Austen who was not then in strong health, performed the short journey on a feather-bed, placed upon some soft articles of furniture in the waggon which held their household goods.'[8]

The Rectory, to which those goods and Mrs Austen were taken, and in which Henry and his siblings grew up, no longer exists, but according to the 1821 Glebe Map,[9] it was situated in 'the corner of Home Meadow' close to the junction of Steventon Road and Church Lane, now called Church Walk.

The overwhelming sense is of a rectory in gentle, beautiful and pastoral isolation. The nearest town, with a population in 1800 of about 2,500, was Basingstoke, 7 miles away, whilst Overton, a village on the London to Exeter road, and famous for its annual sheep fair and a silk mill, was 3 miles distant. In Steventon itself, the church and the Manor House at the far end of Church Walk formed a community like a small, self-contained hamlet, distinct from the main village. When George Austen arrived, he would not have expected the parish to be a place buzzing with excitement or intellectual delight.[10] If things of the intellect and the spirit were required, then the Rectory family would have to provide them for themselves, which, of course, eventually, they did.

It was at Steventon Rectory that Henry was born. Whether a midwife was present at his birth is not recorded, though since the early sixteenth century it had been a requirement that midwives were to be licensed by the diocesan bishop.[11] However, whilst the regulations were clear, obedient observation of them did not always exist. In Henry's case, it could have been that it was a female family member or friend, or even a local male physician, who attended his birth and cared for his mother, Cassandra. But following customary practice, provided the birth had proceeded properly, Henry's mother would have had a month-long 'lying-in'. Quite soon after the birth, Cassandra (Leigh) Austen would have been required to take part in a service called 'The Thanksgiving of Women after childbirth commonly called The Churching of Women'. It would have been conducted by her husband George, the Rector. The brief service was about giving thanks for the safe delivery of a child.[12] One of the prayers began: 'O Almighty God, we give thee humble thanks for that thou hast vouchsafed to deliver this woman, thy servant, from the great pain and peril of childbirth.' Whilst thanksgiving was at the heart of the service, there were also traditions, especially in the countryside, that said a woman should not go outside her house until she had been 'Churched'.

The social reasons for Churching were obvious: in the eighteenth century, 20 per cent of mothers died in childbirth. In such circumstances, it is not surprising that giving thanks for safe delivery was part of the religious framework of the country. Complications of childbirth could include obstructions and infections; the latter, puerperal fever, was usually caused by parts of the placenta remaining in the womb and becoming gangrenous, leading to sepsis, fever and death.

But when we consider Henry's birth there are other elements in the eighteenth-century childbirth process that deserve our attention, such as the preparation of clothing needed to enable Cassandra (Leigh) Austen to feel comfortable and 'disguised' during her pregnancy. Eighteenth-century clothing could be adapted relatively easily to the pregnant woman; for instance, stomachers could be widened, and aprons could be used to cover gaps in clothing as the months passed, and side lacing could be loosened.[13]

It is likely that for reasons of social decorum, Henry's mother, in the later stages of her pregnancy, might have found her social life curtailed – less visiting, for example, though that would not have been easy in Steventon, anyway. And then she had to give thought to the clothes needed for the birth itself and for the lying-in. Obviously, the quantity and availability of extra clothes depended on the wealth of the family but, no doubt, once Henry was born, hand-me-down clothes from his older brothers, plus bassinet and bed clothes, would have featured.

In brief, Cassandra (Leigh) Austen's preparations for the birth of Henry, as for all her other children, would have needed some degree of forward planning, including the place, if any, for the nursery. In the days before the birth and immediately afterwards, the house would have been reorganised to allow the necessary privacy for the birth itself. But once the delivery had been safely achieved there would have been rejoicing and relief. One can imagine the older brothers, James, aged 6, George, aged almost 5, and Edward, aged 4, being escorted quietly into the bedroom to be given a first look at their new baby brother, Henry, and then being told to go outside to play, perhaps much to their boyish relief. And then, once it had become clear that Cassandra had no post-natal medical problems, the life of the family could gradually settle back into its normal pattern.

Chapter 2

Growing up in the Rectory

So, what was the Rectory like in which the Austen children grew up?

As we have seen, the Rectory in which Henry was born was demolished in the 1820s and no ground plan exists, but there are memories and sketches of the house, enabling us to picture it. If we follow Benjamin Lefroy's[1] (1791–1829) sketch, we can see that it was a three-storey house that had two dormer windows in the roof at the front; below them were three sixteen-paned windows, and on the ground floor, a central door surrounded by a latticework porch, which was flanked by two casement windows on either side. The front door opened directly into a small parlour, and there was a dining room and best parlour. There were ten bedrooms, three of which were in the attic; there was a back kitchen, plus the Rector's study towards the rear of the house. So, which bedroom was used as the birthing chamber for Henry is necessarily speculative. But it can be assumed that the entire household, including Henry's older brothers, would have been aware of extra and unusual activity during and after Henry's birth. The Rectory was small enough and crowded enough to ensure that everyone was aware of the tensions and anxieties surrounding the birth of a baby.

It is possible that Philadelphia Hancock,[2] Mrs Austen's sister-in-law, would have been present for the days preceding Henry's birth, and for the birth itself. She is mentioned as being at Steventon for Henry's younger sister Cassandra's birth in 1772. Writing to Mrs Walter in advance of Cassandra's birth, Mrs Austen said, 'I begin to be very heavy and bundling as usual, I believe my sister Hancock will be so good as to come and nurse me again, for which I am sure I shall be much obliged to her, as it will be a bad time of the year for her to take so long a journey.'³ No doubt, she would have been comforted by Philadelphia's presence, along with other close friends and supporters. Whether Mrs Austen gave birth in a bed, in which case, subsequently, there would have been much laundry work involved in washing the blood-stained sheets, or in a birthing chair, can only be a matter of conjecture.

Childbirth, of course, had a significant impact upon the day-to-day running of the house. Sarah Fox, an acknowledged expert in eighteenth-century midwifery, describes the preparations that were made. For instance, linen swaddling bands had to be aired in front of the fire, and then those who were attending the birth had to ensure that the fire was kept burning so that the caudle could be warmed. Caudle was a hot drink made with milk and eggs sweetened with honey or sugar; sometimes it contained thickening agents such as wheat flour, and to give the drink a more palatable taste, ale, wine or spices such as ginger could be added. The recipes for caudle varied from place to place, but one of the characteristics of eighteenth-century births was the smell of caudle throughout the house. It was consumed not only during the birth itself by the midwife and her helpers, but was also provided for the nourishment of the mother during her period of lying-in.⁴

What Henry's older brothers made of all this, including the all-pervasive odour of the caudle, can only be imagined.

So, there was Henry, the youngest of four brothers, taking his place in the family. His life after that can only be surmised. If Cassandra, his mother, followed the teaching of eighteenth-century medical textbooks, then the age at which weaning happened would have been between eight and twelve months.⁵ It varied from family to family and was dependent upon the mother's health.

However, it was the Austen family practice for the mother, Cassandra, to suckle the babies at home before handing them over after three months to someone she described as 'a good woman at Deane'.⁶ The 'good woman' was Elizabeth Littleworth; she and her husband John acted as foster parents. Henry lived with them in their cottage for his first year. Following customary practice, as a baby, Henry would either have been bound tightly in swaddling bands of cloth, or, because the fashion was changing, more likely he would have been dressed in a long, lace-trimmed dress, under which was a pilcher – a kind of extra layer of the nappy to absorb urine – and next to the baby's skin would have been a 'clout', a thick layer of cloth acting as a diaper or nappy.[7]

Once Henry could walk, he returned from the Littleworths' to live at the Rectory. Mrs Austen, in one of her regular letters to Mrs Walter,[8] wrote on 8 November 1772, 'My little boy is come home from nurse, and a fine stout little fellow he is, and can run anywhere, so now I have all four at home, and sometime in January I expect a fifth, so you see it will not be in my power to take any journeys for a while.'

Henry, now running about the Rectory, would have remained in a dress, the dress being shortened as he grew to enable him to move more easily, until he was breeched at about 4 years of age. Mrs Austen, writing to Mrs Walter on 20 August 1775, reported: 'Henry has been in breeches some months and thinks himself near as good a man as his brother Neddy,[9] indeed no one would judge by their looks that there was above three years and a half difference in their ages, one is so little and other so great.'[10]

It is sad to note that Mrs Austen did not mention Henry's other brother, George,[11] who was almost 5 years old at the time of Henry's birth. George is believed to have suffered from epilepsy and may also have been deaf and dumb. He was boarded out locally and remained separate from the family for the rest of his life.[12]

But with his two older brothers James and Edward at home, what games might Henry have played as he began to leave his early childhood behind? Possibly, the boys had sets of tin toy soldiers (known as 'flats' because they were not three-dimensional), cards, a toy drum, marbles, a spinning top and probably a rocking horse, and for outdoor games, a hoop, perhaps, and a kite. Plus, of course, in the Rectory, books. Unfortunately, we do not have records of the books used by the Austen children, but their little library might have contained popular books such as *Lessons for*

Children by Anna Laetitia Barbauld, or Mary Cooper's *Tommy Thumb's Pretty Song Book*, one of the first anthologies of English nursery rhymes, and maybe they also had encouraging books of morally uplifting and didactic poetry, such as Isaac Watts's *Divine Songs Attempted in Easy Language for the Use of Children*.

We know that Jane Austen read a number of books,[13] including William Cowper's poem in six volumes, *The Task*, published in 1785, Eliza Haywood's *The History of Miss Betsy Thoughtless*, a novel published in 1751, and Sarah Scott's utopian novel *Millenium Hall*, published in 1762. Whether any of these would have been read by Henry and his brothers is a moot point, but it is safe to assume that their mother would have read to them when they were small and before they entered the schoolroom.

J.E. Austen-Leigh describes Mrs Austen as a woman who 'united strong commonsense with a lively imagination, and often expressed herself, both in writing and in conversation, with epigrammatic force and point'.[14] Language and its use seems to have been a powerful characteristic of the family, and although George Austen's own library frequently receives comment, the early influence of Cassandra does not receive the same attention, but as a lively and witty woman, her influence upon Henry, his brothers and sisters should not be ignored.

As the Austen children grew up it is likely that they would have read and enjoyed Daniel Defoe's *Robinson Crusoe*, published in 1719, and Jonathan Swift's *Gulliver's Travels*, of 1726, and maybe its spin-off, the first children's periodical ever created, entitled *Lilliputian Magazine*, by John Newbery, published in London in 1751. How the Austen family obtained its books is, again, a matter of conjecture. It seems reasonable to assume that they could have arranged the purchase of books from London printer/publishers, such as John and William Taylor at The Ship[15] in Paternoster Row, or from the well-regarded publishing house of Cadell and Davies,[16] based in the Strand. But nearer to the Austen home, there were printers/publishers/booksellers in Winchester, such as William Clarke, whose name appears on books from 1682 to 1710, and John Sadler, who published the first edition of the *Hampshire Directory* in 1784, or, slightly nearer to Steventon, William Pinnock, born in Alton in February 1782, who founded a printer's and stationer's in that town. He became highly successful and opened premises in London, an achievement that resulted from his lucrative business printing catechisms.[17] Of course, the family might have bought books from Hatchards, founded in Piccadilly in 1797, the oldest bookshop in London.

Whatever the source of the books might have been, in the long winter evenings in a room flickering with candles and firelight, George Austen read books aloud to the family. It was the time when the constraints of rectory life could be released by stories that fired and enlarged the imagination. And if George followed eighteenth-century practice, the reading aloud would have involved exaggerated facial expressions, dramatic use of the arms and hands, and loud and soft modulations of the voice. Some neighbourhoods had what were called 'spouting clubs', places where a group would gather to hear stories read aloud, the more (melo)dramatic the better. It is unlikely that Steventon would have had such a club, but we know that George belonged to a 'gentleman's club' in Basingstoke and perhaps in that town a 'spouting club' might also have excited the neighbourhood.

Once Henry was of an appropriate age to begin 'school', he would have joined James and Edward (Neddy) in his father's study to be taught by him. No one knows who instructed the boys in the art of writing; perhaps it was their father, or their mother (she was known for her 'admirable hand, both powerful and interesting'),[18] or maybe it was a clerk living in the village. It was a clerk, for example, who taught Bishop Charles Sumner to write when he was a child in Kenilworth in the 1790s. The clerk described Sumner as the 'most ink-spillingest boy I have ever taught'. Was Henry equally messy?

If their father or mother or a clerk taught the Austen boys penmanship, it is likely that they would have used one of the classical teaching texts of the eighteenth century: George Bickham's *The Universal Penman*

(1741), a book replete with examples of handwriting, and filled with moral exhortation, such as:

> Children like tender Oziers take the Bow
> And as they first are fashion'd always grow
> For what we learn in Youth, to that alone
> In Age are by second Nature prone.[19]

Henry and his brothers would have had to learn how to cut a quill,[20] for steel pen nibs were not invented until the first decade of the nineteenth century. And so, we can imagine, with much smudging of ink on paper and scratching with his quill, his lips moistened by his tongue, Henry would have developed the concentration necessary to develop a 'good hand'.

As well as the actual skills of learning to write legibly in English roundhand, the boys would have been required to learn and translate both Greek and Latin texts, such as Aristotle, Plato and Cicero. They would have been taught some mathematics, and maybe a globe in the school room or the study would have been used to teach them the rudiments of geography. And then, outside the schoolroom, when Henry was about 7 years old, he would have been taught to ride and would have learnt the basic principles of how to look after a horse. His younger brother Francis was a keen rider and bought his own pony when only 7 years of age. Because it was a chestnut, he called it 'Squirrel', and dashed around the countryside in a specially tailored scarlet riding jacket. Riding and caring for horses were important accomplishments, not least for boys growing up in the countryside. And if Henry had been allowed to accompany one of the servants in taking his pony to the village blacksmith to be shod, he would have been entranced by the soft hiss of the bellows and the deep roar of the flames in the forge, and watched the sparks flying upwards in an arc as the red-hot horseshoe, held in a pair of tongs by the muscular, leather-aproned blacksmith, was hammered on the anvil into the correct shape.

But the three boys were not learning on their own. There is some evidence that George and Cassandra Austen looked after George, the

3-year-old motherless son of Warren Hastings, the Governor General of India, who had been introduced to the Austens by Philadelphia Hancock, George Austen's sister. Sadly, little George died three years later of what was described as a 'putrid sore throat'. Mrs Austen declared that the little boy's death 'had been as great a grief to her as if he had been a child of her own'.[21] What is certain is that George and Cassandra Austen, like many other clergy families at the time, took in older paying pupils. Between 1773 and 1796, that is, for twenty-three years, the Rectory was loud with the noise of the boy pupils,[22] including, for example, Fulwar and Tom Fowle (who later became Cassandra's fiancé),[23] and the two other Fowle brothers, William and Charles, the sons of one of the Lloyd sisters, Eliza, and her husband, the Reverend Fulwar Craven Fowle.[24]

In a charming letter written on 12 December 1773, and addressed to his sister, George Austen mentions a couple of his pupils with warm and concerned affection, but not before he has dealt with more humdrum and personal matters:

> I thank you for your kind letter and the receipt [recipe] for Potato Cakes, I have not yet found time to try it but dare say they must be very nice and light ...
> My little girl [a reference to Cassandra] is almost ready to run away. Our new Pupil, Master Vanderstegen has been with us about a month, he is near 14 years old, is very good tempered and well disposed. Lord Lymington[25] has left us, his mamma began to be alarm'd at the hesitation in his speech which certainly grew worse and is going to take him to London in hopes a Mr Angus ... may be of service to him.[26]

Teaching was a way for George Austen to eke out the family income, and for an academically inclined clergyman, as he was, it was preferable to farming the glebe, though in the case of the latter, Thomas Knight had generously leased 200 acres to George. It would have significantly improved his income. He earned £230 per annum as an incumbent and so the £35 per annum that he charged for each of his boarding pupils would have been a welcome addition to the family's purse. By the 1790s, the fees had increased to about £65 per annum. The teaching regime was obviously financially successful and in addition to that income, by the time he retired, he was also receiving about £900 per annum from tithes.[27] That sum, translated into twenty-first-century terms, was the equivalent of just under £100,000.

All of that was in the future, but for now, George Austen had a growing family to support, and the paying pupils meant that Henry and his brothers and sisters grew up at the Steventon Rectory not only with each other for company, but they also had the boarding pupils to play and fight with during term time. There were two terms each year: one from February until June, the other from August until Christmas. As the Steventon Rectory was a boys-only establishment, it is not entirely surprising that in spring 1783, when Jane was 7 and Cassandra, her sister, was 10, they were sent off to boarding school[28] at Mrs Cawley's in Oxford, where, amongst other subjects, they learnt French, music, dancing and sewing. Mrs Cawley was the widow of Ralph Cawley, the Master of Brasenose, and was related to the Austens – her brother was married to Cassandra (Leigh) Austen's sister. But there were other Austen relations and connections in Oxford. James Austen, Henry and Jane's oldest brother, went up to Oxford to St John's College in 1779 when he was 14, so he was there when Jane and Cassandra arrived, and also in Oxford was their great-uncle, Theophilus Leigh (1691–1785), who was Master of Balliol. He had a reputation as a wit;[29] for instance, only three days before his death he was told by some of his friends that a particular colleague was going to get married. The colleague had been seriously ill and claimed to have cured himself by eating many eggs. The friends of the Master joked that the man had been egged on to marriage, whereupon the Master replied, 'Then may the yoke sit easy on him.'[30]

The appointment of Theophilus Leigh as Master had not been without its critics. It was said that the Balliol Fellows could not agree amongst themselves who should be Master and so decided on Theophilus

Leigh, a Fellow of Corpus. He was reputed to suffer from poor health and the Balliol Fellows decided that he would be unlikely to last long and that would give them time to decide upon his successor. He had the last laugh: he remained Master for fifty-nine years.

A story is told of James Austen arriving in Oxford as a raw undergraduate and deciding that he ought to visit Theophilus Leigh, his great-uncle. Accordingly, he wore his academic gown for his formal visit and when he entered the Master's room, he began to divest himself of his gown. The 80-year-old Theophilus Leigh greeted his great-nephew by saying, 'Young man, you need not strip, we are not going to fight.' The story entered Austen family folklore. Unsurprisingly, there is no record of Jane and Cassandra visiting this formidable man.

But what did Jane and Cassandra make of their Oxford school? It is possible that the famous description of a girls' school in *Emma* captures something of their experiences:

> Mrs Goddard was the mistress of a school—not of a seminary, or an establishment, or anything which professed in long sentences of refined nonsense, to combine liberal acquirements with elegant morality, upon new principles and new systems, and where young ladies for enormous pay might be screwed out of health and into vanity, but a real, honest, old-fashioned boarding school, where a reasonable quantity of accomplishments were sold at a reasonable price, and where girls might be sent to be out of the way, and scramble themselves into a little education, without any danger of coming back prodigies.[31]

It could be, however, that the reference to schools in *Emma* was also influenced by Reading Ladies' Boarding School, to which Jane and Cassandra were sent early in 1785. There the curriculum was almost identical to what they had experienced at Mrs Cawley's, but they returned home to Steventon in December 1786 because their father could no longer afford the fees. And that was the end of their formal education. From now on, it would be their father and mother who would teach them.

Meanwhile, Henry, aged 8 and without the company of his oldest brother, now in Oxford, remained at the Rectory with Edward. It must have seemed a little quiet without the noise of their older brother, James, but perhaps the company of the boarding pupils would have compensated.

It is not difficult to imagine that one of the great events of 1784 would have caught their imagination. That great event was the ascent in a balloon from Moorfields in London made by Vincent Lunardi in September of that year. News of the daring feat would have arrived at the Rectory in *The Gentleman's Magazine*, which reported the event in breathless tones:

> The aerial voyage which had been much talked of, and long expected, took place. It drew an innumerable multitude of all ranks, together, to the ground from whence the balloon was to be launched ... a buzz and a hollow murmur ran through the crowd. The mob were on tip-toe, ready to mount the cock-horse of their own sagacity and to trample the impostor with all his apparatus into the earth who had the outlandish impudence to tell them he could fly through the air ... when on a sudden a cannon was heard (the appointed signal), and the machine was seen to move, but in a reeling course expressive of some defect. A few moments passed in dreadful apprehension ... and the balloon was seen to rise with all the majesty that heart could wish to the astonishment of millions.[32]

But, despite the excitements of interruptions caused by sensational national events, there was still more mundane learning to absorb from the Reverend George Austen. He was not only an erudite man, but we can imagine, from the results of his work seen in his daughters and sons, that he must have been an inspiring teacher.

We cannot leave the Rectory there, however, without giving thought to what it must have been like for Henry's mother, Cassandra (Leigh)

Austen. She had arrived at Deane Parsonage after her wedding to George Austen in April 1764. From the fashionable swagger, elegance and bustling noise of Bath she had moved with her new husband to a house in a remote, quiet and tiny village in North Hampshire.

We can picture the new bride being trundled in a carriage through the narrow muddy lanes, passing a few cottages ('This is my parish,' exclaims George, proudly) until the carriage comes to a halt outside the Vicarage at Deane ... the Steventon house was not ready for her arrival. But once the final move to Steventon Rectory was made in 1771, she had to get things organised. There were the servants to manage, perhaps as many as nine,[33] including a washerwoman and a dairymaid. For a young mother with little boys, it must have been a daunting logistical task. And then later, she had the daily exhausting business of caring for those boys as well as running and provisioning the household. And from 1771, when Henry was born at Steventon, until 1779, she gave birth to a further two sons and two daughters. In addition, once her husband began to take student pupils she had to think of their care, their clothes, their food, their ailments and their travel arrangements. Perhaps the time she spent feeding the Rectory chickens gave her a moment of respite for herself. Or there could have been a fleeting moment for daydreaming when she gazed out of the window and saw the sheets flapping in the wind on the washing line, though it is more likely she spent that time wondering how the laundry woman would be able to get the sheets dry, and hoping against hope that none of the children in her care would sleep in damp bed linen. Or maybe, less prosaically, with a couple of carrots in her pocket, she visited the field where the two carriage horses grazed, and, leaning on the gate feeding the carrots to the horses and stroking their muzzles, she had a brief time to herself. She must have been a formidably efficient organiser and although in her letters Jane suggests that her mother, later in life, was something of a hypochondriac, Cassandra (Leigh) Austen's desire for a bit of comfort, having dedicated so much of her life to her own children and to the children of others, is entirely understandable.

Chapter 3

The Political and Intellectual World of George Austen, Henry and Jane's Father

In the remoteness of the Rectory, Henry Austen was subject for the first seventeen years of his life primarily to his mother and father. They were the sun around which he orbited. Their influence upon him must have been enormous. In addition, naturally, there were social conformity pressures resulting from his relationships with his siblings, the boarding pupils, and the domestic servants. There might have been some pets, perhaps a cat or two to deal with vermin, and maybe even a dog. Was it a pug? There is only one dog mentioned in Jane's novels and that was a pug. It's Lady Bertram's dog in *Mansfield Park*. But apart from rare social occasions, the arrival of family visitors, and weekly attendance at church on Sundays, outside influences on Henry would have been minimal. It was a constrained but lively universe in which he lived. If he had been born in much poorer circumstances, the need to work, even if it had only been crow-scaring in the fields, would have been forced upon him from a much earlier age. But because he was part of a relatively well-off family there was no need for outside employment. The Rectory, therefore, and its surrounding glebe, were, for the most part, the limits of his world. His mother would have provided the steady domestic rhythm of the household, the meals, the bedtimes, and the moments of fun, but it was his father who was the most high-profile influence, not only as a parent, but also as his teacher, and as a clergyman. There was no getting away from him, even on Sundays. In such circumstances, if we are to get to know and understand Henry, we must first get to know a little more about his father.

George Austen had been born in 1731 to William Austen (1701–37), a surgeon of Tonbridge, Kent, and his wife, Rebecca Hampson (1693–1732), the widow of William Walter Hampson of Frant, Sussex. George's mother, Rebecca, died when he was only 1 or 2 years old, and his father, William, died less than five years later. It meant that George and his sisters, Philadelphia (1730–92) and Leonora (1732–83) were placed in the care of their uncle, Francis Austen (1698–1791). George had had a motherless and fatherless upbringing and that must have left its mark, notwithstanding the care given to him by his relations. Might it have left him with a desire when the time came for marriage, to create a kind of ideal family, close, respectful, teasing, and lovingly affectionate?

George Austen was born at an interesting time in the developing story of Britain. Just twenty-five years before his birth, the Act of Union had taken place. It was an Act in which the Scottish and English parliaments were merged to create the new legislative body of the Kingdom of Great Britain. A new flag was created, the Union Jack, in which the English Cross of St George had the blue and white saltire of Scotland added to it.[1] A few years later, in 1740, when George Austen was 9 years old, the words and music of 'Rule, Britannia!' were heard for the first time and being 'British' was becoming a way of declaring one's allegiance to the new political and military entity called 'Great Britain'. It is likely, therefore, that George would have imbibed this new form of confident, outward-looking patriotism.

These political developments were not entirely without controversy. When George Austen was 14, in July 1745, Charles Stuart landed in Scotland in an attempt to take the English throne. He and his largely Scottish Jacobite army, supported by the French, defeated an English army at Prestonpans in September, but one year later, in April 1746 they were roundly defeated by a much larger English army at the Battle of Culloden. That English army of some 7,000 men was under the leadership of the Duke of Cumberland (1721–65), the youngest son of King George II (1683–1760). The Jacobites fled and were harried by the English army, and Charles Stuart, with a £30,000 reward on his head for his capture, made his way during a five-month period towards the Hebrides, eventually taking a small boat and escaping to Skye, and thence to France. The hauntingly lovely and romantic 'Skye Boat Song' commemorating this event was not written until the late nineteenth century.

There were darker social consequences resulting from Culloden. The Highland 'clearances', which had begun before the Jacobite rising, now accelerated, and thousands of people were displaced; the land that they had tended was taken by wealthy landowners and was given over to sheep-rearing. The displaced people either moved to the coasts to be employed as fishermen and kelp collectors or they emigrated.

The population of Scotland at the time was about 1.3 million; in England and Wales, it was about 6.8 million. London's inhabitants numbered about 650,000; it was by far the biggest city in the country, and its population would increase by a further 300,000 in the next fifty years.

So, in the background of George Austen's early life, apart from the personal sadness of losing both his parents, were these turbulent political and social circumstances. How far he was aware of them, we cannot know, but at 14 years of age and as a pupil at Tonbridge School, he must have heard about the Battle of Culloden, even if he was less aware of some of the larger trends in population movement that were helping to reshape the country.

We can see some of those forces of change if we look at Thomas Gainsborough's (1727–88) painting of *circa* 1750: *Mr and Mrs Andrews*. The wealthy couple, Robert Andrews and his wife Frances, are seated beneath a sturdy oak (the patriotic song 'Heart of Oak' was written only nine years later, in 1759). Behind them are some of the 3,000 acres of Suffolk that Robert Andrews owned. In the middle-distance, sheep are grazing in an enclosed field;[2] nearer to hand, the wheat has been cut, but the wheat had been planted in neat rows – a sign of the use of a seed drill, invented by Jethro Tull in 1701.

Agricultural changes and industrial changes – James Newcomen had invented the first steam engine in 1712 – were beginning to change the character of Britain. Meanwhile, George Austen had become a pupil at Tonbridge School, his place paid for by his kindly and wealthy uncle, Francis. What might George have studied there?

We are fortunate that a letter has survived that was addressed to the Bishop of Rochester. It reveals what the curriculum of the school was in 1770:

> I flatter myself that my plan of education quite corresponds with the sentiments of your friend, being entirely a classical one and to qualify youth for the university ... I find it indeed necessary to have a French master in the house, and a dancing master attends the school from London once a week ... There is a very good writing master in the town greatly under my own direction who attends my school; every day after classical hours.

It is safe to suppose that George Austen, about thirty years before that letter was written, would have studied a similar curriculum dominated by Greek and Latin texts, with the addition of some mathematics, plus tuition in writing. It was limited, as many school curricula were at that time, but George was fortunate. St John's College, Oxford, had a fellowship reserved for a pupil from Tonbridge School, which meant that in 1747, George, aged 16, went up to Oxford, where he automatically became a Fellow. It was a very different process of gaining a place at Oxford from what we are used to in our own day. George was an undergraduate for three years and was awarded his BA on 12 February 1751. What had been the curriculum in Oxford that he was required to follow?

Edward Gibbon's searing critique of life at the university in the eighteenth century is well known: 'To the University of Oxford, I acknowledge no objection, and she will as cheerfully renounce me for a son, as I am willing to disclaim her for a mother. I spent fourteen months at Magdalen College: they proved the fourteen months the most idle and unprofitable of my whole life.'[3]

Whether one view such as that is a fair representation of life at Oxford need not detain us, but it was true, for example, that noblemen were not obliged to study for a degree but could obtain one by fiat, and gentlemen commoners were awarded an MA, without any form of examination, if they had been in residence for two and a half years.[4] And it is also true that there was some louche behaviour, largely centred on the consumption of alcohol: 'In 1761, Dyer of New College bet Mr Williams 2s 6d that he would drink three pints of wine in three hours and write out six verses from the Bible correctly, but he was so 'immensely drunk' that he 'could not write for his life'.[5]

The curriculum, such as it was, consisted of some mathematics, some physics, Greek and Latin texts, plus moral philosophy, logic, and ancient history, but there were no written exams and very few, if any, professorial lectures. The entire 'testing' process consisted of 'disputations' between one student and another, overseen by a tutor, and those disputations could easily be 'fixed'. In fact, no one failed. It was all very lax. In any case, the number of students graduating from Oxford in the eighteenth century was in rapid decline. In the 1750s, the numbers were down to 200 per year.[6] It was in that milieu that George Austen, given the nickname 'the handsome Proctor', was educated.

It seems that it was no better at Cambridge: as Leedham-Green neatly says, 'it was ... possible for a young scallywag to come away from the University with a BA and precious little else except advanced skills in drinking and driving a coach and pair.'[7]

But, despite the drinking, and the employment of servants brought from home by the wealthy, and the keeping of horses for alleged reasons of 'health' (they were frequently used instead for racing),[8] there were some developments that perhaps hinted at a more disciplined and promising future. In 1749, for example, the Radcliffe Library was opened. Its purpose was to acquire modern books in all faculties and languages that were not in the Bodleian Library. Earlier in the eighteenth century, two new colleges had been founded: in 1714, Gloucester Hall was refounded as Worcester College, and in 1740, Hart Hall became Hertford College. Were these signs of real reform, or would the university continue in its debauched and dissolute ways?

There were stirrings – of a moral kind, which later would have a significant influence upon the nation. Those stirrings began in 1744, only three years before George Austen arrived in Oxford, when John Wesley preached a powerful sermon at St Mary's, the university church, in which he compared the early life of the Church with the situation in Oxford in his own day. The sermon began innocuously enough, with a gentle introduction to the inspiring behaviour of the first Christians as described in the Acts of the Apostles, but it was not long before Wesley was accusing the city and the university of failing in its moral duty to follow more closely the teachings of Christ:

> Let it not be said that I speak here, as if all under your care were intended to be clergymen. Not so: I only speak as if they were all intended to be Christians. But what example is set them by us who enjoy the beneficence of our forefathers? – by Fellows, Students, Scholars; more especially those who are of some rank and eminence? Do ye, brethren, abound in the fruits of the Spirit, in lowliness of mind, in self-denial and mortification, in seriousness and composure of spirit, in patience, meekness, sobriety, temperance; and in unwearied, restless endeavours to do good in every kind unto all men, to relieve their outward wants, and to bring their souls to the true knowledge and love of God? Is this the general character of Fellows of Colleges? I fear it is not. Rather, have not pride and haughtiness of spirit, impatience and peevishness, sloth and indolence, gluttony and sensuality, and even a proverbial uselessness, been objected to us, perhaps not always by our enemies, nor wholly without ground? O that God would roll away this reproach from us, that the very memory of it might perish for ever.

John Wesley (1703–91) was a generation ahead of George Austen at Oxford. He became an undergraduate of Christ Church in 1720 and graduated in 1724. In September 1725, he was ordained as a deacon at Christchurch and in 1726 he became a Fellow of Lincoln College. In 1727, he left the college to become his father's curate at Epworth and Wroot, Lincolnshire, but was invited back to Lincoln College in 1729 to be a Teaching Fellow. Meanwhile, his brother Charles (1707–88) had come up to Oxford in 1726 and was meeting with a few friends for Bible study and prayer. John became part of that group, which assembled daily from 6 am to 9 am to pray, to read the Psalms, and to study the New Testament in Greek. As a personal discipline, members of the group fasted twice a week and attended Holy Communion services weekly, unlike their fellow students who were required to receive Communion on only three days of the year. They were mocked by many and were given unflattering nicknames such as 'Holy Club', and 'Bible Moths', but the name that stuck was 'Methodists'. They began to involve themselves in practical Christian social action and in 1730 started to visit Oxford's Castle Prison. Compared with their hard drinking, horse-racing fellow students they were noticeably disciplined, rigorous in their Bible studies, and eager to lead devout Christian lives.

In 1735, John and Charles Wesley sailed for Georgia, USA, where John ministered to the settlers in the new colony and Charles became Secretary to the Governor. It was not a successful venture, but they had been deeply influenced by some Moravian settlers whose faith and devout lives had impressed them. And so it was that when they returned to England, they attended a Moravian meeting in Aldersgate Street, London. At that meeting, on 24 May 1738, John Wesley heard someone reading Martin Luther's Preface to the Epistle to the Romans. It touched him deeply and he later recalled his experience in words, which have since become treasured by Methodists and others:

> About a quarter before nine, while he [the preacher] was describing the change which God works in the heart through faith in Christ,

I felt my heart strangely warmed. I felt I did trust in Christ, Christ alone for salvation, and an assurance was given me that he had taken away my sins, even mine, and saved me from the law of sin and death.[9]

It is regarded as one of the seminal moments in the Evangelical Revival, a movement that also encompassed the new American colonies and is known in the USA as the Great Awakening. It emphasised personal holiness, the need for repentance, personal salvation, and a wrathful but merciful God. Those themes would have been in play amongst some of his fellow students, when George Austen was in College.

In England, the reaction of many to the Evangelical Revival was to deplore what they described as 'enthusiasm'. Dr Johnson, in his *Dictionary* of 1755, defined it thus:

A vain belief of private revelation; a vain confidence of divine favour or communication. Enthusiasm is founded neither on reason nor divine revelation but rises from the conceits of a warmed or overweening brain.

For its opponents, 'enthusiasm' was regarded as a term of sardonic and alarmed abuse and was a very long way from ideas of Deism and Providence, which were the predominant concepts in mainstream Anglicanism. As a committed Anglican, it is likely that George Austen was more influenced by that intellectual tradition than by the 'enthusiasm' of Wesley and his successors. He was, in fact, part of a much broader consensus. As David Cecil says, describing religious belief in the eighteenth century, a good Christian was a person who did his duty according to the state of life to which he had been called by God, which included his duties to neighbours and to whoever was his or her superior.[10] In short, society was hierarchical, and everyone should know and adhere to his allotted place in the pecking order. Which might be a fine sentiment for those at the top of the social pyramid, but not so helpful or encouraging to those of much lower rank. And it was to those kinds of people that John Wesley spoke so eloquently and so effectively.

In contradistinction to the Wesleyans, one of the most influential books in the eighteenth century was about the place of reason in religion. Written by Matthew Tindal (1657–1733), it was entitled, *Christianity as old as the Creation, Or, The Gospel, a Republication of the Religion of Nature*. In the preface of that book, published in 1730, Tindal set out his purpose:

> THE Author of the following Sheets, makes no Apology for writing on a Subject of the last Importance; and which, as far as I can find, has nowhere been so fully treated: He builds nothing on a Thing so uncertain as Tradition which differs in most Countries; and of which, in all Countries, the Bulk of Mankind are incapable of judging; but thinks he has laid down such plain and evident Rules, as may enable Men of the meanest Capacity, to distinguish between Religion and Superstition; and has represented the Former, in every Part, so beautiful, so amiable, and so strongly affecting; that they who in the least reflect, must be highly in love with it; and easily perceive, that their Duty and Happiness are inseparable. Whether he has succeeded in this Noble, and Generous Attempt, the Reader will be better able to judge, if he reads with the same Freedom, and Impartiality as the Author wrote.[11]

The very rhythm of the phrasing of that preface sets the tone of the book. The argument that follows is orderly, cool, and quietly judicious.

The book ran into many editions and was popular amongst Anglican clergy. However, the intellectual ethos of that age was formed not only by writers such as Matthew Tindal, but also by the philosopher John Locke (1632–1704). In his influential book *An Essay Concerning Human Understanding*, Locke emphasised the importance of reason. In Chapter 10 of Volume 2, headlined 'Of our knowledge of the existence of a God', he wrote:

Though God has given us no innate ideas of himself, though he has stamped no original characters on our minds wherein we may read his being: yet, having furnished us with those faculties our minds are endowed with, he hath not left himself without witness, since we have sense, perception, and reason and cannot want a clear proof of him, as long as we carry ourselves about with us. Nor can we justly complain of our ignorance in this great point, since he has so plentifully provided us with the means to discover and know him, so far as is necessary to the end of our being and the great concernment of our happiness.[12]

Locke was also critical of the concept of 'enthusiasm', arguing that although humankind had the faculties of reason and faith, there were some people who lived and taught that 'enthusiasm' superseded reason 'whereby in effect it takes away both reason and revelation, and substitutes in the room of them the ungrounded fancies of a man's own brain, and assumes them for a foundation of opinion and conduct'.[13]

There was a further element in this intellectual climate, which was to do with conduct and right behaviour in society. We can see a delightful cameo of this in *Mansfield Park*.

Jane Austen revealed through the character of Edmund Bertram that as a clergyman he should see himself as a 'gentleman' serving his society rather than as a chosen servant of God.[14] For Edmund, the clergyman's main obligation was to undertake 'the guardianship of religion and morals, and consequently of the manners which result from their influence. ... The manners I speak of, might ... be called conduct, perhaps, the result of good principles.'[15]

Was this a description of how George Austen saw his vocation? Jane Austen returned to a discussion of what the term 'gentleman' might mean a few years later, in *Persuasion*.[16]

In what follows, Mr Shepherd and Sir Walter Elliot, who is outrageously snobbish, are trying to remember the name of a curate they once knew. The answer is supplied by Anne Elliot, Sir Walter's long-suffering daughter.

> 'You mean Mr Wentworth, I suppose,' said Anne.
> 'Wentworth was the very name! Mr Wentworth was the very man. He had the curacy of Monkford, you know, Sir Walter, some time back, for two or three years. Came there about the year 18—5, I take it. You remember him, I am sure?'
> 'Wentworth? Oh! ay,—Mr Wentworth the curate of Monkford. You misled me by the term "gentleman". I thought you were speaking of some man of property: Mr Wentworth was nobody I remember; quite unconnected; nothing to do with the Strafford family. One wonders how the names of many of our nobility became so common.'

There is no need to discuss this eighteenth-century intellectual, social and moral English world any further, and we should acknowledge that we cannot know with any certainty what the content of George Austen's theological and spiritual thinking might have been. Unfortunately, none of the sermons he preached when he was the incumbent of Steventon survive. There is, however, a brief record, collected by his son James, of the biblical texts he used. All are New Testament texts, including, for example, Matthew 4, 1: 'Then was Jesus led up of the Spirit into the wilderness to be tempted of the Devil.'[17]

However, it seems reasonable to maintain that George Austen was in that Anglican tradition that acknowledged the high significance of Reason in religion and the importance of Morality in society. It was within that late eighteenth-century milieu in the Rectory and the church at Steventon that Henry and his siblings were brought up. There can be no doubt that they were influenced deeply by it. We can see it, for example, in the quotations above from *Mansfield Park* and in the prayers that Jane herself composed; the following prayer written by Jane suggests that 'enthusiasm' was eschewed and was not part of her spiritual vocabulary, but she was profoundly aware of the ineffable majesty and transcendence of God, and consequently of herself as a sinner.[18]

> Give us grace, Almighty Father, so to pray, as to deserve to be heard, to address thee with our hearts, as with our lips. Thou art everywhere present, from thee no secret can be hid. May the knowledge of this teach us to fix our thoughts on thee, with reverence and devotion that we pray not in vain. Look with mercy on the sins we have this day committed and in mercy make us feel them deeply, that our repentance may be sincere and our resolution steadfast of endeavouring against the commission of such in future. Teach us to understand the sinfulness of our own hearts and bring to our knowledge every fault of temper and every evil habit in which we have indulged to the discomfort of our fellow-creatures, and the danger of our own souls. May we now, and on each return of night, consider how the past day has been spent by us, what have been our prevailing thoughts, words, and actions during it, and how far we can acquit ourselves of evil. Have we thought irreverently of thee, have we disobeyed thy commandments, have we neglected any known duty, or willingly given pain to any human being?
>
> Incline us to ask our hearts these questions oh! God, and save us from deceiving ourselves by pride or vanity. Give us a thankful sense of the blessings in which we live, of the many comforts of our lot; that we may not deserve to lose them by discontent or indifference.

If that prayer symbolises not just Jane's own innermost disposition, but reveals the spirit of Steventon Rectory and the family's daily evening prayers led by George Austen, can we not assume that Henry, her brother, might have shared similar underlying spiritual convictions?

Chapter 4

Improvement, Enclosures and Livings

In the previous chapter, in discussing the eighteenth-century milieu in which Henry, Jane and their siblings were brought up, we were trying to demonstrate the ways in which that intellectual and moral climate might have affected them through their father's teaching and his personal moral code. But there is yet a little more to add.

George Austen spent seventeen years as a Fellow of St John's College, was awarded his BA, MA and BD, and 'whilst doing so, taught Logic, Greek, and Natural Philosophy, i.e. science and was one of the University Proctors'.[1] It must have been a pleasant enough life; he had congenial company, a non-strenuous teaching timetable, the pleasures of riding, lively conversation, and, it should be noted, he was not an 'enthusiast'.

The main objective of the college in the eighteenth century was the education of the Fellows; the older Fellows taught the younger ones, but the practical purpose of the college was to turn out Church of England clergy, at which the college succeeded, but there was a catch: if a Fellow had not been ordained within ten years of entering the college he would be expelled.

So, George, not wishing to be expelled, was made a deacon in 1754 by the Bishop of Rochester and was ordained as a priest one year later. Two years after that, in 1757, the Seven Years War began – an armed struggle in Europe and the Americas between two opposing alliances. On the British side was Prussia, on the enemy's side was an alliance consisting of France, Spain, Saxony, Sweden and Russia. It was a war about the expansion of influence and territory, especially in the Americas, and, of course, about global power and international trade, as well as, in Europe, a struggle for supremacy in the Holy Roman Empire. Prussia emerged out of the war as one of the new and major players in Europe, and in the Americas, Britain gained control of much of what had been known as New France, plus Spanish Florida, and some of the Caribbean islands.

During much of the period of that war, George Austen was a Fellow of his college – a huge cultural distance from the brutalities of war on the Continent and in the Americas. As a Fellow he was required to be unmarried, and he remained in that state for the next nine years. Interestingly, in 1760, he 'became a Trustee of a slave plantation in Antigua at the request of one of his former pupils, James Langford Nibbs'.[2] Whilst such a decision is vehemently deplored in our own age, at the time it seemed to many to be the accepted order of things. However, some legal cases in Scotland in 1755 and 1769, plus some significant antislavery voices, including John Wesley's 1774 publication *Thoughts Upon Slavery*, were beginning to raise the profile of the abolitionist cause. What George Austen's views were on the subject, we simply do not know.

But perhaps, as a Fellow of his college, his thoughts were beginning to turn in a more personal direction ... towards marriage and family. His eye fell on Cassandra Leigh (1739–1827). Her uncle, as we have seen, was the Reverend Dr Theophilus Leigh (1693–1785), Master of Balliol. Might he have been involved in the matchmaking? Or was it Cassandra's brother, James Leigh? He studied Civil Law at St John's, and although he was younger than George Austen, they would have known each other well.

Cassandra Leigh had the good fortune to be a direct descendant of the sister of Sir Thomas White, the founder of St John's, which meant that any children she might have could rightfully claim a place at the college as Founder's Kin. It was a right that was later exercised by two of her sons, James and Henry. In addition, Cassandra Leigh had other useful connections. Her grandfather, Theophilus Leigh (1643–1724), was the Squire of Adlestrop, Gloucestershire, and had married the sister of the Duke of Chandos. Her own father, the Reverend Thomas Leigh (1676–1764), became the Vicar of Harpsden, Oxfordshire, in 1731, having been a Fellow of All Souls, Oxford, and her mother was Jane Walker, who was part of the Perrot family. And just to add to this confusion of Leighs,

Perrots and Austens, the Reverend Thomas Leigh, the younger brother of James Leigh, a later Squire of Adlestrop (and Cassandra Leigh's first cousin), later inherited Stoneleigh Abbey, to which George and Cassandra Austen's children went on visits. Thomas Leigh had married Mary, his cousin, the daughter of Theophilus Leigh of Balliol. And to complete a tiny fragment of the complex family tree, the Reverend Thomas Leigh was Henry Austen's godfather. But let's return to George Austen.

On 26 April 1764, George Austen and Cassandra Leigh were married at St Swithin's, Walcot, Bath, a city basking in its fashionable status in the eighteenth century and one to which the Austen family returned from time to time, and to which George and Cassandra eventually retired. St Swithin's, a Saxon foundation, had been severely damaged in a storm in 1739 and had had to be rebuilt. The architect chosen for the rebuilding was the churchwarden, Robert Smith, and it was in his new church that George and Cassandra plighted their troth. After the wedding, George and Cassandra, the newlyweds, took up their new life in the parish of Steventon but, as we have seen, lived for a while in the Parsonage of Deane because the Steventon house was not yet ready for occupation.

Steventon Rectory was not as grand as might be imagined but George Austen 'improved' it as the years passed. The first improvement was to create a gravel semi-circular drive called a 'sweep' for carriages to come to the Rectory door.

'Improvement' was one of the powerful catchwords of the late eighteenth century and was applied to houses and to grounds. There were plans, for example, for Steventon Rectory to develop a small plantation of trees, but should it be an orchard, or should it be composed of trees that had a pleasing, picturesque beauty?

In a letter to her sister Cassandra, written on 20 November 1800, thirty-six years after her parents had moved into the Rectory, Jane Austen wrote: 'A new plan has been suggested concerning the plantation of the right-hand side of the Elm Walk—the doubt is whether it would be better to make a little orchard of it, by planting apples, pears and cherries, or whether it should be larch, Mountain Ash and acacia.'

And one of the most fashionable things to create, that is, to 'improve', even in a Parsonage garden, was a shrubbery,[3] as Fanny Price rhapsodises in *Mansfield Park*:

'This is pretty, very pretty,' said Fanny, looking around her as they were thus sitting together one day: 'every time I come into the shrubbery, I am more struck with its growth and beauty. Three years ago, this was nothing but a rough hedgerow along the upper side of the field, never thought of as anything or capable of becoming anything; and now it is converted into a walk, and it would be difficult to say whether most valuable as a convenience or an ornament ....'[4]

Somehow, the notion of 'improvement' has cast its golden shadow across the late eighteenth century. Visitors to properties in the care of the National Trust, for example, often think that what they are seeing is a typical English landscape, but that landscape might well have been artfully contrived, a result of 'improvement', and that might have been a direct consequence of enclosure.[5] The golden shadow had an ugly side. Land legally enclosed was frequently the only land upon which the village poor and agricultural labourers could graze their few cows and sheep; furthermore, the 'open-field' system of agriculture was also placed under the terms of the Enclosure Act of 1773. And this meant that strips of land that were not contiguous could be pulled together to create larger, hedged and demarcated fields. The deprivation of that common land and of the 'open-fields' inevitably led to increased rural poverty and hardship, as journalist and politician William Cobbett (1763–1835) pointed out frequently in his rumbustious and polemical fashion. In addition, poorer tenant farmers who leased their land were subject to similar deprivation as they were unable to meet the new lease commitments. Those so deprived, the poor and small tenant farmers, had to seek work elsewhere and there was an inevitable population drift towards towns.

The enclosure process is rarely mentioned in Jane Austen's novels; instead, the sweeping lawns, the decorative trees, and the carefully created fashionable 'prospects' were the favoured background setting for her characters. However, we might be able to see her own moral qualms about enclosure in a speech that she places in the mouth of John Dashwood in *Sense and Sensibility*. She allows him to exhibit his own moral failures – greed and self-centredness:

> The inclosure of Norland Common, now carrying on is a most serious drain. And then I have made a little purchase within this half year; East Kingham Farm, you must remember the place, where old Gibson used to live. The land was so very desirable for me in every respect, so immediately adjoining my own property, that I felt it my duty to buy it. I could not have answered it to my conscience to let it fall into any other hands. A man must pay for his convenience; and it has cost me a vast deal of money.[6]

Some clergy, whom one might have expected to have had a concern for the poor and to have remonstrated about the consequential poverty, applauded enclosure, seeing it as an important and necessary means to increase agricultural production by new methods, and, of course, the clergy also benefited from an increase in the tithes that resulted. However, it should also be noted that the land that a clergyman 'owned' by virtue of being an incumbent was subject to the Parliamentary Act, which required land to be improved, to be enclosed with hedges, and to be properly drained and managed. Those improvements cost money, and whereas a normal landowner could foresee that by investing in enclosure, he and his heirs would gain financially in the long term, in the case of the clergy who did not own the land personally but only by virtue of their office, the costs of improvement could be considerable and might bring benefit only to their successors. It was a tricky moral dilemma.

There can be no doubt that enclosure and its legal enforcement in the Enclosure Act of 1773 marked a huge economic and social change in the country; as Easton points out, 'It marks the change from thinking of land in terms of community use to designating land for individual use. Enclosure demarcates private property.'[7]

The preamble to the Act makes all too clear what its fundamental purpose was:

> Whereas there are in several parishes and places in this kingdom several wastes and commons, and several open and common fields, which, by reason of the different interests the several land owners and occupiers, or persons having right of common, have in such wastes, commons and fields, cannot be improved, cultivated or enjoyed to such great advantage for the owners and occupiers thereof, and persons having right of common, as they might be and are capable of if an improved course of husbandry was to be pursued respecting such open and common fields in each parish respectively, and such wastes or commons of pasture were to be properly drained or otherwise amended.

There was a slight change to the Act in the following year, 1774, in which Parliament required petitions for enclosure to be affixed to the door of the parish church annually in August and September. It is not difficult to imagine George Austen with hammer and nails in hand, fixing those notices to the door at St Nicholas, Steventon. As a result, he would have been acutely aware of which landowners in his parish would increase their landholdings by enclosing common land and adjusting the 'open-field' system. In the late seventeenth, and in the eighteenth century, about 21 per cent of England had been affected by enclosure; the rest had been enclosed earlier and thus, although George Austen affixed the official notices to the church door, those notices might have had little effect because much of the enclosure of lands in that part of Hampshire had been happening piecemeal over the previous 100 years.

In theory, the poor could object to enclosure, but as those objections had to go through the hands of lawyers and the cost of lawyers was beyond the reach of the poor, legal objections were few.

Enclosure, then, was a fact of life in late eighteenth-century England. It reshaped the landscape, increased the wealth of some and seriously impoverished others.

This was the social and political context in which rural clergy such as George Austen and his family lived. But the clergy also had their own more limited personal, cultural and social situations with which they had to deal.

It can sometimes appear that the trajectory of families in rectories was smoothly upwards. But that was not necessarily so. For example, the description of the Reverend George Austen's life as a young man makes it sound as though the progress from an Oxford Fellowship to a living was straightforward. It was not. There were about 11,600 livings in total, but these were 'owned' by a variety of organisations and individuals: over 2,500 belonged to bishops and cathedral chapters; approximately 600 were in the hands of Oxford and Cambridge colleges; 1,100 livings were in the gift of the Crown (in reality, the gift was exercised by the prime minister); more than 5,500 livings were in the hands of wealthy individuals who had purchased the advowson precisely so that they could award the living to whomsoever they chose; and the remainder were held by a variety of sources. So, in order to get a living, you either needed a wealthy relative who owned the advowson, or you needed to be a relative or close family friend of a bishop or the Dean and Chapter, and, in the case of Oxbridge colleges, you were sometimes chosen by election.[8] But not everyone had the ability or the connections to prosper as a clergyman. About 1,000 livings were worth less than £100 per annum, and another 3,000 were only capable of paying something between £100 and £150. It was a system that was not entirely healthy. But, for the most part, the Austen clergy were at the better and happier end of the spectrum, though as we shall see, Henry, when he eventually became a curate in Farnham in 1822, earnt only £75 plus £35 in so-called surplice fees.

It needs to be made clear that in the eighteenth century there was no central body in the Church of England that was responsible for the pay of clergy. Each clergyman received his income from two possible sources: first, there were tithes that were legally bound to be paid by some parishioners, that is, 10 per cent of the product of all cultivated land in the parish should be paid to the clergyman. However, there were serious caveats. Some clergy did not feel adequate to the task of asking for what was, in law, rightly theirs. In many parishes the clergyman and local landowners came to an agreement that commuted tithes into a regular cash sum based on an estimated yield of produce per acre[9] – but how could the parson be certain that the estimated yield was correct; could that yield not go up in good times, and down in bad times? The second item in a clergyman's stipend came from the glebe that he owned as the incumbent. The glebe could consist of many acres, or very few, depending on the history of the endowments of the parish. From that glebe, depending on how alert the clergyman was to local demand, he could grow crops for sale, or use it as pasture to graze cows, sheep and pigs. Or he could lease it to a local farmer and collect the annual rent. Any money the clergyman made from his glebe was legally his. The glebe at Steventon was originally just 3 acres, but George Austen's patron, Thomas Knight I, as we have seen, gave him the opportunity to take a lease on a further 200 acres. And thus, George Austen employed a steward to look after and manage his glebe. Interestingly, Chawton, the parish in which Jane Austen lived for the latter part of her life, had over 60 acres of glebe associated with it. There was a third element in clergy pay, or rather, lack of it. Some patrons of livings were also impropriators who were legally entitled to the 'greater tithes', that is, the tithes paid on cereal crops, which left the clergyman with the 'lesser tithes', which amounted to 10 per cent of products such as chickens, fruit and eggs.

It was a complicated system. Some clergy were accused of spending more time in farming their glebe than in their clerical duties; others found the glebe system burdensome and did all they could to lease their glebe to local landowners, trusting that the landowner would play fair by them – a trust that was sometimes abused.

As we have seen, George Austen became Rector of Steventon because of the largesse of Thomas Knight I. St Nicholas, the parish church, had been constructed in the thirteenth century but there have been minor alterations since; for example, the spire was added in the nineteenth century, but the church as it is now is essentially the same as that in which George Austen ministered and in which his wife and family worshipped. The parish was small and rural. The church could only seat seventy-five to eighty souls. George had taken over the living from his cousin Henry Austen, who was his predecessor – it was how the system of Church appointments worked in the eighteenth century; family connections, or connections with wealthy families who owned the advowsons of livings, were sought after and nurtured.

In *Northanger Abbey*, the choleric General Tilney boasts about the living into which he has placed his son:

> The house stands among fine meadows facing the south-east, with an excellent kitchen garden in the same aspect; the walls surrounding which I built and stocked myself about ten years ago, for the benefit of my son. It is a family living, Miss Morland and the property in the place being chiefly my own, you may believe I take care that it shall not be a bad one.[10]

There is a similar illustration of this process concerning livings in *Sense and Sensibility*, the novel that Jane Austen first wrote as an epistolary story at Steventon sometime between 1795 and 1797, but which was only published anonymously in 1811 when its author was described as 'A Lady'. In that novel, Elinor Dashwood, one of the main characters, is trapped into a complicated conversation with Lucy Steele, a manipulative, unintelligent young woman desperate to improve her own social status. Lucy Steele has secretly been engaged to Edward Ferrars for about four years. The conversation, led with cunning by Lucy, who, incidentally, is unaware that Elinor had also fallen in love with Edward, has now turned to his future prospects. Lucy says:

> I will honestly tell you of one scheme which has lately come into my head, for bringing matters to bear; indeed, I am bound to let you into the secret, for you are a party concerned. I dare say you have seen enough of Edward to know that he would prefer the church to every other profession; now my plan is that he should take orders as soon as he can, and then through your interest which I am sure you would be kind enough to use out of friendship for him, and I hope out of some regard to me, your brother might be persuaded to give him Norland living; which I understand is a very good one, and the present incumbent not likely to live a great while. That would be enough for us to marry upon, and we might trust to time and chance for the rest.[11]

Unfortunately, the living of Steventon, unlike the fictional Norland, was not initially a wealthy one, and with a rapidly growing family (five children had been born in the nine years following the wedding, and three more would soon follow), George Austen and Cassandra were beginning to feel the financial pinch. 'He had already sold off in parcels his £800 worth of South Sea annuities and it was at this time that the family finances reached a crisis. Mrs Austen's brother, James Leigh-Perrot [he had added the name "Perrot" in the belief that he would thereby receive a fortune from a major bequest – which he did] came to the rescue.'[12] He paid £300 into George Austen's bank account in February 1773. It must have been received with humbling gratitude. But he received more family help soon afterwards because the Living of Deane, the next-door parish worth £110 yearly, came to him from his wealthy uncle, Francis Austen. Sighs of relief all round.

Henry Austen, aged 2, while all these financial dealings were taking place, would not have been aware of the way in which household budgets were being stretched. Nevertheless, when he was older, he might have picked up some of the details of those difficult financial years. Was it his awareness of this, of the poverty that could trap an impecunious clergyman, that led him as an adult into banking? Or might it also have been his knowledge that as there were no clergy pensions, the only way for a clergyman to receive an income if he felt forced to retire would be to hire a curate to take over his living who would then be required to pay the retired incumbent the normal stipend, leaving the curate to survive on whatever was left? Either way, the children of Steventon Rectory would have been shrewdly observant of the financial complexities involved in collecting tithes and managing the glebe; in short, taking Holy Orders might have had relatively high status in the late eighteenth century, but it was by no means risk-free.

All that has been outlined above was the social, political and religious context in which Henry had been raised, and which helped to shape the person he was, but one other typically eighteenth-century trend must also have impacted upon his sensibility, and that was the matter of 'taste'. David Cecil describes 'taste' as being about learning and discrimination: 'learning and discrimination were acquired through a thorough grounding in the established and classical tradition of scholarship and the arts.'[13]

Whilst that kind of learning and the appreciation of the finer things in life can rightly be attributed to eighteenth-century gentry, and wealthy families, for example, could send their male offspring on the Grand Tour, such discursive learning and appreciation would not have been open to the poor in society, though, of course, it was the poor who created, fired and decorated the Wedgwood pottery that was so sought after by the people of 'taste'.

Henry and the Austen family fitted elegantly into the 'taste' category, for we know that Jane Austen visited the Wedgwood showroom in London and that her brother Edward had a set of Wedgwood; we also know from a letter written by Jane to Cassandra on 6 June 1812 that Chawton had some Wedgwood pieces: 'On Monday I had the pleasure of receiving, unpacking and approving our Wedgwood ware.'[14] It would seem that within their financial limits, the Austens regarded 'taste' as a civilising element of life.

And according to James Austen-Leigh, Jane Austen's nephew, she herself embodied good taste in her manner of dress and in her way of conducting herself: 'In person, she was very attractive; her figure was rather tall and slender, her step light and firm and her whole appearance expressive of health and animation.'[15]

But now it is time for us to move our attention away from the family and concentrate upon Henry and his life. As we shall see, his life turned out to be very unlike what one might have expected of a child growing up in an isolated rural rectory.

The question is, was his future career a subtle act of rebellion against his own background or was it a continuation of themes that were present within the Austen family?

Chapter 5

Henry Austen: Oxford University and *The Loiterer*

As we have seen, Henry Austen received his initial education from his father, but because of the Founder's Kin rule at St John's College, Oxford, in 1788 he was able to enter as an undergraduate without any preliminary examination or discussion. The curriculum he followed would have been very similar to the one his father had undertaken.

It would be interesting to know whether his father wrote a serious and encouraging letter to Henry on his arrival at the university, as he had done to Francis when the latter went to sea aged 14. That letter contains the following paternal advice:

Your behaviour, as a member of society, to the individuals around you may be also of great importance to your future well-being, and certainly will to your present happiness and comfort. You may either by a contemptuous, unkind and selfish manner create disgust and dislike, or by affability, good humour and compliance, become the object of esteem and affection; which of these very opposite paths 'tis your interest to pursue I need not say.... Your conduct, as it respects yourself, chiefly comprehends sobriety and prudence. The former you know the importance of to your health, your morals and your fortune. I shall therefore say nothing more to enforce the observance of it. I thank God you have not at present the least disposition to deviate from it. Prudence extends to a variety of objects. ... She will teach you the proper disposal of your time and the careful management of your money.[1]

It was advice that encapsulated the importance the eighteenth century gave to manners and gentlemanly conduct and would certainly have been of use to Henry later in his life, as we shall see.

When he went up to Oxford, his oldest brother James was already ensconced. He had gone to Oxford in 1779 and had graduated with a BA in 1783 and an MA in 1788. He stayed on as a Fellow until his marriage in 1792. Henry and James, therefore, overlapped for four years. They saw a great deal of each other and together, on 31 January 1789, they launched a weekly journal.

It's not difficult to imagine the heady and excited preliminaries to this venture. They called their journal *The Loiterer* (a 'knowing' reference to Samuel Johnson's *The Rambler*, published from 1750 to 1752, and a series of his essays known as *The Idler*,[2] published from 1758 to 1760). But *The Loiterer* was not the only, or even the newest college-based weekly journal. Some Etonians had launched their journal, *The Microcosm*, in 1786. One year later, Thomas Monroe edited the *Olla Podrida*, which also was a weekly. James and Henry, it would seem, were following a fashionable student trend. *The Loiterer* continued in print until 20 March 1790. Twenty-nine of the essays were written by James; Henry contributed nine, and the rest were written by valued friends. It was not simply an Oxford undergraduate *jeu d'esprit* with a local readership; it was, in fact, sold by booksellers in London, Bath, Reading and Birmingham, and in London the distributor was Messrs Egerton, who later became Jane Austen's publisher.

The purpose of the journal, as described by James, was 'to emulate other well-known periodicals, not only the urban but also the provincial ones ... and to supply [our] countrymen with a regular succession of moral lectures, critical remarks, and elegant humour'.[3] It feels a trifle self-conscious, not to say patronising and pompous, but it is saved by its wry reference to 'elegant humour'. The title-page motto was 'Speak of us as we are', which was suitably enigmatic and sounds as though it might have been an Austen family joke.

The journal was in keeping with James's reputation as a classical scholar of good taste. He had, after all, provided witty prologues and epilogues for family plays and other theatrical entertainments at Steventon, and had written some poetry. Furthermore, the practice of writing and of reading literature was one of the family's lively accomplishments and critics have noted that the style and content of *The Loiterer* bore a close resemblance to Jane Austen's juvenilia.[4] Critics have also highlighted the close relationship between the wit of *The Loiterer* and Jane's novels. Henry, in particular, is singled out for praise: 'Henry's quick wit and tongue-in-cheekiness shed light on our understanding of the caustic prowess of his younger sister.'[5]

Henry's essays are amused reflections on life at Oxford. His first essay was number 8 in the journal and was published on 21 March 1789. It pretends to be the ruminations of a former student, H. Homely, who, it was alleged, had pursued a rackety and self-indulgent time at university and ended his life as a clergyman in Yorkshire. The opening sentences, purporting to be a letter from the clergyman to the journal's editor, reveal the style and format of the essay that follows:

> As I understand that your design is, by a weekly distribution of wit and advice, to amuse and instruct the University of which I was once a member, and as I have already perceived that you have resolution enough to expose the vices and follies, which have sprung up in a soil so friendly to each, I hope you will not despise the communications of one who in a former part of his life was a considerable sufferer from both.

Following this prologue, the 'contributor' outlines the hopes, follies and enjoyments that he experienced:

> I was the only child of honest though not wealthy parents, who discovering in me early symptoms of very extraordinary abilities (a discovery which parents frequently make) could not prevail upon themselves to deprive the literary world of so promising a genius; and therefore, instead of breeding me up to assist my father

in his shop, they were determined to make a scholar of me. To this end I was sent at the age of nine to the free school of the town in which we resided, where in the succeeding nine years I completed my classical education; that is, I could construe Latin pretty well with an *Ordo Verbarum*, and generally knew Greek when I saw it. At this juncture I had the good fortune of being recommended by the Master of our School to the Head of —— College in Oxford and soon after had the inexpressible pleasure of being elected to a scholarship worth at least £15 per annum.

Language is not adequate to express the joy which spread itself through my family at the news of such an unlooked-for acquisition of fortune; and I need not say that both my father and my mother thought it an indispensable duty to accommodate their common hope to the theatre of science, that they might see me take possession of my estate and make my first entrance on the world.

This account of a poor student from a modest background extolling his good fortune is, of course, humorous, as seen, for example, in the aside about the hopes of all parents ... but there is also a satirical undertone that is discomforting. Was not Henry himself extremely fortunate, through no effort on his part, to have been awarded a place at his college? Should he have chosen a shopkeeper's son as the butt of his heavy-handed joke? Perhaps it can be put down to a youthful lack of maturity.

Henry's essay continues with the shopkeeper's son rejoicing in the freedom he was experiencing:

I had scarcely convinced myself that it was not all enchantment, when on looking about me, I concluded from several reasons that I was the happiest man alive. In the first place I was totally my own master and might do what I pleased; that is, I might do nothing at all. Secondly, I was convinced that I had money enough to last for ever.

But the writer falls into bad company and naïvely begins to lend money to his friends, and to live a life of intemperance and idleness:

> and when I took my degree, I was as emaciated and as much in debt as a peer of the realm. I had lost everything which I ought to have preserved; I had acquired nothing but habits of expence [*sic*], which long outlived the means of gratifying them, and a relish for indolence when I had my bread to earn.

One can see that any undergraduate reading this account would perhaps have recognised his own moral and personal failings. It is also possible that such an essay would have been enjoyed and relished and would have promoted some lively discussions over late-night candlelit claret in students' rooms. It was indeed an essay that fulfilled the objectives of *The Loiterer* to provide 'moral lectures'. So, was this critique of university life a way in which Henry (and James) could bring about some much-needed changes? In short, was the journal more radical than it appeared to be on the surface? Was it even a lower-key version of what John Wesley had been saying forty-five years earlier?

The narrative of the shopkeeper's son continues with him gradually losing his friends who had gone down from Oxford, followed, melodramatically, by the death of his father and subsequently, his mother. So, what was he to do? He had taken Orders a little time previously, and therefore he set off to Yorkshire to find himself a curacy – a quest in which he was eventually successful. His rector was not resident in the parish and, in any case, was involved in a long legal dispute with the local squire. The field was open, therefore, for the curate to go about his duties assiduously, duties that were by no means arduous. He cultivated a friendship with the Squire and married the Squire's sister. Fortune was with him, because the Rector died and the Squire appointed the curate to the living, which was worth about £300 per annum, and that, plus his wife's private income, ensured that they had a comfortable and pleasant existence.

He concludes his life story by asking his student readers to learn from the mistakes he made and not to repeat them.

It is indeed a moral tale, though it does not ask any serious ethical questions about the fact that the young man, notwithstanding his dissolute and spendthrift time as a student, had so easily become a providentially well-off vicar. It is a quintessentially eighteenth-century retelling of the story of the Prodigal Son but omitting any mention of the repentance evinced by the character in the original narrative. Whether this epistolary essay in *The Loiterer* can be used to reveal anything of the inner moral world of the young Henry Austen is a matter for debate. But one can see that it must have received some interesting reactions from his student contemporaries, and perhaps that was all he set out to achieve.

One of Henry's other essays (number 27) is about the nature of education. It opens with a carefully crafted piece of irony:

> When I observe how universal this wish for Children is, as well amongst those who have fortunes to bequeath as those who have their own bread to earn, I am not a little surprised at finding few or perhaps none who are considerate enough to recollect that the simple possession of Offspring ought to be but half their care, and that how to manage them when obtained is a business of equal importance; since it is evident that they may prove plagues as well as blessings, and disgraces as well as ornaments. So frequently does it happen that in embracing an Heir, we totally forget the duty of educating the Boy, and so apt are we to imagine that after the immediate risques [*sic*] of Child-birth are over, nothing more needs to be done, or to be endured, and that beauty of person, elegance of mind and goodness of disposition are only to be wished for and to be obtained.

The essay continues with a critique of Rousseau, whose influential book *Émile, or On Education* had been published in 1762 and had caused quite a stir. But Henry asserts that he has a much better educational plan, and with his tongue firmly in his cheek, declares:

> I could say much more in praise of me and mine, but modesty (which has always been my foible) forbids it, and I hurry to put my Readers in possession of my Plan, which I venture to affirm, will induce all the married part of them, to remove their Sons from Winchester, Westminster or Eton and place them (with a salary of £200 per annum) under the direction of the Loiterer.

Presumably, such a statement raised a smile or a knowing chortle amongst his readers. His critique of Rousseau's educational ideas is gently mocking. Then he turns his attention to the educational philosophy of Madame de Genlis, who had argued in her epistolary novel *Adèle et Théodore* that education should fit a young woman for her role in society rather than being constricted to the domestic scene. What looks like a step forward in emancipation was hindered, however, by her insistence that a young woman should be subject first to her mother and then to her husband.

Henry satirises de Genlis's ideas and again argues, with tongue in cheek, that a young woman should be 'early taught the use of Cards, and the propriety of Gaming. She will of course soon play a good game of Whist or Cribbage, and by always winning increase her portion or improve her jointure.'

Henry's third essay, number 32, published on 5 September 1789, is also written as though it was created by someone other than himself. It is about potential matrimony, and the perils of unlooked-for courtship. It is addressed to the Editor of *The Loiterer*, and opens thus:

> Sir, you have from the beginning of your work most generously offered protection to the oppressed and consolation to the unfortunate; may I hope that to the latter you will also distribute your advice, for indeed the writer of this is most thoroughly in

want of all you can bestow: an assertion you will hardly have the boldness to doubt, when I inform you that a Woman and Matrimony (at least the thoughts of it) are the causes of my current complaint.

Is there not just the tiniest hint here of Jane Austen's famous opening line of *Pride and Prejudice*?

It is a truth universally acknowledged, that a single man in possession of a good fortune, must be in want of a wife.

That novel, published in 1813, some twenty-four years after Henry's piece in *The Loiterer*, bears a family relationship to his essay, though Jane's wit and polish have a much lighter and more amusing touch than Henry's heavier, self-conscious style.

His essay continues with the letter writer's slightly vain self-description:

I am a middle-aged Man, perhaps about 35, or perhaps a little more. An inch they say is a good deal in a man's nose, but a year or two is nothing in the age of one blessed with sound Lungs and active Limbs.

Which is followed immediately by a reference to possessions and inheritance, the preoccupation of many eighteenth-century gentlemen:

I inherited from my Father an Estate of about £1,000 a year; to which having been considered an heir ever since the moment of my birth, I was never suffered to waste my time, injure my health and load my memory by learning the vocabulary of Dead or even Living Languages. To confess the truth, the chief of my erudition was collected from my Aunt's Bible and the most constant objects of my succeeding studies, have been Bartlett's Farriery, or the

> Racing Calendar. I shot, I hunted, I fished like other young Squires. I was rather good natured than agreeable, moderately temperate and only extravagant in Pointers and Horse-flesh.

It is a neat bit of characterisation, stereotypical but amusing for all that. The letter writer continues by describing his life as untroubled and pleasing:

> My estate was unincumbered, my constitution unhurt, my person uncontrolled; I was rich, healthy and unmarried.

The two triplet phrases are nicely balanced but then comes the melancholic conclusion:

> I sigh when I look back on such days, and when I reflect that in all probability such days will never return.

The reason for his melancholy is explained a couple of paragraphs later: he feels that he might be manoeuvred into marriage, and then all his freedom and self-indulgent idleness will be curtailed. He goes on to explain that a cousin has written to him inviting him to stay for a few days. He regards this seemingly innocuous invitation as a potential trap, for his cousin has some unmarried daughters. Once he has arrived and has had breakfast, he becomes aware that the daughters are planning a dance on the following evening. It is a prospect that fills him with alarm:

> The idea of attending Women to a Ballroom, and of being obliged to dance with them whether I would or no, struck such a panic into me, that I could scarcely swallow a cup of chocolate.

The daughters come rushing into the room where he is dining, and behaving immodestly, as he sees it, begin to flirt with him. He is hotly embarrassed but is spared further discomfiture because his cousin takes him for a two-hour stroll around his estate. The conversation is initially about the fine trees growing there but soon the cousin steers the conversation to the subject of his daughters' marriages. Later that evening, at dinner, the aforesaid daughters reappear, but this time carefully coiffed and made-up. So amazed is the writer by their transformation that he does not know where to look. The young ladies continue to flirt with him:

> From this moment began the long-premeditated attack. All the batteries of ogles, sighs and smiles were at once opened upon me, which engaged so much of my attention that I presumed not to eat another mouthful, and being at the same time closely wedged in, between the Curate of the Parish (who dined with us) and the leg of the table, I might with truth be said to suffer at once, the horrors of a famine and a blockade.

Again, some elements of Jane Austen are present here: the embarrassed guest, the flirtatious sisters, and the absurdity of the hero being wedged between the curate and the table leg. Of course, Jane would have used a similar social setting, a dinner table, and similar characters, but the humour would have been more subtle.

After further descriptions, he returns to the story:

> Miss B did not seem to have partaken of any share of her sister's shrewish looks, on the contrary, when her eyes (by accident) met mine, she smiled and simpered and looked down quite modestly, to be sure she did not blush, but they say that the London ladies put something on their cheeks which you cannot see the blushes through. Nor were her conversation and behaviour less pleasing than her looks, for she enquired most kindly after my health, seemed quite sorry that such near relations had not been sooner acquainted and expressed a great wish of improving the acquaintance.

Another long walk follows in which the young lady apologises that she needs to hold his arm lest she stumble. All is going well. He almost falls in love with her but then a puff of wind disturbs the tresses of her fashionably constructed hairstyle, and the spell is broken. He congratulates himself on his lucky escape but once he has returned home, he receives a letter from his cousin, who proposes to call on him in the company of his daughters. What is he to do? He concludes with a cry of faux despair:

> Oh! the torture of being loved against one's will, and being married in spite of one's self!!

One can guess that this story with its simple plot but with the beginnings of real characterisation would have been enjoyed not only in London and Oxford but also in Steventon. Did Jane consciously or unconsciously learn something of the craft of writing from Henry, her favourite older brother?

His subsequent essays in *The Loiterer* (numbers 37, 47, 48, 51 and 57) are more ponderous than this one, and do not contain much wit, nor are they lightened by sharp observation. However, essay number 32 has moments of such light-hearted fun and satire one can imagine that Henry, in the right mood, would have been good company.

There is an interesting postscript to this brief survey of Henry's essays in *The Loiterer*. Immediately following his essay number 8, on 28 March 1789, a response was published from someone using the penname 'Sophie Sentiment'. It opens with a rebuke to the editors:

> I write this to inform you that you are very much out of my good graces, and that, if you do not mend your manners, I shall soon drop your acquaintance. You must know, Sir, I am a great reader, and not to mention some hundred volumes of Novels and Plays, have, in the last two summers, actually got through all the most entertaining papers of our most celebrated periodical writers from

the *Tatler* and *Spectator* to the *Microcosm* and the *Olla Podrida*.
… I assure you that my heart beat with joy when I first heard of your publication, which I immediately sent for, and have taken in ever since. I am sorry however, to say it, but really Sir, I think it the stupidest work of the kind I ever saw, not but that some of the papers are well written; but then your subjects are so badly chosen, that they never interest one.

The author goes on to berate the editors for their inability to write about subjects that might interest 'the fair sex'. So, who was 'Sophie Sentiment'? It is generally agreed[6] that the writer was none other than Jane Austen herself, aged 13. In other words, the essay was an in-house family joke, a young sister enjoying the process of pretending to be cross and teasing her older brothers. But inside the joke was a real criticism: *The Loiterer* was indeed an intensely masculine venture that did not take cognisance of the fact that some of its readers were women.

Chapter 6

The Oxford Militia

Henry spent a total of five years in Oxford. After he was awarded his BA in June 1792, he stayed on for one more year an as Assistant Logic Tutor, having been awarded a scholarship and a stipend by his college.[1] It suggests that he was an able and natural teacher. But now, aged 22, he faced a major decision. If he was not going to continue in academia, what should he do? The obvious answer, his father might have asserted, was that he should take Holy Orders and enter the Church, just as his older brother James had done. James had been ordained as a deacon on 10 December 1787 by the Bishop of St David's, and following curacies at both Stoke Charity and Overton, Hampshire, on 27 March 1792 he married Anne Matthew at Laverstoke; his father, George Austen, conducted the marriage service. Anne was the 30-year-old daughter of General Matthew, who had been Governor of Grenada. He settled a generous sum of money on Anne, and this, combined with the £300 per annum that James received as the Vicar of Sherborne St John, meant that he and his wife had a comfortable life. Unfortunately, tragedy soon struck. James and Anne had a baby daughter whom they named Anna Elizabeth. She was born in 1793, but her mother Anne died just two years later, in 1795.

The memorial tablet in St Nicholas, Steventon, describes her death as 'having exchanged this Life for a far better' and includes this tribute:

As the Innocency of her Heart,
Simplicity of her Manners,
And amiable unspotted Tenour of her Life in every Relation
Will render her Memory ever dear to her surviving Friends

So the humble and pious Resignation
Eminently manifested at that trying Period
When departing with what was most dear on Earth
Will always be considered by them
As an Example
Of Christian Fortitude
Which, although they can scarcely hope to Equal,
They will yet endeavour
To imitate.

Naturally, the Austen family, whilst grieving the loss of Anne, rallied around James. Anna, the toddler, was taken to live with George and Cassandra Austen, her grandparents, and with her two aunts, Cassandra and Jane, and the rest of the family.

Steventon was only 8 miles distant from Sherborne St John, which meant that James could see his parents, his sisters, and his little daughter very frequently. But to make those visits easier he soon moved to Deane. His parish of Sherborne St John had within its bounds The Vyne, a great house owned during the Tudor period by the Sandys family but held in the eighteenth century by the Chute dynasty, descendants of Challoner Chute, a Speaker of the House of Commons. He had purchased The Vyne in 1653. James was the vicar of the parish for the next twenty-eight years, until, in 1801, he succeeded his father as Vicar of Steventon. Jane Austen knew the Chute family and referred to them in some of her letters.[2]

Henry, then, might have followed family tradition and settled into a languorous existence as a country vicar. James, for example, was a quintessential hunting parson who had his own pack of hounds, but who also gradually collected the livings (and the income) of several parishes: Stoke Charity in 1788, Overton in 1790, Sherborne St John in 1791, and the curacy of Deane in the same year. Deane had been a living that George Austen had received from his wealthy uncle, Francis Austen, in 1773, but he now allowed James to live in the Parsonage because it was so close to Steventon. It had previously been let to Martha Lloyd, the widow of a clergyman whom George knew. She had two unmarried daughters, rather winsomely named Mary and Martha – they were great friends of Jane and Cassandra Austen. But now the Lloyds had to leave the Parsonage so that James could move in. It can't have been easy, but that was the uncertainty for many clergy families. When the clergy husband died, the widow and family, unless they had substantial private means, had to throw themselves on the mercy of friends and relations. As it happens, just two years after the death of Anne Matthew/Austen, in 1797, James married Mary Lloyd and they went on to have two children: James Edward was born in 1798, and Caroline Mary Craven in 1805.

Collecting livings was part and parcel of eighteenth-century clerical life, with its concomitant joys and sorrows, but while this genteel game of ecclesiastical 'Monopoly' was taking place in England, considerable turmoil had erupted in France. Since 1787, France had been riven by increasingly angry social and political factions and then, in July 1789, the Bastille, a powerful symbol of royal tyranny, was stormed. Although Britain had remained neutral during these internal French troubles, by 1793, with its allies, it was taking part in a conflict that later historians have dubbed the 'War of the First Coalition'. In December 1792, King George III (1738–1820) called out the Militia, of which the Oxfordshire Militia was a part.

In such circumstances, perhaps Henry wondered whether he should *not* go into the Church but instead, follow his younger brothers' examples and put on a military uniform. Charles, in 1791, aged only 12, had gone to the Royal Naval Academy and by 1794 was a midshipman on board HMS *Daedalus*;[3] Francis, his older brother, had joined the Royal Navy in 1786, when he was also 12 years old, and after a period at the Royal Navy Academy in Portsmouth had joined HMS *Perseverance*[4] on the East Indies station, and in December 1789 had become a midshipman on HMS *Crown*.[5] Both brothers eventually became admirals. But perhaps it was the influence of his older brother, Edward, that suggested another route, for Edward was a captain in the Godmersham and Molash

Company of the East Kent Volunteers and had written a long, patriotic poem about his men. This is the opening verse:

> Ye Patriot Soldiers whom loyalty praises,
> In the sacred defence of your county to fight,
> Stand at ease for a moment and pile up your arms
> While Gratitude pays hospitalities rite.[6]

It seems that none of the Austen family could resist putting pen to paper, even if it resulted, as in this case, in doggerel.

So, which path should Henry follow? Should it be the gentle way of life as a country vicar, which was the route that James had taken, or should he tackle something more obviously patriotic and heroic, following the examples of his younger brothers, Francis and Charles, and his older brother, Edward?

Unfortunately, we do not have any evidence about the debates Henry must have had in his own mind about what he should do; suffice it to say, he chose Edward's middle and safer way. In April 1793 he decided to join the Oxfordshire Militia.

The county militias were not an active fighting force; they were more like the Home Guard, regiments whose primary purpose was to keep order in the nation, and defend the country if invasion threatened. Unlike the Regular Army, they could not be ordered to serve abroad.[7] They were placed under the leadership of the Lord Lieutenant of each county, but were under the nominal command of the sovereign.[8]

The Oxfordshire Regiment of Militia (Fourth Battalion, Oxfordshire Light Infantry, to give it its formal title) had come into existence on 26 March 1778, following a Royal Warrant issued by King George III. A letter accompanying the warrant was addressed to the Lords Lieutenant of the fifty counties of England and Wales. It was a call to action. In Oxfordshire's case, the letter was sent to the 4th Duke of Marlborough, George Spencer (1739–1817), and it was soon followed by instructions from the King about ammunition:

> Our Will and Pleasure ... is that out of the Stores remaining within the Office of our Ordnance under your Charge you cause a proper quantity of Powder, Ball and Flints to be forthwith issued and delivered to such Person or Persons as shall be duly authorised to receive the same for the use of our said Militia; and you are to take the usual Indents for the same and to insert the Expense thereof in your next Estimate to be laid before Parliament.[9]

Following the issue of the Royal Warrant and letter, the traditional county system of deputy lieutenants[10] had swung into action: sixteen of them met in Oxford on 28 April 1778, and decided that instructions should be given to the constables and other officers of each Hundred to draw up lists of men aged from 18 to 45. Eight days later, a further list was created of the numbers of men required from each Hundred; thus, for example, Bampton Hundred had 1,347 men who were theoretically available, but they were ordered to provide 56. In total, the county of Oxfordshire had to provide 538 men for the regiment. Those men had to fulfil certain criteria: they had to be 18 to 45 years of age and not less than 5 feet 4 inches tall. If a poor man within those categories had three children born in wedlock, he was exempted from service. But the list of exemptions rapidly grew; so, for instance, members of the universities of Oxford and Cambridge were exempt, as were clergy, articled clerks, apprentices and seafarers. In taking account of those exemptions, the remainder were selected by ballot, but even so, if a man was chosen, it was possible for him to elect a substitute. Once chosen, the men of the Militia had to serve for five years, but those over 35 years old only had to serve for two years. Their pay and the costs of the regiment were met by a charge on property owners of the county and by government funds. In addition, the county taxpayers were required to provide allowances for wives and children under the age of 10 who had been left behind. The system, unsurprisingly, was fairly haphazard and led to much querulous debate about the burden that was placed on the taxpayers. And, again, unsurprisingly, there were riots in some villages and towns over the choice of the men required to serve. The lists compiled by the parish constable of those chosen to join the militias were, in some places, subject to seizure by angry rioters.[11] It seems that whilst on paper, the creation of the militias had the appearance of being a straightforward, logistical matter, the reality was quite otherwise.

Further changes in the make-up of the Oxfordshire Militia were made in July 1778 when the deputy lieutenants subdivided the regiment into companies, trying to ensure that men from neighbouring villages served in the same company. Most of the companies were headed by a captain assisted by lower-ranking officers, and the rank and file consisted of approximately fifty-eight men per company.

Having completed that part of the task, there was more work to be done before the militias could be ready for service. For the moment it was imperative that the lines of command in the regiment should be made clear. On 25 May 1778, instructions had been issued that the Duke of Marlborough was to be colonel of the Oxfordshire Regiment, assisted by John Caillaud as lieutenant colonel, and Lord Viscount Parker as major. There were to be five named captains, one captain lieutenant, and five lieutenants. It was strictly hierarchical and followed accepted social norms, thus, for example, the five captains all held the suffix, Esq., whereas the lieutenants held the suffix, Gent. But the appointment of the various ranks of militia officers was also dependent on property qualifications, and some of the prospective officers, like men in the other ranks, were very reluctant to serve, claiming that their landholdings would suffer by their enforced absence. The result was that there was often a shortage of officers in each regiment and an even greater shortage of those who were competent. The problem was exacerbated because a commission in the Militia did not have to be bought, and therefore, some very unlikely, unsuitable and impecunious young gentry joined up as junior officers (subalterns) in the hope that by doing so they might one day obtain a commission in the Regular Army.[12] Because many junior officers in the Militia were felt to be inept, and the other ranks lacked training, it was decided that the only way to strengthen the backbone of the militias was to transfer a few Regular Army officers who would bring, it was hoped, some discipline and order to proceedings. They did not need any property qualifications to be appointed. Frequently, Regular Army officers were appointed as adjutants, to provide the commanding officer with military expertise and the necessary administrative skills.

The militias, however, were not without their social and moral complexities. As J.R. Western says: 'Paying and equipping any military unit in the eighteenth century was largely a business venture on the part of the officers. They received funds from the government and supplied themselves and their men with what they needed, making a profit if they could.'[13]

Having completed the logistical shape of the Militia, the next most pressing task was that the financing of the regiment had to be considered. And thus, it was agreed, that a Contingent Account should be drawn up by the Militia's paymaster twice each year, on 24 June and 24 December. That account needed to include a budget for the regimental hospital, an allowance for the transport of ammunition, plus an allowance for stationery and postage, and there was another detail – the account had to allow a Marching Allowance of one shilling for every mile that the companies marched, as long as it was also recorded where they had marched to and from. The account was to be signed off by the paymaster and then had to be submitted to the War Office.

Another meeting was held in Reading in October 1778, at which the number of drummers was decided (sixteen plus a drum major) and each company was to have a 'fifer'.[14] At the same meeting it was agreed that a small band should be formed, which, of course, required a music master to teach and drill the motley musical crew. Interestingly, the entire regiment was required to be inoculated against smallpox, although conscientious objection to the procedure was allowed.

It was in April 1793, fifteen years after the original formation of the Oxfordshire Militia, that Henry enlisted as a lieutenant. It was a decisive moment in his young life. But from the perspective of the Militia, compared with the reluctance of many to join, Henry's ready willingness must have been noted and been welcomed by the senior officers. Two months earlier, in February 1793, France had declared war on England. Later that same year, the Oxfordshire Regiment was instructed to accompany 1,000 French prisoners from Southampton to Salisbury. In 1794, the regiment was stationed on the Downs at Brighton,[15] where a camp of over 10,000 men had been created. Such tented camps included several militia regiments and were designed for training purposes: the men were taught how to drill, how to form up in squares and how to fire their weapons, and were inspected by their senior officers. It was a massive logistical exercise, which required the tents to be set out in lines in a pattern that replicated the regimental formation when it was on parade. There was a need for food, drink and latrines, plus washing facilities. The administration and coordination between regiments that lay behind such camps was considerable.

And it was this organisation with its mixture of strict hierarchical rules and rural casualness that Henry had joined. No doubt, he enjoyed the officer's uniform, for which, like all officers, he had had to pay, and as a young man of 22, must have enjoyed the admiring glances of people in Oxford and other towns when he sauntered through. What might his sisters Jane and Cassandra have made of their debonair officer brother?

Chapter 7

Henry's Promotion and Marriage

That same year, 1794, having only joined the Oxfordshire Militia one year earlier, Henry was promoted to be Acting Paymaster. It was a significant and important promotion because it meant that he was responsible for the finances of the regiment. And those finances were a mixture of the simple and the extremely complex; for example, for items of clothing, 'each private was to receive 30s per annum, drummers received £2 per annum and sergeants £3. 10s.'. All the other ranks needed to be clothed on joining up and then re-clothed each succeeding year, which meant that a deal had to be made between the regiment and the purveyors of uniforms – and it was from the clothing allowance, and the deals made, that profits could be made by senior officers. 'Each man was to receive a waistcoat, breeches, shirt, roller, and a pair of shoes and stockings.'[1] Then, in addition to the clothing arrangements, there were other logistical matters to be handled. If the regiment was required to march to a new posting, they were allowed to have one wagon to transport all their kit but could, in law, requisition wagons as long as the regiment paid the owner one shilling per mile for a four-horse wagon, or 9d per mile for a four-horse cart.[2] The requisitioned carts and wagons could only be used for one day, could carry loads of no more than 30cwt, and at the end of the day had to be returned to their owners. The combination of government funding, requisitioning of transport, the variety of payments to the militia soldiers and officers, the constant arguments about the inadequacy of clothing, and the fact that there was usually a year's gap between the order and payment for clothing being placed and the clothing arriving – all of this meant that Henry, as Acting Paymaster, would have been involved in complicated bookkeeping and a tense financial balancing act. To be a paymaster required the person appointed to have financial acumen and a high level of negotiating skills. Presumably, Henry fulfilled those criteria and brought to the role his famous charm and his head for figures. But he spotted a further opportunity and began to develop a subsidiary, unofficial job; he began to act as a private banker for some of his fellow officers. It was a shrewd if risky move. But that combination of shrewdness and the enjoyment of risk was a characteristic that Henry carried into his life after he had completed his regimental service, as we shall see.

In 1795, the regiment moved to Newhaven, where a serious riot occurred over the poor remuneration of the soldiers and the price they were having to pay for meat, flour and bread. The riot was not aimed against the officers but against the local shopkeepers, who were alleged to be charging high prices, but it was soon put down and two of the ringleaders, Edward Cooke of Witney and Henry Parish of Chipping Norton, were court-martialled and sentenced to be executed by firing squad. Those who were considered lesser ringleaders were sentenced to being given punishment by lashing. One was sentenced to 1,500 lashes, four others, 1,000 lashes each, and one, 500 lashes.

Before his execution, Edward Cooke (also known as Edward?) wrote a letter to his brother:

Dear Brother, This comes with my kind Love to you, and I hope you are well. I am brought very low and weak by long confinement and been in great trouble. Dear Brother, I am sentenced to Death and must Die on Saturday the 13th of June, and I hope God Almighty will forgive me my sins.

I never was nobody's foe but my own, and that was in Drinking and breaking the Sabbath, and that is a great sin.

I have prayed night and day to the Almighty God to forgive me and take me to heaven, and I hope my prayers be not in vain. I am going to die for what the Redgment [sic] done. I am not afraid to meet Death, for I have done no harm to no person, and that is a great comfort to me: there is a just God in Heaven who knows I am going to suffer innocently. Dear Brother, I should be very glad to see you before I Depart this Life. I hope God Almighty will be a Guardian over you and all my relations, and I hope we shall meet in heaven, where we shall be ever happy without End.

So, no more from the hand of your loving and Dying Brother. Edward Cooke.[3]

The Gentleman's Magazine[4] described the preliminaries of the execution:

The Oxfordshire Regiment marched on Friday night last, at eleven o'clock from Seaford to attend the execution ... the hour of Four was the time appointed to assemble. On the march the Regiment halted; and twelve men who had taken part in the riot were called out, when the Commanding Officer ordered them to fix their flints and prepare to execute the sentence. This was done to demonstrate to the men that state of obedience in which the officers were determined to hold them; and by this measure they felt more pointedly the folly of their former conduct, when those persons whom they had before made their leaders, were now to suffer death at their hands.[5]

The entire process was carefully stage-managed. The regiment was formed up on two wings at the place of execution. Forming a barrier at the rear of the two wings, on the rising ground of the valley, were 3,000 mounted cavalry, plus Horse Artillery. *The Gentleman's Magazine* continued: 'From the disposition of the ground and from the arrangement of the troops a more magnificent and more awful spectacle was never exhibited in this country.'

Before the execution, the lesser punishments of public lashings were carried out: the 1,500 lashes had been commuted to 300, and those sentenced to 1,000 lashes had had their punishment also reduced to 300. In the stillness of the morning, the sound of the whips biting into the bodies of the prisoners must have echoed around the valley. The chances of survival after such vicious punishment must have been extremely limited. If the bodies could withstand the shock, the wounds would have been subject to infection. All the while, the two waiting to be shot looked on. Then it was their turn. *The Gentleman's Magazine* reported:

> They walked along the vale in slow and solemn procession, accompanied by the clergyman who had conscientiously devoted his time to them from the moment the sentence had been made known, and they were fully prepared to meet their fate. Upon approaching the fatal spot, with resignation and religious confidence, they kneeled down upon their coffins with cool and deliberate firmness. When the one who was to drop the signal said to his comrades, 'Are you ready?' Upon the reply being made he dropped a prayer book; and the party did their duty at about 6 yards distance. One of them not appearing to be entirely dead was immediately shot through the head.

It was a carefully choreographed execution, designed to quell any further disobedience, but it was brutal, and the sounds and sights of the lashings and the sound of shots being fired would have seared themselves into the minds of the onlookers. It must have been a grim experience, and for Henry, the contrast between the harsh justice administered in the South Downs valley and the genteel charms of Steventon Rectory, the warmth of his family and the wit of his sisters, must have been disquieting. Might it have been this disturbing experience that led him, in January 1796, to consider joining the Regulars?

We can glimpse the way his mind was moving in a letter that Jane wrote to Cassandra on 9–10 January 1796.[6] Jane describes a ball she had attended the previous night and talks teasingly of taking James with her: 'We were so terrible good as to take James in our carriage, though there were three of us before; but indeed he deserves encouragement for the very great improvement which has lately taken place in his dancing.'

She also mentions Henry, who had been at the ball, but he had left for Harpsden, near Henley-on-Thames, the home of Mrs Cassandra Austen as a child; her father, the Reverend Thomas Leigh, had been the rector there for over thirty years, but the parish was now being looked after by Henry's cousin, the Reverend Edward Cooper (1770–1833) as the curate.

Jane's letter continues with news of family and friends, but also states: 'Henry Is still hankering after the Regulars, and as his project of purchasing the adjutancy of the Oxfordshire is now over, he has got a scheme in his head about getting a lieutenancy and adjutancy in the 86th, a new-raised regiment, which he fancies will be ordered to the Cape of Good Hope.'

Note that, as was the common practice, Henry purchased the adjutancy. But it is in the next sentence that we can get an inkling of Jane's wry understanding of Henry: 'I heartily hope that he will, as usual, be disappointed in this scheme.'

There is a note of humorous but exasperated fondness in what Jane writes. Clearly, Henry was a confident, not to say, over-confident young man full of ideas and bubbling with energy who was always looking forward to a newer and better project.

Jane got her wish; Henry did not join the Regulars but instead stayed with the Militia and was soon moving to a new camp at Sheerness, and relocated with them from there to Chelmsford Barracks.

Henry's life with the Oxfordshire Militia, however, does not seem to have been overly demanding. In a letter written by Jane on 1 September 1796, when Jane was staying at Rowlings in Kent, she tells Cassandra:

> Henry leaves us tomorrow for Yarmouth, as he wishes very much to consult his physician there, on whom he has great reliance. He is better than he was when he first came, though still by no means well. According to his present plan, he will not return here till about the 23rd, and bring with him, if he can, leave of absence for three weeks, as he wants very much to have some shooting at Godmersham.[7]

Henry's Promotion and Marriage   67

On Monday, 5 September, Jane reports him as having been at a dance in Goodnestone, so he must have achieved his desire of being given leave of absence from his regiment. But, to be fair, there was also concern about the time that the other ranks were spending on regimental duties away from home, a concern that became particularly acute at harvest time when their help in their families' fields would have been necessary. In some cases, for example in Sussex in 1801, a detachment of that county's militia was allowed to return home to help with the harvest.[8]

Meanwhile, for Henry, romance was in the air. It centred on a woman called Mary Pearson, who was a naval captain's daughter based in Greenwich. In the summer of 1796, Henry went to stay with her family, and it was arranged that she should travel to Steventon to meet the Austens. Jane Austen makes a characteristically caustic comment about Mary Pearson in a letter she wrote to Cassandra on 18 September: 'If Miss Pearson should return with me, pray be careful not to expect too much beauty ... my Mother I am sure will be disappointed, if she does not take great care.'[9]

How and why the relationship with Mary Pearson ended is not clear. But that it did, is not open to doubt.

Claire Tomalin highlights Henry's tendency towards vacillation:

He was not entirely committed to the militia ... Much as [Jane] loved Henry, she was clear-sighted about his not always realistic ambitions and his vacillations, although even she may not have known that he was simultaneously pursuing a quite different plan to become a clergyman in nearby Chawton. He was also involved in complicated dealings and was about to pay off a debt to his father.[10]

Perhaps it was on the rebound from his relationship with Mary Pearson, and the breakdown of that relationship, that Henry began to think again of his older cousin, Elizabeth 'Eliza' de Feuillide (1761–1813), as a possible life partner, and in November 1796 he went to see her. She was the only daughter of Philadelphia Austen (1730–92) and her husband, Tysoe Hancock (1723–75), who was the son of the Reverend Thomas Hancock, Vicar of Hollingbourne, Kent. Tysoe Hancock had trained in medicine and sailed to India in 1745 to serve with the East India Company. In 1752, Philadelphia Austen had sailed to India on what was commonly called the 'fishing fleet', i.e. she was 'fishing' for a wealthy husband. In 1753, she married Tysoe Hancock, who was twenty years older than she was. By 1758, Tysoe Hancock had progressed to become a surgeon in Madras, and he and Philadelphia moved to Bengal, where they became friends with Warren Hastings (1732–1818), who was then the governor. In December 1761, after eight years of marriage, Tysoe and Philadelphia became the proud parents of Elizabeth, who was named after Hastings' stillborn daughter. He became Eliza's godfather. And as a result, rumours began to swirl concerning the identity of the father of Elizabeth: was it Tysoe Hancock or was it Warren Hastings? The fact that Warren Hastings settled upon Eliza a trust, which had an income of £700 per annum, only added spice to the gossip.

In 1765, Philadelphia and Tysoe Hancock returned to England with their daughter, Eliza, who was 4 years of age. Unfortunately, the family hit financial problems and Tysoe had to return to India to earn more money. His health was poor, but he remained determined to send as much money as possible back to England for Eliza's future. He appointed the Reverend George Austen as one of the trustees of a fund set up for her. But Tysoe Hancock never returned to England to see his daughter: he died in Calcutta in November 1775.

His death meant that Philadelphia and Eliza, now aged 14, who were living in England, had to make decisions about how they were to live. They were fairly well off. Liza had her trust fund monies, and Philadelphia had been left over £8,000 by her husband.[11] It gave her the freedom to travel and so she and Eliza decided to go to the Continent. They travelled in Germany and Flanders but finally settled in Paris in 1779, because the cost of living was cheaper there. It also meant that

Eliza could attend a finishing school. It was a decision that set off an interesting chain of events. This is how Claire Tomalin describes it:

> Someone presented Eliza to the thirty-year-old Jean François Capot de Feuillide as a wealthy heiress, related to 'Lord Hastings', and presumed to have more expectations from him, and he was presented to her as an aristocrat with large estates in the south. Both descriptions had an element of truth, but neither was entirely true ... he had no title, and Eliza's claim that she was becoming a Countess by marrying him was based either on fantasy or, more likely, on some misrepresentation.[12]

But marry him she did. He had purchased 5,000 acres of marshy land at Le Marais (the word means 'swamp'), near Guyenne, which he believed gave him the right to style himself 'Count'. And from their marriage onwards, Eliza referred to herself as 'Countess'.

Unfortunately, in 1782, Philadelphia's health began to falter, and she and Eliza made several visits back to England, where Eliza's title 'Countess' added a certain frisson to social occasions and, no doubt, much fluttering of fans to hide the whispered gossip at dances in great houses. They travelled backwards and forwards between England and France and in 1786, Eliza and the Count had a son, whom she named Hastings. Presumably, the choice of name was significant. She returned to England, where she lived for the next two years.

It was during that same year of 1786 that she spent Christmas with the Austen family at Steventon. Henry, aged 15, and James, aged 20, were enchanted by her. She was an older, sophisticated woman who had had an exotic life: she had lived in India, had travelled in Germany and France, and was married (wasn't she?) to a French count. What could be more captivating? Compared with the humdrum rural and isolated life of the Rectory, she embodied the excitements of imaginary worlds. From that moment on, both James and Henry developed a crush on her. And it could be said, to use a cliché, that Henry thereafter carried a torch for her.

While staying with the Austen family at Steventon that Christmas, Eliza took a lively and flirtatious part in the family theatricals. Putting on plays was one of the family's happy traditions. Eliza perhaps needed these exciting events to distract herself from worrying about her baby son. He was showing signs of failing to develop normally and was subject to epileptic seizures.

On returning to London after such an escapist time in Steventon, she was faced with a further challenge: her godfather, Warren Hastings, was under political pressure, the charges being that he had mishandled his rule as Governor General of India, had abused his position, and had not behaved properly in his management of various local wars. Further, he had antagonised some influential members of the council that had been created to provide checks and balances around his leadership. It was alleged that he had gained considerable personal wealth from his direction of the East India Company. There were some powerful figures in England who were determined to cut him down to size, but on his return to Britain in June 1785, Hastings thought that he could handle and defuse the criticism he was facing. It was not to be. The political opposition to him grew and on 7 May 1787, he was arrested by the Sergeant at Arms to face the charges against him in the House of Lords. Nine months later, in February 1788, he was impeached.

This was the background to Eliza's life in London after the rural Christmas festivities with the Austen family. It cannot have been an easy time for her. Warren Hastings and his wife, however, were very kind. They invited Eliza and her mother to their house in St James's Square and ensured that mother and daughter could use their private box at the opera.

But maybe, even in those heady social and political times, Eliza's thoughts might have strayed towards her cousin, Henry. She had seen something in him that attracted her, for later, when he was a student at Oxford, she wrote to a female friend extolling his looks, 'Henry is now rather more than six feet high, I believe', and added, 'and is certainly endowed with uncommon abilities.'[13]

In 1788, Eliza returned with her mother to Paris, where she met up with her husband, and little Hastings saw his father for the first time. But the situation in France was becoming even more troublesome, and, in any case, the Count was suffering from a fever and continuous financial difficulties. Eliza, her 4-year-old son Hastings and her mother decided to return to England and settled in Orchard Street, London.[14] It was a curiously nomadic existence that mother and daughter had embraced over the previous nine years and must have occasioned conversations at Steventon, where the Austens were, by contrast, firmly rooted in the Hampshire countryside.

But Philadelphia, George Austen's sister, had been ill for some time and died in 1792. It meant that Eliza was now on her own.

Meanwhile, the Count, who was a Royalist, stayed in France and in the chaos of the Revolution, in 1794, as he attempted to escape to England, he was arrested in Paris and was guillotined. It meant that Eliza had to consider what her future as a widow might be. She had her income from the trust fund, it is true, but her little boy was a sickly child, suffering from epilepsy and other maladies. The future for her was uncertain.

In a letter to her cousin Phylly[15] on 3 May 1797, Eliza wrote about Henry:

> Captn Austen has just spent a few days in town; I suppose you know that our Cousin Henry is now Captain, Paymaster and Adjutant. He is a very lucky young man and bids fair to possess a considerable share of riches and honours ... I believe he has given up all thoughts of the Church, and he is right, for he certainly is not so fit for a parson as a soldier.[16]

It is a statement that between the lines hints at a developing relationship between Eliza and Henry. And at some point in 1797, Henry, who had always been more than half in love with her, offered her a proposal of marriage.

Eliza did not tell her godfather, Warren Hastings, about the proposed marriage until a few days before the wedding. Hastings was then living at Daylesford, near Cheltenham, and Eliza wrote to assure him that Henry had a 'comfortable income' and went on to describe his character: 'the excellence of his heart, temper, and understanding, together with his attachment to me, his affection for my little boy, and disinterested concurrence in the disposal of my property, in favour of this latter'.[17]

And so, to Henry's delight, despite the difference in their ages – he was ten years her junior – Eliza and Henry were married in Marylebone Parish Church,[18] London, in December 1797. He was still in the Militia as a captain and an adjutant, and she was a wealthy young widow with a 9-year-old child who was subject to convulsions and fainting fits.

It is interesting to compare Henry's marriage to Eliza with the courtships and marriages in Jane Austen's novels where prospective marriages are sometimes, but not always, about wealth and land, and therefore, about local hierarchy and power.[19] For example, in *Persuasion*, Lady Russell tries to persuade Anne Elliot to marry her cousin, William Elliot, and reminds Anne that thereby she would become 'Lady Elliot' and would live in Kellynch Hall. Anne Elliot rejects the idea because intuitively, she does not trust her cousin. In short, she rejects the seductive possibilities of Title and Land. And by agreeing to marry Captain Wentworth, as well as recognising his personal qualities, perhaps it is implied by Jane Austen that commerce (flourishing internationally because it was protected by the Royal Navy) and gentlemanly behaviour were not inherently incompatible. Is this a moment when a new and rising 'gentlemanly' class begins to move into the foreground of national life?[20] By contrast, Elizabeth Bennet in *Pride and Prejudice* falls in love with Mr Darcy and through marriage to him will become the chatelaine of Pemberley and its thousands of acres – with not a mention of commerce anywhere.

When Henry married Eliza, although she was relatively wealthy, had a title and, theoretically, owned land in France, it was not a marriage about gaining power arising from the ownership of land in England; it was rather, from Henry's perspective, a romance in the courtly love tradition. His teenage infatuation with his delightful cousin had now come to head-spinning fruition later in his life. And from Eliza's perspective, it was a marriage that meant she would gain a kind man as a husband and a kind father for her disabled son. Moreover, with Henry's amused delight in social occasions, the marriage might result in a shared and loving social happiness.

One year after that marriage, in a letter to Cassandra on 25 November 1798, Jane Austen wrote about Henry's blossoming career: 'I suppose you have heard from Henry himself that his affairs are happily settled. We do not know who furnishes the qualification.'[21]

By 'qualification', Jane Austen was referring to the fact that Henry had managed to persuade the powers that be in his regiment that he was creditworthy as an adjutant. He had to provide 'financial guarantees, both personally and from two other sureties to a total of £2,000, as a safeguard against misappropriation of regimental funds'.[22]

At a guess, one can assume that one of his sureties was his wife, Eliza.

The state of the nation at this time was one of high anxiety: invasion was expected. Meanwhile, in 1798, a rebellion had broken out in Ireland. The Oxfordshire Militia was ordered to embark for Ireland to join the regular troops who were already there. For the Regimental Adjutant and Paymaster, Henry Austen, and his colleagues, such a move would have required extra work and careful coordination of transport, money and supplies. The fact that in that same year the French had invaded Ireland at the behest of the rebels lent further urgency to the situation. From Henry's perspective it must have been satisfying that the rebellion in Ireland was eventually contained and put down. It accounts for the fact that one year later, in October 1799, the Secretary of State for War wrote to the commanding officer (at that point it was Colonel W. Gore-Langton) offering the Oxfordshire Regiment the opportunity to remain in Ireland until Christmas. It is not certain when the regiment actually returned to England, but it was either in December 1799 or January 1800 that it was disembodied, i.e. stood down.

Henry had been with the Oxfordshire Militia for almost seven years. It had not all been marching, manoeuvres and living in tented camps; indeed, because of his friendly relationship with the colonel, he was able to take periods of time away from the regiment. In November 1794, as we have seen, Henry 'took three weeks' leave and spent time with his family. He was able to be at the Rectory for his sister Jane's nineteenth birthday to see her receive the gift from her father of a mahogany writing desk with a drawer for paper and a glass ink-stand.'[23]

So, Henry had made the best of his opportunities in the Militia. He had gained promotion, developed his administrative and financial skills, and had ensured that he had plenty of time for rest and recreation. And perhaps most importantly of all, in a culture devoted to knowing and cultivating influential people, he had developed a network of relationships with his fellow officers. Equally important was the fact that as an administrative officer, at no point had he had to face the enemy. But what was he to do now? He was 28 years old, a married man with a delightful, socially extravert wife, and was stepfather to her ailing son. Should he think again about entering the Church (despite what Eliza said) or should he make use of his newly found skills in finance? Unfortunately, there is no extant documentation that can help us to understand his inner motives – unlike in the novels of his sister where, as Alexandra Mullen states: 'One of Austen's greatest gifts was to capture her characters in the process of thinking.'[24]

It was a significant moment in Henry's life. Certainty, and the close relationships forged in the regiment, would have to give way to radical uncertainty. Could he use the relationships he had developed to forge a new career?

Chapter 8

The Lure of Finance

Henry was granted paid leave in 1800 to think about his future. He had the regimental accounts to complete and so re-joined the regiment on the Isle of Wight in November. It was there he discovered that the auditors of his accounts were entirely satisfied with them – all very satisfactory.

That same month, on a visit to Steventon, he must have been aware of potential changes in his father and mother's lives. George Austen, the great *paterfamilias*, decided that it was time to retire. That momentous decision also meant he had to decide where he and his wife and their two unmarried daughters, Jane and Cassandra, should live. It seems that without consulting them, George Austen and his wife decided on Bath, perhaps because Mrs Austen's brother, James Leigh Perrot, and his wife lived at 1, Paragon for several months of the year, but there were many other things to consider. Jane wrote to Cassandra on 3 January 1801:

> My Mother looks forward with as much certainty as you can do, to our keeping two Maids – my father is the only one not in the secret – We plan having a steady Cook, and a young giddy Housemaid, with a sedate middle-aged Man, who is to undertake the double office of Husband to the former and sweetheart to the latter … there are three parts of Bath which we have thought of as likely to have houses in them – Westgate buildings, Charles Street and some of the short streets leading from Laura Place or Pulteney Street.[1]

As is frequently the case with Jane's letters, it is difficult to disentangle reality from wit.

At the same time as making the decision about Bath, George Austen arranged that his oldest son, James, should take over as Curate of Steventon, but George presumably would retain some of the tithe to provide income for his retirement.

Meanwhile, Henry was still pondering his career after the Militia. He had gained considerable experience in the Militia's financial underpinnings, and he knew about supplies and the canny negotiations required to obtain the same. And so, it is to the complexity of these dealings that we must now turn in order to discover what his talents might have been as an administrator and financial officer.

In the eighteenth century, the Regular Army (not the Militia) was paid in the following way. The Estimates were presented to the Treasury by the Paymaster General. The Treasury then paid a lump sum into his bank account. The Paymaster General issued payments in cash to each regimental agent as required, who, in turn, issued payments to the regimental paymaster. The next link in the chain were the captains, who paid their men.

The system was then reversed: the captains reported to the regimental paymaster; the regimental paymaster to the regimental agent, and the regimental agent to the Paymaster General. The captains accounted to the regimental paymaster; he in turn to the agent; and the agent to the Secretary at War. When the Secretary at War had accepted the accounts of all the agents, the Paymaster General refunded any balance due to the Treasury.[2]

Of course, this system was open to serious abuse. Thus, for example, the Paymaster General, a politician, could delay paying the regimental agent and by putting the lump sum on deposit could cream off the interest. He might also send only a portion of the lump sum to the regimental agent and keep the remainder for himself. The sums involved were huge. Lord Holland, for example, when he was Paymaster General, had annual balances in his personal account of almost half a million pounds.

If that kind of mismanagement and misappropriation happened at national level, it is reasonable to assume that similar sleights of hand were also operating at regimental and militia level. At the same time, recruitment for the Regular Army necessitated the offering of bounties. In 1798, the bounty for recruits was three guineas, with a further two guineas allotted to the recruiting officer. And there was even a system that ensured that the more men an officer recruited, the more his own pay and rank would increase.

In the militias it was subtly different – at least, in principle. The Militia was regarded in some ways as the personal property of the Lord Lieutenant and his commanding officer, and was financed by a county-based Land Tax. This was paid by all persons owning land and property, at a rate of between two and four shillings in the pound. The taxpayers were not only the aristocracy and country landowners, but also local farmers, tradesmen and shopkeepers. The rate of tax was set by Parliament each year in a Land Tax Act. However, the oversight of the collection of the tax was carried out not at national but at local level by 'commissioners', usually gentry, whose names were incorporated in each Land Tax Act. The actual collection of tax was carried out by local farmers and tradesmen. Again, the system was open to evasion, fraud and abuse of all kinds.

The financing of the regiment was extremely complex. For instance, although the government supplied some equipment, the militias were responsible for that equipment's storage and repair, and although the arms and armaments supplied were supposed to last for twelve years, in some instances the arms and armaments were defective from the beginning or wore out long before the twelve-year limit. And this was not the only complexity with which Henry had to deal. As we have seen, the actual arrangements for the pay of officers and other ranks were not a simple matter, either.

When a private joined the regiment, he was given the bare minimum of clothing, but no overcoat was provided for when he was on guard duty. As a result, if the Militia by chance had a few greatcoats, they had to be shared between the soldiers, and when there were not enough greatcoats to go around, it was just too bad. Then, once the private had been paid (he received 8d per day), certain sums of money were automatically deducted from his wages. These deductions were called 'stoppages'. In 1792, a Royal Warrant decreed that over a one-year period, the maximum amount that could be deducted should be no more than £3. 5s. 5d., and from this amount and his weekly pay, the soldier was supposed to provide himself with a pair of gaiters and stockings, two shirts, two pairs of gloves, a forage cap, and pay for the replacements when the originals wore out. He also had to supply himself with combs, clothes brushes and pipe clay, and had to pay for washing, and shoe repairs, and pay three shillings per week for food. It was a chaotically bureaucratic system.

What all this reveals is that the overall financial system in the militias was extremely complicated, requiring meticulous bookkeeping (or sleight of hand?), and in the case of the Oxfordshire Militia, the business was overseen and administered by Henry Austen. Clearly, when Eliza had referred to his 'share of riches and honours', it is reasonable to assume that that reference might have meant he was operating as his immediate seniors were doing, that is, creaming off percentages of the regimental income. It was simply the way the entire system operated.

His sister Jane might also have also been aware of the system because she was completely *au fait* with Militia matters. In *Pride and Prejudice*, drafted in 1796–7 but not published until 1813, she states that two of the Bennet sisters, Catherine and Lydia, were excitedly aware of the Militia, which was headquartered nearby:

At present, indeed, they were well supplied both with news and happiness by the recent arrival of a militia regiment in the neighbourhood; it was to remain the whole winter, and Meryton was the headquarters.

Their visits to Mrs Philips were now productive of the most interesting intelligence. Every day added something to their knowledge of the officers' names and connections. Their lodgings were not long a secret, and at length they began to know the officers themselves. Mr Philips visited them all, and this opened to his nieces a source of felicity unknown before. They could talk of nothing but officers.[3]

And Jane herself went to balls at Basingstoke, where three of the companies of the South Devon Militia were billeted and whose officers were sought after as dancing partners. It was the Minuet that began each ball, as James Austen Leigh writes: 'it was a slow and solemn movement, expressive of grace and dignity, rather than of merriment. It abounded in formal bows and curtsies, with measured paces, forwards, backwards and sideways, and many complicated gyrations. It was executed by one lady and gentleman, amidst the admiration or the criticism, of surrounding spectators.'[4]

Jane loved dancing and frequently writes about dances in her novels, including a wonderfully witty and sardonic piece in *Emma*:

> It may be possible to do without dancing entirely. Instances have been known of young people passing many, many months successively, without being at any ball of any description, and no material injury accrue to either body or mind; but when a beginning is made – when the felicities of rapid motion have once been, though slightly felt – it must be a very heavy set that does not ask for more.[5]

During 1794–5, Henry's own militia, the Oxfordshire Regiment, was stationed not far away at Petersfield, Hampshire, and three of the companies were billeted at Alton, Farringdon and Chawton.[6] But whether Henry or Jane attended balls in those places is not recorded.

At a more granular level and away from the gaiety of dances and the fun of dalliances, it is important to realise that there were private offices in London specialising in selling officer commissions. The most prestigious of these was an office called Cox and Greenwood, named after the two cousins who ran it. An entry in the ledgers of Hoare's Bank on 15 October 1796 reveals that Henry paid them the large sum of £300.[7]

That was probably for the purchase of a more senior Militia post. In short, like all his fellow officers, Henry was gaming the system. And although the Oxfordshire Militia was formally stood down ('disembodied') in 1799/1800, administrative and financial tasks remained. Henry was officially appointed to be the Militia's agent. He would 'continue to administer pay and half-pay for the Oxfords at the rate of two pence in the pound for the whole payroll plus pay of one soldier at sixpence a day, and could also provide banking services for its officers including lucrative interest on loans'.[8]

It was the beginning of a new career, which required not only financial acumen but a shrewd appreciation of the relationship between risk and reward. If Henry made a loan, for example, to a fellow officer, could he be certain that the loan would be repaid including interest, as agreed? He also needed to be aware of what we today call 'commodification', that is, the process of treating anything, be it a service, an object or an opportunity, as a commodity that can be bought or sold.

The eighteenth century was aware of and practised commodification in various parts of national life, for example, in the commodification of parishes. Thus, the arrangement made for James to take over Steventon from his father involved treating the parish as an income-generating commodity. In the same way, so it was with Henry's new business as an agent for the Oxfordshire Regiment: everything was treated as though it were a commodity and therefore was open to being bought, sold and traded. Nevertheless, capital was needed to underpin this new venture. It seems likely that some of Henry's money from his time in the Militia, plus money deposited by Eliza in their joint bank account, provided the capital base. And thus began 'H. Austen and Co.' of Cleveland Court, which being close to St James's and Pall Mall, conveyed a sense of status and probity. It was a suitably impressive address for his new office and was a symbolic statement about his new career. He had made his decision. He had not chosen the Church of England; instead, he had decided to become a military agent. He was building on his experience in the Oxfordshire Militia and, no doubt, relied on many of the contacts he had made in that chapter of his life. There was something of the risk-taking entrepreneur about him.

Writing from Steventon to Cassandra on 25 January 1801, when Cassandra was staying at Godmersham, Jane mentioned Henry's new place of work: 'I dare say you will spend a very pleasant three weeks in town. I hope you will see everything worthy of notice, from the Opera House to Henry's office in Cleveland Court; and I shall expect you to lay in a stock of intelligence that may procure me amusement for a twelvemonth to come.'

In order to signal the sense of social distinction, Henry and Eliza leased a house at 24, Upper Berkeley Street, near Portman Square, staffed by her loyal and beloved French maids and cook.[9] So, we might imagine Henry dressed as a gentleman, making his way with confidence and maybe an understated swagger, to his new office. He had succeeded as an officer; he had a wealthy wife; and the world lay at his feet. And to prove and display his wealth, he also owned a barouche with four horses, and employed a coachman to drive it.[10] Style was all.

But tragedy struck. On 9 October 1801, Eliza's son, Hastings de Feuillide, died. It must have been an awful blow for Eliza, and a great sadness for Henry and for the French servants who had so assiduously cared for him. The funeral and burial took place at St John-at-Hampstead, where the little boy was interred in the same grave as his grandmother, Philadelphia Hancock.

Henry himself had been seriously ill just prior to his stepson's death, and so it must have felt as though the wheel of fate had suddenly turned downwards. But Henry was not in his new agency venture entirely on his own, and in any case, in law, he, rather than Eliza, was the inheritor of the estate of his late stepson. And that might have resulted in a further inflow of capital.

Henry had two partners in the new agency: first, Henry Maunde, whose family were based around Leominster in Herefordshire (he was a former officer with the Oxfordshire Militia who had succeeded Henry as Paymaster); and second, a man called Charles James (1758–1821), who was more of a 'sleeping partner', but who had the advantage of being a protégé of Lord Moira and the Royal household. The risks in the new business were, therefore, shared. At least, that is the appearance on the surface.

On 3 November 1801, a quasi-legal document was drawn up between the partners. It was headed 'Articles of Agreement between Charles James Esq., Henry Thomas Austen Esq. and Henry Maunde Esq.'. That the heading places Charles James as the first in the list suggests that he was the most influential and significant of the three. In that document, one of the paragraphs states, 'Henry Thomas Austen and Henry Maunde make themselves responsible for their attendance at the office and the correct management of accounts' and highlights Charles James's powers: 'I have at all times a perfect right to enter the said office and inspect all papers and accounts.'[11] The document implies that Charles James, although a sleeping partner, was a powerful personality lurking in the background, and that Austen and Maunde were somehow subordinate to him. Had Charles James invested in the new agency? Or was he useful to Austen and Maunde because he was a man with contacts in all the right circles? It is all rather opaque, and the tone of the document is decidedly cool, not to say, threatening.

Charles James is a singularly elusive character. A published poet, he was also the author of several books on military matters. He had trained as a lawyer at Gray's Inn but switched to Lincoln's Inn under the name 'Charles Simpson', which he later petitioned to change back to 'James' because he said that he had entered his uncle's surname by accident. He was fluent in Latin and French and had been educated at the Jesuit College in Liège. He was a supporter of the French Revolution (his friends nicknamed him 'Jacobin James') and had published in London in 1793 a document entitled 'An Extenuation of the conduct of the French Revolutionists'.[12] It is intensely and unreadably flowery. Also in 1793, he had served as a captain in the West Middlesex Militia; two years later, in 1795, he transferred to the North York Militia and somehow during those years had become known to Lord Moira, for whom he had a high regard and who became his patron. In fact, Lord Moira appointed him as his confidential agent and financial adviser. When Moira became Master of the Ordnance, he appointed Charles James as his 'French Secretary', a suitably ambiguous title with an unspecified role.[13]

Because of his Jacobin leanings and his fluency in French, some have suggested that Charles James might have been a spy; others are less sure. So, why did Henry Austen and Henry Maunde have anything to do with him? Or, expressed another way, what did Charles James hope to gain by creating a business liaison with the two agency partners, Austen and Maunde? Was it just to obtain easy and unquestioned loans for his patron, Lord Moira? Or did Charles James consider Austen and Maunde to be innocents abroad who could be manipulated for his own ends?

An undated letter[14] written by Henry Austen to Charles James, who was living at 105, Great Portland Street, reveals the way that the agency was working:

> Dear James,
> As you and I need not use superfluous ceremony on topics perfectly understood between us, I beg to inform you that if you can get a respectable Field Officer to give the usual certificate for a young friend of ours and for whom I will answer on my reputation, who is desirous of purchasing a commission and whose money is lodged, I will pay you ten pounds [?] [writing illegible] on the Gentleman's being gazetted ... Let us meet as soon as you can. I shall be at home this evening and if you will drop in, the matter may be settled immediately.

Isn't there something hasty and possibly clandestine in the tone of this letter? It reads like an under-the-counter arrangement with risky implications. It has none of the open warmth and affection, for example, of letters that Henry sent to his family in Steventon. Would they have approved of what he was doing? Does it give us some insight into another and carefully hidden side of Henry's character?

Be that as it may, let us return to the agency. As the prospects of peace in the struggle with Napoleon seemed about to be realised (the Peace of Amiens of 1802 formally signified this), it meant that the normal work of the agency would necessarily suffer. In short, the regiment would need fewer things. What was to be done? Henry and his partners became 'half-pay' agents, that is, they were responsible for paying officers who remained on half-pay and who received payment every six months, but if those officers did not live in or near London (and the pay was only distributed in London), they could appoint an agency to collect the pay on their behalf, for which service the agency would charge six pence in the pound.[15] It was not perhaps the way that the partners had foreseen how their new agency and embryonic bank would operate, and it was unlikely to have been as remunerative as they had hoped, but perhaps something else would turn up. Henry was not deterred. He was always bubbling with confidence.

Chapter 9

Henry's Success and Luck

As we have seen, the two main partners, Henry Austen and Henry Maunde, were in the business of providing financial services to the Militia regiments that had been disembodied, but they were also buying and selling commissions to officers. It had to be slightly under the counter because, as Douglas Allen says, 'all purchases were technically subject to the approval of the Crown and the king reportedly paid close attention to the granting of commissions, especially at the higher ranks'.[1] Whilst the buying and selling of commissions was theoretically illicit, it was nevertheless known about and commonly practised, and indeed was only finally and formally abolished in Great Britain in 1871.

Jane Austen herself knew about the purchasing and sale of commissions and explored the whole business of settling debts and paying for commissions in *Pride and Prejudice*[2] when Darcy pays off Wickham's debts and a commission for Wickham is purchased.

It was a subtle, class-based system: anyone wishing to join the most prestigious regiments, for instance, one of the Guards regiments, had to pay the highest rates, but anyone purchasing such an officer post was required to sign an affidavit denying that they had any transaction with the agency. It meant that Austen and Maunde, who were also navy agents, were sailing close to the wind (no pun intended). It would be interesting to know if Jane and Cassandra knew in detail what was going on. It is difficult to believe that two such perceptive young women would not have had an inkling.

But as peace became, for the moment, more likely, Henry Austen and Henry Maunde had to seek other forms of trade to support their business. Henry accompanied Eliza to France to see if she could recover some of the lands belonging to her late husband that had been confiscated during the Revolution, and while he was there, he began to investigate the wine trade. Might that add another profitable product to his portfolio? Certainly, it seemed a possibility, but everything depended on the fragile peace actually holding.

It didn't. The Peace of Amiens was broken in May 1803, which meant that the military agency side of the business received a timely boost. They moved offices to Canon Row, near the Houses of Parliament, and were successful in obtaining the agency for two more regiments, the Nottinghamshire Militia and the North Devon Militia (the South Devon Militia had been billeted at Basingstoke in the mid-1790s – was there a connection with Henry Austen at that point?). The colonel of the North Devons, Lord Boringdon, was to become an Austen family acquaintance a few years later and was associated with an infamous scandal.

Two years after the move to Canon Row, Henry Austen and Henry Maunde moved offices again. This time it was to Number One, The Courtyard, Albany, close to Piccadilly. It was yet another highly prestigious address. Charles James, the third, sleeping, partner, moved into one of the new apartments nearby; meanwhile, Henry and Eliza moved to a new house: 16, Michael's Place, Brompton, an up-and-coming fashionable part of London, which only fifty years previously had been a place of market gardens and horticulture.

But then there was a family death. George Austen had been described as 'suffering from oppression in the head with fever, violent tremulousness, and the greatest degree of Feebleness'.[3] On 21 January 1805, he died, in Bath.

In a letter from Jane to her brother Frank, on Monday, 21 January 1805, Jane wrote:

Our dear Father has closed his virtuous and happy life, in a death almost as free from suffering as his Children could have wished ... Being quite insensible of his own state, he was spared all the pain of separation, and he went off almost in his sleep ... My Mother bears the Shock as well as possible; she was quite prepared for it, and feels all the blessing of being spared a long Illness.[4]

George was buried in the crypt of the rebuilt St Swithin's, Walcot, the church in which he and Cassandra Leigh had married in 1764. There were two pressing questions to be dealt with after the funeral: first, would Mrs Austen decide to move somewhere else as soon as possible?

As the lease on the rented house in Bath still had three months left to run, the decision was made to remain where she, Jane and Cassandra lived for the time being. It was a sensible decision, for it gave Mrs Austen and her daughters time to quietly grieve, and by walking the elegant streets of Bath and through visiting friends, enabled them gradually to come to terms with their loss.

The second question concerned money. How would that be handled? It was natural that Mrs Austen should look to Henry, who, despite what he described as his own 'precarious income', assured his mother, and his sisters, Jane and Cassandra, that £50 would be sent to them by him every year. It was hardly munificent, and Henry obviously hoped that his other brothers would rally to the cause. James added a further £50, and Edward was expected to offer another £100 a year.

It might be that these inter-family decisions prompted one of the classic episodes in *Sense and Sensibility*, when John Dashwood (the son of his father's first wife), and his wife, Fanny, are debating the sum of money that Mr Henry Dashwood had left in his will to his daughters by his second wife – Elinor, Marianne and Margaret. The sum was £3,000. However, Fanny Dashwood protests that the sum is too great because it would deprive their own son, Harry, of his future inheritance.

'It was my father's last request to me', [said] her husband, 'that I should assist his widow and daughters.'

'He did not know what he was talking of, I dare say, ten to one but he was light-headed at the time. Had he been in his right senses, he could not have thought of such a thing as begging you to give away half your fortune from your own child.'

'He did not stipulate for any particular sum, my dear Fanny; he only requested me, in general terms, to assist them, and make their situation more comfortable than it was in his power to do so. Perhaps it would have been as well if he had left it wholly to myself. He could hardly suppose I should neglect them. But as he required the promise, I could not do less than give it: at least I thought so at the time. The promise, therefore, was given and must be performed. Something must be done for them whenever they leave Norland and settle in a new home.'

'Well then, let something be done for them; but that something need not be three thousand pounds. Consider', she added, 'that when the money is once parted with, it never can return. Your sisters will marry, and it will be gone for ever. If, indeed, it could ever be restored to our poor little boy …'

'Why, to be sure,' said her husband, very gravely, 'that would make a great difference. The time may come when Harry will regret that so large a sum was parted with. If he should have a numerous family, for instance, it would be a very convenient addition.'

'To be sure, it would.'

'Perhaps, then, it would be better for all parties if the sum were diminished one half. Five hundred pounds would be a prodigious increase to their fortunes!'

As the conversation between husband and wife continues, the total to be given to the mother and her daughters is gradually whittled away. And beneath that argument lies a deeper theme: the contrast between head and heart, between the desire to be generous because of family affection and the devious desire to hold on to what one has. It is a point that Ruth apRoberts makes: 'As literalism was developing in the late eighteenth century, along with the evangelical movement, the most current philosophical dichotomy was the intellect-emotion one, pre-eminently the Sense and Sensibility of Jane Austen.'5

Whilst *Sense and Sensibility* was written long before the Reverend George Austen's death, Jane Austen was all too aware of how precarious her own financial situation was, because it depended upon the largesse, or otherwise, of her brothers. The sense of dependent helplessness must have been worrying.

And as for Henry, his own financial uncertainties could not have been too far from the forefront of his mind. One month after his father's death, he was nurturing the aristocratic networks on which some of the income of his agency depended. He met Lord Moira, a well-connected, Irish-born aristocrat who had close links with the Prince Regent, himself a charming but extravagant spendthrift, and had loaned him thousands of pounds. Moira had served with some distinction in the army, seeing action in several battles during the American War of Independence. He kindly gave Henry a letter of introduction to Lord Nelson, whose baby daughter Horatia, incidentally, had been baptised at Marylebone Parish Church in 1801. Those links with Lord Moira were to lead eventually to financial difficulties for Henry because he had lent Moira large sums of money. It was a rackety but headily exciting part of society in which Henry was now moving. He himself was charming, good looking, tall and apparently successful – but perhaps his pleasure in being associated with the Prince Regent's 'set' might have led him to ignore what should have been a banker's natural caution.

His brother, Frank, had been successful too in his naval career. He was now captain of HMS *Canopus*, an eighty-gun, third-rate ship of the line that had been captured from the French at the Battle of the Nile in 1798 and had been recommissioned by the Royal Navy. In the Battle of San Domingo in the Caribbean in 1806, HMS *Canopus* had been involved with others in capturing five French ships of the line. It was a notable victory, which carried with it significant prize money for the victors.

Accordingly, Frank, having married when he was in England on leave, and having stayed with his mother and his sisters, Jane and Cassandra, at Southampton,[6] felt confident enough in his brother Henry's abilities to invest some of his money in the agency. That agency turned itself into a bank and because of Frank's investment, renamed itself as 'Austen, Maunde and Austen'. It was another step on the ladder of success for Henry.

But success also needs luck. And the luck for Austen, Maunde and Austen was that following the death of Prime Minister William Pitt in January 1806, a new government was formed. Nicknamed 'the Ministry of All the Talents', it was led by Lord Grenville (1759–1834), who had been Paymaster to the Forces in 1784–9. The government included several of Henry's influential friends as ministers. Lord Moira, for example, became Master of the General Ordinance, and his former colonel, Lord Charles Spencer (1740–1820), the second son of Lord Charles Spencer, 3rd Duke of Marlborough, became Master of the Mint. It seemed that things could only get better for the new bank and its principals. They had capital, they had important connections in society, and they could now boast of having had several years of experience in the military and financial fields. Henry could afford to take out a £2,000 insurance policy and was also able to invest well over £6,000 in government consolidated annuities (known as Consols), a form of government debt. Henry was now signalling that he was a sophisticated banker and could talk with ease about financial matters that were beyond the understanding of the man in the street.

That same year, Henry and Maunde were able to add two more regiments to their portfolio: the Derbyshire Militia, and the 4th Garrison Battalion, based in Jersey. It added further to Henry's collection of influential friends: the colonel of the Derbyshires was George Cavendish, brother of the Duke of Devonshire, and the colonel of the 4th Garrison Battalion was a man called Sir Charles Hastings. The latter was not related to Warren Hastings, but they were good friends.

The process of Henry Austen and his banking colleagues at this stage in their careers is like watching a set of playing cards being laid out on a table: new cards are dealt, old ones are held in the hand, and the value of the game seems to increase on an almost daily basis. Did he wonder how long it could last? Or was he so confident of his skills and the wealth of his wide-ranging network that failure did not enter his mind?

His confidence must have been sky-high, because later in 1806 he became a partner in three country banks and was the London correspondent for two more, the Horwood Well Bank[7] in Wincanton, Somerset, and the Buxton and High Peak Bank in Derbyshire, which had close connections with the Duke of Devonshire and the Derbyshire Militia. Was he overstretching himself? One of the country banks he founded was at Alton, near Steventon – it was called Austen, Gray and Vincent, and operated from a private house that had previously been a galleried inn. Like other country banks it issued its own banknotes and had local partners, of whom Henry was one. The second country bank, called Austen, Blunt and Louch, was based at 13, Market Square, Petersfield, a small market town, and the third bank was at 93, High Street, Hythe in Kent, where Henry Austen's partner was William Stevens Louch.

It would be incorrect to view Henry Austen's entrepreneurial banking ventures as though they were unique to him. They weren't. The banking system in the eighteenth century had developed rapidly so that by the end of the century it exhibited 'a version of the five key elements that are associated with specialised and sophisticated financial systems: sound public finances and debt management; stable monetary arrangements; a variety of banks, both domestic and international; a central bank; and a well-functioning securities market'.[8] All of this meant that although there were virtually no country banks in 1750, by the end of the century there were, some estimates suggest, about 230, and some even claim that by 1800 there were over 400. Henry's expansion from an agency into a bank was part of a bigger trend.[9] But those country banks were not stand-alone concerns; they needed the larger banks and agents in

London to have access to capital markets, and the London agent could act as a receiver of the country bank's surplus, or, on the contrary, could act as a source of capital for the country bank, if needed. Henry was placing himself at both ends of this system. In addition, it should be noted that the local collectors of Land Tax and Excise duties needed a strong place to safely deposit their tax collections and a trustworthy means of transferring their dues to the government. A subtle part of this was that a tax collector had access to public sums of money and could borrow at a discount. It was in the country banks' interest, therefore, to have a good relationship with the tax remitters so that, if necessary, they could turn to them if they needed credit or, if the banks had been used for deposits of cash by tax remitters, that cash could provide a cushion against sudden runs on the bank.

The burgeoning of this financial system in the last decades of the eighteenth century meant that there were many agencies besides Austen, Maunde and Austen that were operating in the financial markets. In short, there was competition.[10] And further, one of the key factors in the relationship between the country banks and their London agents was a reliable and swift means of communication. It meant inevitably that at the London end of the banking system, clerks[11] were needed who had the education and the ability to deal with an increasing amount of complex mail containing instructions from the country banks. And at the same time, the London agency needed information from the country banks to ensure that they were not becoming overdrawn and could alert them if it perceived that the country bank was getting into financial trouble.

In comparison with Henry's small agency and bank, the Bank of England was heavily dependent on an army of clerks to operate its complex systems. By the 1780s, the bank employed over 300 clerks – 'five times the number employed by the Admiralty and the Treasury'.[12] How many clerks Henry employed is not known, but he must have had some. Whether or not those clerks followed the example of some of their Bank of England confrères in having a second occupation is again unknown, but that clerks were essential to the workings of even a small bank cannot be gainsaid. At the Bank of England, a clerk needed a guarantor behind him to assure the employer that the clerk was honest and trustworthy; it would be interesting to know if Henry made similar demands on the clerks whom he employed.

It should be remembered that Henry Austen's bank, located in the West End of London, was not a City bank. Whilst initially there were some differences between City banks and West End banks – the West End banks tended to be more relational and exclusive, dealing, for instance, with the aristocracy and landed gentry rather than with merchants and trade – the differences gradually disappeared, though banks such as Coutts and Hoares still maintain their exclusive West End presence today. As Turner explains:

> In general, their lending became ever more focused upon bond and mortgage to landowners and lawyers, while investments would be in securities such as Bank of England, East India and South Sea stock and tea warrants. Discounting was not significant, and reserve ratios could be reduced as clients' demand for their money was more predictable than that of merchants.[13]

Interestingly, George Austen and his family banked with Hoares Bank, as did Eliza's mother, Philadelphia Hancock, and Henry Austen and Eliza banked with Drummonds Bank, which had been founded by Andrew Drummond, a former silversmith, in 1712/13 at Charing Cross. Drummonds initially had a largely Scottish clientele and allowed silver and gold jewellery to be used as collateral when their owners sought a loan. In its first decades it remained a relatively small bank but rapidly increased its reach when Richard Cox of the military agency went into partnership in 1765.[14]

Whilst the creation of Henry's bank followed a trend, it might be significant that it was a relative latecomer to the West End banking scene. Child and Co. had been founded in the 1580s, Goslings in 1650 at the sign of the Three Squirrels in Fleet Street, Hoares Bank in 1672, Coutts in 1692, and Drummonds in 1712. However, the opening of country banks by Henry Austen was part of a late eighteenth-century phenomenon: in Hampshire in 1780, there was only one bank, by 1800 there were thirteen; in Gloucestershire in 1780, there was just one bank but by 1800 there were eighteen; and in Yorkshire in 1780, there were thirteen banks, whereas by 1800 there were forty-four.[15]

These new country banks were subject to limitations: they were not allowed by law to have more than six partners, which meant that they might not have sufficient capital to withstand financial shocks, and perhaps it was not always the case that the partners understood the complexities of the banking processes. It was a potentially unstable situation.

Henry's agency and bank in the West End, however, had some diversity of income: regimental accounts and other matters, including loans to officers, were an important part of the bank's life, but Henry and his partners might have thought that by becoming agents for country banks, they could spread their risk. But would this be sufficient to allay all possible danger? There were other more mundane risks that banks, whether large or small, faced. They had to keep meticulous paper records and find space to store them, and therefore a fire on the premises would be catastrophic. In the City, fire engines were sometimes the responsibility of the livery companies, or the major insurance companies. Outside the City, fire engines and their crews were the responsibility of the parish. What actions might Henry have taken to mitigate fire risk? Similarly, if his bank took deposits of money, where was that money stored? Who had the keys to the safe? Could the partners be certain that none of their employees would surreptitiously defraud the bank by manufacturing duplicate keys and helping themselves to cash?

Unfortunately, in the case of Henry's bank, these quasi-domestic matters are unrecorded, but they indicate that whilst the West End banks were primarily relational in terms of their customers, they still had to be efficient, disciplined and well organised in their back-office functions.

Was there a straw in the wind about such things?

The inexperience of Austen and Maunde was apparent in an initial blunder in 1806. They were, after all, learning on the job. The most bizarre took place when Henry Austen was away establishing the bank in Alton. Henry Maunde issued a promissory note for £200 to an individual calling himself Count Stuarton. The Count promptly vanished, taking the £200 with him.[16]

The partners put out 'Wanted' notices, but to no avail. They had been conned. It must have put the partnership under strain.

This was a critical moment in the life of the young bank but not a catastrophic one. There were further developments to come, as we shall see in the next chapter.

Chapter 10

More Banking Developments and Publications, 1807–1813

In 1807, Henry Austen's bank moved to new premises – yet again. It was the fourth time the agency and bank had moved in little over six years. This time he and his partners chose to locate themselves at 10, Henrietta Street, Covent Garden.[1] They took out a twenty-one-year lease on the building, with an annual rent of £110[2] (roughly equivalent to over £10,000 today). What might have been their reasons for choosing Henrietta Street? According to Clive Caplan, 'The move signified a shift from primarily army agency to primarily banking, with the new location providing easier communication with provincial farmers and traders coming into London to do business.'[3] If Caplan is correct then the proximity of Henrietta Street to the Golden Cross coaching inn (where Charing Cross Railway Station now stands) might have been a significant factor. It was where stagecoaches from various parts of the country arrived: coaches from Kent, Yorkshire, the Midlands, and the South Coast would clatter into the yard. It was a massive terminus, with stabling for seventy-eight horses. Stagecoaches from the west of England frequently used Hatchett's Hotel and White Horse Cellar, a coaching inn on the corner of Albemarle Street, as their London terminus, but that was about a mile from Henrietta Street, and stagecoaches from Surrey tended to use the Talbot Inn in Southwark – an even greater distance from Covent Garden, as was the Swan with Two Necks in Cheapside, which served Basingstoke, amongst other places.

But perhaps Henry was following a fashionable trend, because there were already associations with banking in Henrietta Street. Number 5, a house a few doors away from number 10, from 1732 to 1782 had been the home of Mr Anthony Wright, a banker, and during the early part of the nineteenth century both number 5 and number 6 had housed banks. Number 10 had been constructed in 1726 and in the early eighteenth century it had been leased to a linen draper. Obviously, it was a smart and prestigious street (the stucco that now adorns the outside frontage was a mid-Victorian addition). However, although the street was fashionable, it should not be forgotten that it was less than 100 yards (90 metres) from Covent Garden, which was not only famous for its flower and vegetable market but in the eighteenth and early nineteenth centuries was known for its trade in prostitution. There was even a publication entitled *Harris's List of Covent-Garden Ladies*, which had been published regularly from 1757 until 1794, when it was closed down. And so, when Henry and his partners chose Henrietta Street for their new premises, and when Jane Austen went to stay with Henry there, they could not have been unaware of the reputation of Covent Garden for the sex trade. It was a trade that was taking place in the nearby streets and taverns. Wealth and poverty and the exploitation of women and children existed side by side.

But perhaps the proximity of the new premises to the City and the Bank of England would have been a more important determining factor. The Bank of England, founded in 1694, was expanding rapidly in the eighteenth century as it dealt with government debt. 'By 1763, the combined total of the funded and unfunded debt stood at £133 million, and at the end of the war with America, at £245 million. By 1819, following the conclusion of the Revolutionary and Napoleonic wars, the debt stood at £844 million.'[4] The bank, with its imposing façade, was becoming more and more significant in the British economy. It stood, as Anne Murphy explains, 'at the apex of Britain's financial architecture', a symbol of Britain's reliability, inventiveness and probity. Henry must have been aware of the colossal national debts and also of some of the financial instruments that were being deployed, and so, perhaps, as trading in debt became normalised, it might have put any potential problems he had in his own bank into perspective. But did he actually understand some of the new financial instruments?

Whatever might be the answer to that question, the fact is that on the political front, 1807 was a momentous year. On 25 March, the King, George III, placed his signature on an Act of Parliament: the Act for the Abolition of the Slave Trade. It was the culmination of all that William Wilberforce (1759–1833) and his colleagues had fought for over so many years. Whilst it meant that trading in slaves became illegal for British ships, it did not mean that slavery itself ceased. All that happened, at least initially, was that slave trading was taken up by other nations. The debate around the economic effects of abolition is too complex to be investigated here, and how, if at all, such a change impacted Henry Austen's bank is impossible to tell, but he and his colleagues must have wondered how the Abolition Act would affect their business.

Nevertheless, despite these big political events, Henry seemed to have been in expansionary mood. There is a hint in one of Jane's letters (15 June 1808) that as well as his financial interest in trading in wine, Henry might have been considering branching out into the brewing business, but it was an idea that did not receive sufficient backing and was therefore dropped. But on the family front, other ideas were in train. Henry and his brother Edward were considering finding a house for Jane, their sister Cassandra, and their mother somewhere in the Alton area. But sadly, that process was interrupted by the sudden and unexpected death of Edward's wife, Elizabeth, on 10 October 1808. Edward was bereft but necessarily had to make arrangements for his eleven children to be educated and cared for.

Writing to Cassandra, who was staying with Edward at Godmersham during this sad time, Jane expressed her own profound sadness and sympathy over their sister-in-law's death:

> We have felt, we do feel for you all ... and for dearest Edward, whose loss and whose suffering seem to make those of every other person nothing – God be praised that you can say what you do of him – that he has a Religious Mind to bear him up, and a Disposition that will gradually lead him to comfort.[5]

On 12 October, Henry went to Godmersham to be with his brother. In common with all the Austen siblings, they were very close, and that meeting must have brought some solace to Edward, though his loss, as Jane had implied, was profound.

Once the funeral and mourning period began to ease everyone's grief, Henry found himself faced with a work problem. In December 1808, his bank lost the agency of the 4th Garrison Battalion. How much this mattered from a financial perspective is difficult to tell but it must have been a disappointment and will have added to Henry's concerns. But he had the Godmersham family to think about, and Jane, in a letter to Cassandra on 27–28 December 1808, refers to a visit that Henry proposed to make to his brother: 'I hope he [Henry] comes to you in good health, and in spirits as good as a first return to Godmersham can allow. With his nephews he will force himself to be cheerful, till he really is so.'[6]

It's a nice insight into Henry's enthusiastic character.

Early in 1809, Jane was in high spirits about Henry's banking career, stating admiringly that its progress was 'a constant source of satisfaction'.[7] It was one of her typically throwaway remarks in a letter otherwise filled to overflowing with news and gossip, but presumably it was a fair assessment of how she regarded the bank and its prospects. Certainly, the bank was increasing its reach, because it took on a new partner, James Tilson, the brother of John Henry Tilson, lieutenant colonel of the Oxfordshire Regiment. The Tilson family were landed gentry in Watlington Park in Oxfordshire and James had been a friend of Henry's in the Militia.[8] It was how things worked; networks of friends and acquaintances were crucial to many enterprises, including banking. And the apparent success of Henry's bank was reflected in the fact that he bought a box at the Pantheon opera house in Oxford Street.[9] He gave the impression of a man rising effortlessly upwards.

At the same time, there were national matters that had implications for Henry and his partners. The louche behaviour of King George III's sons, the Prince of Wales (1762–1830) and his brother, Frederick,

Duke of York (1763–1827), continued to provide material for satirists and newspapers. Frederick had taken as his mistress Mary Anne Clarke (1776–1852), the separated wife of a stonemason. She was an attractive and delightful companion and in 1803 the Duke had set her up in a house in Gloucester Place. She lived in great extravagance, keeping ten horses and twenty servants, and the Duke paid her £1,000 per month; at least, that was the theoretical arrangement, but he was an irregular payer, and it was not long before she was being pressed by her creditors. To hold them at bay she promised to use her influence with the Duke. Amongst other things, this involved the sale of army commissions, and eventually, in 1809, this became the reason why an MP, Colonel Gwillym Lloyd Wardle, brought a case against the Duke to the House of Commons. Mary Anne Clarke testified before the House that she had sold army commissions with the Duke of York's knowledge. As he was Commander-in-Chief of the Armed Forces, the repercussions of her testimony were considerable. Such was the public outcry that the Duke of York was forced to resign his position as Commander-in-Chief and broke off his relationship with Mrs Clarke.

As we have seen, Henry had also been involved clandestinely in selling army commissions, so the case against the Duke must have caused him some personal anxiety. Would his own sales techniques be brought into the light of day? Might this mean that the sale of army commissions by his bank should be put to one side?

Further rumours around the relationship between Mary Anne Clarke and the Duke began to circulate, and she threatened to publish the letters that she and the Duke had exchanged. When this came to the notice of the Duke's close friends, it was decided that if she would agree not to publish, she would be rewarded with a lump sum of £7,000 and an annual pension of £400. An agreement on these terms was reached, though one copy of the letters was deposited for safekeeping with Drummonds Bank.[10]

During all these background political uncertainties, Henry and Eliza felt sufficiently wealthy that they could move house again. This time they chose 64, Sloane Street, Knightsbridge, an enviably fashionable address.[11]

The bank appeared to be thriving. It lent £2,000 to Lord Charles Spencer in March 1810. That sum today would be the equivalent of over £150,000 or almost £400,000, depending on the way the underlying maths are calculated. Either way, for a small private bank, it was a not inconsiderable loan.

But 1810 had more significant financial difficulties in store. Ever since paper money had been introduced a few years earlier, there was distinct unease in the press and amongst some commentators about the relationship between gold and paper money. Many people simply did not trust the paper money, seeing it as worthless. And they did not trust the people involved: William Cobbett called them the 'Paper Aristocracy'. There were strident calls for the government to build up stocks of gold because it was a tangible and 'real' source of value. In September, the Percival government had to take out a massive loan to cover the costs of the war with France, and that caused widespread alarm, but also in September, the suicide of a banker called Abraham Goldsmid, a man heavily involved in the contract to raise the loan for the government, meant that panic set in in the markets. It was an economically perilous time.[12] Several country banks failed, including the Horwood Well Bank in Wincanton, with which Henry had connections

Yet, somehow or other, during this financial turbulence, Henry found time to help his sister Jane to get *Sense and Sensibility* published. With his backing and support (in effect, he was her agent), the novel was accepted for publication by Thomas Egerton and was introduced to the public in October 1811.

How did this relationship with Thomas Egerton come about? He was, after all, a well-known, specialist publisher of military and political books whose shop in Whitehall was close to the Admiralty Office, and he had hardly published any novels prior to *Sense and Sensibility*. Perhaps Henry Austen knew Thomas Egerton because *The Loiterer* had been published by him many years previously. Or might it have been, as Kathryn Sutherland suggests, that Henry and Thomas Egerton had a friend in common, the printer, Charles Roworth. Henry used Roworth to print 'reward notices for the apprehension of absconding debtors, and for Egerton a range of military titles'.[13] Whatever the initial and personal connection might have been between Henry and Thomas Egerton, there was a deal to be struck, but the financial exigencies around publishing in the early nineteenth century were complicated. In the case of *Sense and Sensibility*, Jane Austen had to pay the publisher for production and advertising, and, in addition, a 10 per cent commission on sales. It was a bit like today's self-publishing ventures. Egerton, perhaps scenting a successful novel, printed 750 copies, a large print run for a first-time author. Jane Austen's name was not on the cover; instead, the novel was described as written by 'A Lady'. Why did she not want her own name attached to the novel? Possibly, as David Cecil says, 'she was following a convention: born and bred a lady in the purely social sense of the term, she may well have felt it unseemly to present herself, as it were in person, before the public.'[14] David Cecil goes on to speculate that her choice of anonymity was 'her sense of her art as something apart from her private self'.[15] It might be of course that she thought it simply bad manners to put her own name in such a prominent position. Whatever her reasons might have been, it did not detract from the book's success. Soon, there were two positive reviews that launched it into the public domain and by July 1813, the copies were sold out and Jane had earned £140 in profits.[16] That sum is worth over £8,500 today. It was a spectacular achievement.

Henry had backed a winner, and he it was who, through his financial acumen, his contacts and his charm, had ensured that *Sense and Sensibility* would be enjoyed by the reading public. Jane was, of course, delighted, and one can imagine that Henry would have been quietly pleased that his sister's talents were being recognised. She was now a professional author. Writing from Sloane Street, where she was staying with Henry and Eliza, on 25 April 1811, she said: 'I am never too busy to think of S and S. I can no more forget it than a mother can forget her sucking child.'[17]

To introduce Jane to her London friends, Eliza threw a party, inviting eighty guests, of whom sixty-six turned up. Jane wrote a long letter to Cassandra on 18 April, which bubbles with the excitement of the preparations:

> Eliza has plenty of business in her hands just now – for the day of the Party is settled and drawing near – above 80 people are invited for next Tuesday Evening, and there is to be some very good Music, 5 professionals, 3 of the Glee singers, besides Amateurs ... one of the Hirelings is a Capital on the Harp, from which I expect great pleasure.[18]

The party was a great success, though Jane Austen spent much of the time in the hallway: 'The Drawing room being soon hotter than we liked we placed ourselves in the connecting passage which was comparatively cool and gave us all the advantage of the Music at a pleasant distance, as well as that of the first view of every newcomer.'[19]

As well as the party, there were drives in Hyde Park, shopping, visits to the theatre and delicious conversations, but, as E.J. Clery writes: 'what Jane saw at Sloane Street was at times troubling. There was a fragility about Eliza, physical and emotional.'[20] There was, too, a kind of reckless and innocent enthusiasm about Henry. He mixed in raffish society. For example, through Eliza he knew the Comte d'Antraigues, and Jane was taken to meet the Comte, his wife, the Comtesse, Anne de Saint-Huberty, an opera singer, and their son, Julien, a musician. It was all very glamorous. But what none of them knew was that the Comte was, in fact, a spy, a double agent working for the Russians and for the British government. One year after Jane's visit, the Comte and his wife were murdered by their manservant.[21]

Henry moved easily in that upper-class level of London society where scandal was endemic. The year 1811 was, for example, the one in which the Duke of Clarence dismissed his mistress, Mrs Jordan, and their ten children, and then settled them in a house close to Henry and

Eliza.[22] Whether Henry enjoyed such proximity to royalty can only be guessed at, but he seemed to be fizzing with energy. 'At 64 Sloane Street, Henry always had one foot out of the door. When he wasn't on his way to the bank, he was setting out on other business. But Jane cherished his presence.' Henry was soon away off to Oxford. 'He wrote to Jane from Wheatfield Park House, the nearby mansion of Lord Charles Spencer, whose son John was Receiver General of Taxes for Oxfordshire, and she responded: 'Joy! Henry had gained the appointment of deputy receiver.'[23]

It meant that in addition to the buying and selling of army commissions, overseeing his country banks, his wine trade dealings, his agency on behalf of some regiments, and his day-to-day banking activities issuing loans and other such things, he was now involved in the taxation business. It was a diverse portfolio of activities. Could his energy and allure hold all these things together in some kind of ordered and manageable structure? Who was ensuring that these multifarious activities were properly recorded, and the resultant financial figures were being entered into the appropriate ledgers? Could Henry be certain that the loans he made, including one of £2,000 to Lord Charles Spencer the previous year, would be repaid? And there was a loan to the Hon. John Spencer of £7,200, which the latter did not repay, having fled the country to avoid his creditors.

Nevertheless, despite his loan-making and the underlying anxiety in the financial markets, Henry seemed to remain calm and confident. He was either a very good actor, or he really believed that his bank was safe and was built on unshakeable foundations. Maybe it was, because in August 1811, Henry was awarded a new regimental agency, this time for the Royal West Middlesex Regiment. He seemed unassailable.

Chapter 11

Death, Taxes and New Opportunities

Meanwhile, Henry's wife Eliza's health was beginning to be a cause for concern. She went to Ramsgate accompanied by her French maid, Madame Perigord, to take the air. It was a fashionable thing to do. In 1753, Dr Richard Russell (1687–1759) had written a book, *The Uses of Sea Water*, extolling the virtues of sea bathing, which had resulted in seaside towns becoming very popular. Russell was patronised by King George III and his brother, the Duke of Cumberland. In 1769, Dr William Buchan (1729–1805), in his book *Domestic Medicine*, had also recommended the practice of seawater bathing. His book went into numerous editions and retained its influence into the mid-nineteenth century.

Eliza was therefore following established practice, even if there is no mention of her taking part in sea bathing. The air itself was a good and less freezing substitute. But after all the exertions of organising such a grand party for Jane, Eliza was feeling poorly. She had a cold, and after she had returned to London, on a visit to Hyde Park the horses jibbed as they pulled her carriage. Eliza was frightened and got out. Jane explained the situation to Cassandra in a letter of 25 April: 'we were detained in the evening air several minutes—the cold is in her chest—but she takes care of herself, and I hope it may not last long.'[1] But as in that same letter Jane refers to Eliza's cold making 'quiet advisable', perhaps the cold was a precursor of something more serious. One of the other features of Jane's letters written when she was staying with Henry and Eliza in their Sloane Street house is the sense that in addition to Eliza's health problems, the relationship between the two women was no longer quite as happy as it had been years ago in Steventon. And with Henry being so involved in his work, there is also a sense that he and Eliza were drifting apart, whereas his relationship with Jane remained as delightfully warm and strong as ever.

The Austen family really were remarkably close. David Cecil refers to them as having a kind of corporate personality: 'The Austen corporate personality combined qualities not often found together. It was at once affectionate and unsentimental, satirical and good tempered, orthodox and highly intelligent.'[2]

We can also sense this in the relationships that the Austen family had with the next generation. In November 1811, while captain of HMS *Elephant* serving in the North Sea, Francis Austen wrote a sweet letter to his young daughter, Mary Jane, aged between 4 and 5:

> My dear little girl,
> It gave me great pleasure to hear from your Mamma's letter that you had improved so much in your reading as to be able to read eight pages of 'Little Charles'[3] at one lesson, and particularly that you liked it well enough to read it once again to yourself ... I am glad too my dear Child that you said your Catechism so well.

It is the combination of affection, intelligence and a concern for good but understated religious practice that is so typical of the Austen family's values.

Meanwhile, Henry was being remarkably energetic, travelling to Chawton to see his mother, and perhaps while there, overseeing the development of his Alton bank. Then he dashed back to London: so much to do, so many responsibilities, so many relationships to keep sweet – including with a certain William Gore-Langton (1760–1847), MP for Somerset and a colonel in the Oxford Militia.

A letter written by Henry to Major Charles James on 8 April 1811, declares, 'I am very desirous of obtaining your kind attention to the following statement which refers to personages of whom you yourself are by no means unaware ... the eldest son of Colonel Gore-Langton has served upwards of three years ... in the 4th Dragoons.'

As Henry explains, the unnamed son was being forced to return to England because of ill health, 'having been dangerously indisposed'. Henry explains that the son was a very wealthy young man, and 'was not desirous of submitting to the drudgery of a subaltern's duty'. The letter suggests that the young man had no chance of promotion in the 4th Dragoons because he was in tenth place in the list of lieutenants. His father, explained Henry, would be mortified if he thought his son might resign his commission. Henry continues by reminding Major James that Colonel Gore-Langton was an acquaintance of the Prince Regent and suggests that the young man would find a fresh stimulus to service, if he 'might possibly afterwards meet with an opportunity of returning to the Cavalry ... I am well aware', writes Henry, 'that promotion is of late so scarcely [? writing illegible] administered by purchase that I forebear saying, "Money would be no object".' He concludes the letter with, 'I make this communication without the privity of either Colonel Langton or his son.'[4]

It is an intriguing letter because, as so often in his communications with Major James, Henry relies heavily on unspoken but mutually understood assumptions that enable the recipient to read between the lines. It is a wily missive that smells suspiciously of underhand dealings. What it certainly reveals is that Henry was still somehow involved in arranging military commissions.

We can assume that as 1811 turned into 1812, banking remained the chief occupation, with military commissions being handled discreetly. But on 11 May, an event took place in the lobby of the House of Commons that was to have far-reaching consequences. A Liverpool merchant, John Bellingham, who had a longstanding grievance with the government, shot and killed Prime Minister Spencer Percival (1762–1812). Percival had described himself politically as 'a friend of Mr Pitt' rather than as a Tory. He had supported the Peninsular War, was in favour of the abolition of slavery, and had withstood the economic crisis of the previous year. His death shook London and the nation, and meant that a new prime minister needed to be selected.

One of the names that was being talked about for the post was that of Lord Moira. He was a close friend of the Prince Regent and was asked to attend upon the Prince with a view to being appointed. Their conversation was reported in gleeful and gossipy terms in the clubs of London, but the net result was that they could not agree about Catholic Relief for Ireland. Moira, an Irish peer, was strongly in favour; the Prince Regent was firmly opposed. The result was that the choice of prime minister eventually fell upon Robert Banks Jenkinson, 2nd Earl of Liverpool – a Tory.

Lord Moira, instead of becoming prime minister, one year later accepted the wealthy and influential post of Governor General of Bengal. There must have been conversations between Henry Austen and Charles James, his sleeping partner in the bank, concerning the rumours flying around London about Moira's near miss. He was well known to them both.

To a certain extent, Henry and Eliza Austen had tied their own advancement in society to Lord Moira, so the fact that he had failed to achieve the most glittering political post in the country must have caused them some disquiet. But if they had any concerns, they were probably at the level of disappointment rather than anything else. Within a year, their eyes would be opened.

For the moment, the bank carried on as usual, but there was about to be a more personal tragedy for Henry to face. His wife Eliza was clearly ill, though the cause is unknown. Clare Tomalin speculates[5] that perhaps she was suffering from breast cancer, the disease from which her own mother, Philadelphia Hancock, had died.

Henry was in Oxford in February 1813 but hurried home and then went down to Chawton to fetch Jane to be with him as he faced his wife's imminent death. In the last days of her illness, Eliza's beloved French companions, Madame Perigord and Madame Bigeon, were with her and would have brought her much spiritual comfort. Jane was also at the bedside. On 25 April 1813, Eliza Austen died after what Jane described as 'a long and dreadful illness'. She was buried six days later, on 1 May, in the churchyard of St John-at-Hampstead, in the same grave as her mother and son. It is not known who attended the funeral, but Henry himself would have been there.

Eliza's gravestone, refurbished by the London Jane Austen Society in 2014–15, reads:

A woman of Brilliant, Generous & cultivated
mind, just, disinterested & charitable
she died after long & severe suffering
on the 25 April 1813 aged 50
much regretted by the wise & good
& deeply lamented by the Poor

The wording feels formulaic and a little emotionally distanced.

On the day of the burial, Jane travelled back to Chawton with Madame Perigord. It was a compassionate and thoughtful gesture. But even in Jane's formal state of mourning, as they rattled along in their carriage towards Hampshire, she might have been reflecting not only on her late cousin and sister-in-law Eliza, and the fun they had had together in Steventon years earlier, but also daydreaming about her most recent literary triumph. In January 1813, with Henry's help, her second novel, *Pride and Prejudice*, had been published by Thomas Egerton, to whom she had sold the copyright. Did the now famous opening line of the novel still please her? Thinking about it, and the way her two novels were selling, might have eased her sense of loss on Eliza's death.

In mid-May, Jane returned to London to stay with Henry in Sloane Street and wrote about going with him to visit Eliza's grave while she was there.[6] They also went together to a service at Belgrave Chapel in Belgrave Square, to an art exhibition in Spring Gardens in Piccadilly and to one in Pall Mall. Jane does not specify where the gallery was in Pall Mall, but it was almost certainly the British Institution Gallery at number 52. For there, from 10 May to 14 August, there was a retrospective exhibition of paintings by Sir Joshua Reynolds, and Jane, writing to Cassandra in a teasing fashion, refers (as Janine Barchas reveals)[7] to her search for portraits of two characters from her own novels, Mrs Bingley (*Pride and Prejudice*) and Mrs Darcy (Elizabeth Bennet, also in *Pride and Prejudice*).

In her letter of 24 May, she refers to Henry. Once he had returned to Sloane Street, she expected him to be:

> dining out a great deal ... as he will then be alone, it will be more desirable – he will be more welcome at every Table, and every Invitation more welcome to him. He will not want either of us again till he is settled in Henrietta Street. This is my present persuasion – and he will not be settled there, really settled, till late in the Autumn.[8]

Meanwhile, Henry, as well as going to art galleries with Jane, was also thinking of the rest of the Austen family. Jane, in her letter to Cassandra, explains what was going on: 'Henry desires Edward may know that he has just bought 3 dozen of Claret (Cheap) and ordered it to be sent down to Chawton.'[9]

Was this part of his wine trade dealings? Did he enjoy the idea of a clever deal, even on wine?

Once Jane had returned to Chawton, it was not long before Henry's energies were re-engaged with his bank and its affairs.

While Lord Moira was lodging in Portsmouth in April 1813, waiting for the ship that would carry him to India, he wrote himself a loan of £6,000 via six bills of exchange representing £1,000 each, drawn upon the bank of Austen and Co. His agent, Captain John Ridge (whom we shall meet later), had written on three of the bills, 'payable at Messrs Biddulph and Co'.[10] If Moira had had £6,000 in his account with Austen, Maunde and Tilson, then the arrangement would have been lawful, but it seems safe to assume, judging by Henry's reaction to the process, that he did not have that amount in his account and that he was behaving fraudulently. On the most positive reading of Moira's actions, he might have thought that his close ties with Charles James and with Henry entitled him to behave in the way he did, but it was an extraordinary, reckless and morally culpable thing to do, not least when he must have been aware, at a personal level, that Henry had just lost his wife. To place the scale of that debt in contemporary terms, it was the equivalent today of about £590,000.

Henry had had banking dealings with Lord Moira ever since he had first started his agency. In 1803, for example, Henry had arranged a series of loans for him. But the relationship in those early days was not solely about finance, it was about more than that. Charles James, the elusive, inactive (?) partner of Austen, Maunde and Co., was a kind of 'fixer'. He was in regular communication with Moira about Moira's debt problems.[11] At the same time, Charles James was also asking Moira to use his influence at the Admiralty on behalf of Henry's naval brothers, Charles and Frank. Those requests paid off when Charles was given command of a sloop, HMS *Indian*, stationed in Bermuda, but when a similar request on behalf of Frank Austen was put to Moira in 1806 (he was then Master General of the Ordinance), it came to nothing. Perhaps that should have given Henry Austen pause for thought. Was Lord Moira, who was easing his way up the political ladder and who was heavily in debt – was he a good risk? Was he fundamentally trustworthy? The relationship between Henry Austen, Charles James and Lord Moira was laden with risk but was typical of the time, when favours and back-handers were part of the way business was conducted. Everything went well in that system when there was integrity and trust on both sides, but in the case of Moira, his huge debts and slipperiness of character overcame such integrity as he had and were a contributory cause to Henry's later downfall.

When Moira's fraudulent and dangerous action was reported to Henry, it must have come as a terrible blow. And in the quiet hours before dawn, as Henry pondered on what to do, and was replaying in his head all the circumstances that had led up to this potential catastrophe, he might have remembered from his time as a young man in his father's church some verses from the Psalms, and particularly, Psalm 146:3, 'O put not your trust in princes nor in any child of man: for there is no help in them'. If he had taken note of those sentiments, he might not have found himself in the predicament he was now in.

The hurt of the betrayal went deep and was remembered by Henry twenty-six years later when he wrote a letter to Lord Moira's son:

> My Lord, ... Your Noble Father, when he left England for India in 1813 owed me £6,000. ... I was in the habit of lending ... from time to time sums of money on his notes of hand. They had always been duly paid up to the time of his departure. ... Before he sailed, he sent for me into his private cabinet in St. James Place and uttered the following words: 'I have ... given directions to my trustees ... to sell my landed property and pay every demand, although it is like drawing drops of blood from my heart.' ... I reposed implicit confidence in his word. ...
>
> Baron Adams requested a renewal for one year. ... In April 1814 they were not honoured. ... my credit as a banker was impaired ... confidence withdrawn, and business destroyed. ... insolvency ensued in March 1816. ... I lost the Receivership, an office of £1,000 a year. I lost everything. ...
>
> Baron Adams ... repeatedly confirmed your father's promise. The last time he made it, it was in his own chambers at Lincoln's Inn. There were present Wm. Seymour Esqr., a solicitor of eminence, W. Hellyer Esqr., ditto, Mr. Ridge, your father's regimental agent, a Mr. Louch, T.P. Hampson Esqr., ... Myself & 3 or 4 more ... Not omitting a Major James, much in your father's confidence. (I have sometimes feared too much, as the Major was a papist, and had been educated at the Jesuits College at Douay.) Several of the above were creditors of your father and, I regret to say, thro my means.[12]

But in that very same month, the month in which Eliza died, and Lord Moira defrauded him, Henry had had some good news. On 21 April 1813, Henry had visited Lord Charles Spencer at his Oxfordshire home.

John Spencer, Charles Spencer's son, had been the Receiver General of Taxes for Oxfordshire but had incurred some spectacular debts, which he could not pay off. On that visit, a loan of £2,000 to Charles Spencer was made by Henry – perhaps a payment for his putative appointment as successor to John as Receiver General. The loan, of course, was not recorded as being for that purpose, but it was between gentlemen so there was no need for detail; a nod and a wink would suffice. Henry was officially appointed as Receiver General for Oxfordshire on 24 July 1813. It was potentially a very lucrative appointment, and if he could not get any of the money owed by Lord Moira, it would have made up some of the shortfall.

What did it mean to be Receiver General of taxes for Oxfordshire? In essence, it meant that Henry oversaw the collection of taxes from the taxpayers of the city and county. Those taxes were collected every quarter at seventeen collection points by duly appointed local collectors of taxes, who were paid 1.5d. in the pound for their work.[13] The collectors then paid the taxes collected to the Receiver General as he made his way, accompanied by two 'minders', around the county. The collecting process, it has been estimated, would have taken seven to ten days.[14] But there was a snag. The tax was frequently paid in notes to the collectors – notes that were issued by local banks. But, since the Restriction on Cash Payments Act of 1797, those notes were not backed by gold. Furthermore, because the notes had been issued by local banks, a question arose: did those notes have any inherent value? If the local bank had issued those notes without having the capital basis by which to honour them, the results would have been catastrophic. The government, recognising this, decreed that before the notes could become currency acceptable to the government, they had to be converted into a recognisable and legitimate form by the Receiver General. In brief, Henry had to find a bank, even his own (?), which would be able and willing to convert the banknotes into coinage and pass the due sum to the Exchequer. The Receiver General of Taxes, in this case, Henry Austen, was allowed to keep £6,500 as a balance each quarter, after he had handed the remainder to the Exchequer. The balance could then be stored in his bank and could be used as capital for making loans to individuals. In theory, the collection process should have worked well, but it was complicated and wide open to abuse.

It is important to add that Henry did not treat his role as Receiver General as though it were a voluntary, charitable activity. He was paid for his responsibilities. He was entitled to 2d. in the pound for assessed taxes, and 1.5d. in the pound for Land Tax, plus a fixed allowance of £270 for administration and collection expenses. Out of this income he had to pay his clerks, accommodation and travel costs. John Avery Jones[15] estimates that he would have cleared about £800 per annum (worth roughly £90,000 today), and, in addition, he had use of the balance of £6,500 – the equivalent of over £600,000 today.

In Henry's case, what made it more complicated was that he had inherited from his predecessor, the Hon. John Spencer, debts that were much larger than the allowed £6,500 per quarter. For example, at the year end of 1812, John Spencer owed the Exchequer over £34,000.[16] As the office holder of the Receiver Generalship, Henry inherited the liabilities that John Spencer had incurred through his failure to pay the Exchequer the taxes owed. Either Henry did not know at the time he became Receiver General what the scale of those debts were, in which case we can ask why, as Deputy Registrar General, he did not know, or he believed that through prudent management he could handle the situation. What was going through his mind? Was it cool calculation or over-confidence that ruled his thought processes? And, one year earlier, as if this inherited debt was not a big enough problem, two banks, closely associated with relatives of James Tilson,[17] Henry's partner, had gone bust. Boldero and Co., a prestigious bank, went into bankruptcy on 2 January 1812, and Lushington and Co. declared bankruptcy just four days later, on 6 January 1812.

Why does it matter that Boldero and Co. and Lushington and Co. went bust? Because, as John Avery Jones so neatly explains, 'Lushington and Co. owed £200,000 to Boldero and Co., which owed £29,000 to Austen

Right: Henry Austen. (*Courtesy Jane Austen's House, Chawton*)

Below: Pencil drawing of Steventon Rectory by Benjamin Lefroy, 1820. (*Courtesy Jane Austen's House, Chawton*)

Above left: St Nicholas Church, Steventon, Hampshire.

Above right: Interior of St Nicholas Church.

Below left: Memorial to Anne Austen in St Nicholas Church.

Below right: Memorial tablet to the three daughters of the Reverend William and Mrs Mary Knight at St Nicholas Church.

Right: Front quad of St John's College, Oxford.

Below left: Interior of St John's College Chapel, Oxford.

Below right: Upper Berkeley Street, London.

Above left: The site of Henry Austen's first agency on Cleveland Court, St James, London.

Above right: Canon Row: the site of Henry Austen's agency/bank in 1803. (Note Parliament in the background.)

Left: Albany courtyard: the site of Henry Austen's agency/bank in 1805.

Above left: 64, Upper Sloane Street (now refurbished).

Above right: 23, Hans Place.

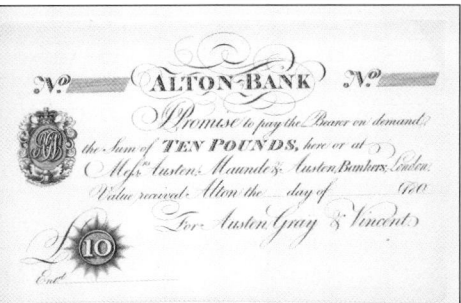

Above: Alton bank note for ten pounds. (*Courtesy Jane Austen's House, Chawton*)

Right: Alton bank.

Left: Jane Austen's House, Chawton.

Below left: Statue of Jane Austen, Chawton churchyard.

Below right: Chawton House.

Right: Henry Austen's ordination as priest, in the Bishop of Salisbury's Act Book.

Below left: St Andrew's, Farnham, Surrey.

Below right: St Mary's Church, Bentley, Hampshire.

Above left: Incised cross on a pillar at St Mary's, Bentley.

Above right: Consecration cross at St Mary's, Bentley.

Left: Henry Austen's grave, Tunbridge Wells, Kent. The faded text reads: Beneath This Stone Are Deposited the Mortal Remains of the Rev. Henry Thomas Austen. Minister of Christ. He was born June – 1771. And Interred Into His Rest March 12, 1850. 'Them also which sleep in Jesus Will God bring with Him.' Thess. IV. 14. (*www.findagrave.com*)

and Co., which owed £48,000 to the Exchequer for taxes collected by Henry as Deputy Receiver which had been deposited with Austen and Co., with part in turn deposited with Boldero and Co.'[18] Fortunately, Henry had made arrangements via Exchequer bills that mitigated the worst of what could have been a disaster for him and his bank colleagues. What he had done was to 'transfer the Exchequer Bills to the Crown as security for the tax money that they could not pay to the Government because of the failure of Boldero and Co.'.[19] It must have been a terribly worrying time, and although the problem had been temporarily solved, it was a foretaste of what was to come. Henry and his partners had successfully managed that particular financial crisis, but the question of the Oxfordshire taxes would come back to bite them a second time a few years later, as we shall see.

Although some of this is necessarily opaque, what we do know is that in order to become a Receiver of Taxes, Henry, in 1813, had had to provide financial guarantors, that is, people who could vouch for his financial integrity. In July, his guarantors, James Leigh Perrott (his uncle and the brother of Mrs Austen), Edward Austen Knight, and others, posted a bond valued at £73,000. It suggests that his guarantors were convinced of Henry's abilities, his rectitude, and his financial skills.

Henry was always close to his fortunate brother, Edward, and spent as much time as he could with him at Godmersham. It was no surprise, therefore, that Henry should look to Edward to be a guarantor. Henry was something of a 'favourite uncle' figure to Edward's children, joining in their games and sharing the family's interest in theatricals and Christmas festivities. Godmersham, at times, was Steventon writ large but without any financial constraints.

In a letter bursting with optimistic sensibility, on 3–6 July 1813, Jane wrote to her brother Frank to congratulate him on his naval posting to Sweden. In that same letter she gives him upbeat news about their brother Edward's successful harvest at Chawton Great House, and then proclaims what has happened to Henry:

> We are in hopes of another visit from our own true, lawful Henry very soon, he is to be our Guest this time – He is quite well I am happy to say and does not leave it to my pen to communicate to you the joyful news of his being Deputy Receiver no longer – It is a promotion which he thoroughly enjoys – as well he may; – the work of his own mind.[20]

It is not clear from this letter whether Jane or the family knew anything of the Moira problem or John Spencer's debts. If Jane did know, she has disguised it extremely well, and if she didn't, it would indicate that the 'true, lawful' Henry had not yet levelled with them. She goes on to speak of Henry's reaction to his loss of Eliza:

> Upon the whole his spirits are very much recovered – If I may so express myself, his Mind is not a Mind for affliction. He is too busy, too active, too sanguine – Sincerely as he was attached to poor Eliza moreover, and excellently as he behaved to her, he was always so used to be away from her at times, that her Loss is not felt as that of many a beloved Wife might be, especially when all the circumstances of her long and dreadful illness are taken into the account. – He very long knew that she must die, and indeed it was a release at last.[21]

She added a delighted postscript: 'You will be glad to know that every copy of S and S has sold and that it has brought me £140.'

In the meantime, Henry, with the help of Jane, had moved house. He left the large house in Sloane Street and moved, in May 1813, to an apartment at the bank in Henrietta Street. It was convenient, and it meant that he could keep a careful eye on the business. More to the point, apart from having the place decorated and painted, there was, as Jane wrote: 'an excellent Dining Room and common sitting parlour—and the smaller one behind will sufficiently answer his purpose as Drawing

Death, Taxes and New Opportunities   117

Room—He has no intention of giving large parties of any kind—His plans are all; for the comfort of his Friends and Himself.'[22]

He was also fortunate that Madame Bigeon and her daughter lived close by and could come to him as often as he needed them.

In September 1813, Henry travelled to Scotland to stay with friends and do some business. According to Jane, he heard *Pride and Prejudice* warmly praised and could not resist letting the cat out of the bag by declaring that the author was his sister. Jane was not entirely amused. She valued her privacy but explained in tones of forgiveness, that 'it was all done from affection and partiality'.[23]

While in Scotland he made loans to a few people and visited quite widely. He travelled back to London via Matlock, where no doubt he also networked, but on arrival in Henrietta Street he was taken ill. In one of her letters (15 September 1813), Jane tells Cassandra that she had had a good journey from Chawton to London,[24] where at Henry's new house they were met by the coachman, Madame Perigord and Madame Bigeon, and the latter had provided Jane and her companions with a 'comfortable dinner of Soup, Fish, Bouillee, Partridges and an apple pie', but she reported that Henry was: 'suffering from a cold in the face which he has been subject to before. He caught cold at Matlock and since his return has been paying a little for past pleasure. —It is nearly removed now—but he looks thin in the face—either from the pain, or the fatigues of his Tour, which must have been great.'[25]

In the same long letter, she refers to Henry having sent a new clerk to Alton. It seems that he was keeping an eye on the financial affairs of his bank there, notwithstanding his facial pain. The following day, in another letter to Cassandra, Jane reported that Henry was suffering from a 'deranged stomach', for which she advised that when Henry came to Chawton, Cassandra should 'keep him in Rhubarb and … plenty of port and water'.[26] In another letter, this time written by Jane while staying in November at Godmersham Park, the main estate of her brother, Edward Austen Knight, she refers to Henry's health again:

Dearest Henry, what a turn he has for being ill! and what a thing Bile is! – this attack has probably been brought on by his previous confinement and anxiety, – but however it came, I hope it is going fast.[27]

It had been a difficult and demanding couple of years for Henry, but perhaps the months and years that lay ahead would be kinder to him.

Chapter 12

Increasing Work and Anxiety, 1814–1816

Despite the difficult times of 1813, Henry had still managed to support Jane's work as a novelist. He had ensured that *Pride and Prejudice* was published in January 1813, and he oversaw the arrangements for *Sense and Sensibility* when it went into a further edition in October 1813. In January 1814, *Mansfield Park* was accepted for publication. It is little wonder that Jane regarded Henry as her favourite brother. He was very kind towards her and generously thoughtful, even to the extent of reading the proofs of *Mansfield Park*, which for such an extravert personality must have been a laborious and tedious occupation, but she records how much Henry enjoyed it.[1]

Is there a subtle reference to their mutual affection in that novel?

'Children of the same family, the same blood, with the same first associations and habits, have some means of enjoyment in their power which no subsequent connections can supply.'[2]

But for Henry, life was about to change. In April 1814, peace was declared between Britain and France, and Napoleon was exiled to Elba, a small Mediterranean island just 6 miles off the Tuscan coast of Italy. Whilst there was much rejoicing in the capital and the country, for Henry it meant that his work as an army agent was bound to be affected negatively. 'The regimental payroll handled by Austen & Co. declined from £112,000 in 1813 to £63,000 in 1814, and £34,000 in 1815, the government naturally being eager to retrench from the crippling expense of the war.'[3] A 50 per cent drop in potential income in one year was serious.

Apart from its effect on the banks, the peace had wider social and economic effects. Soldiers discharged by their regiments had to find work, and agricultural prices fell because grain merchants could obtain cheaper imports of wheat from Europe. Among those discharged by the military was Frank Austen; he had had a 'good' war and had invested some of the money he had made. Naturally, he had turned to his banker brother, who had advised him about potentially useful investments. Together they had made two joint investments, including the investment in Henry's bank, but when the customary seven-year period as a partner was completed, Frank gave up his nominal duties in the bank. With Frank Austen retired, the bank took on its final name: Austen, Maunde and Tilson. In our terms, the brand of the bank, because of its many changes of name since its inception, and its many changes of address, must have been weakened.

Nevertheless, for the moment, all was celebration. Henry was invited to the most exclusive of the celebrations marking the defeat of Napoleon, which was organised by White's at Burlington House. His presence at such a high-powered gathering impressed his sisters and mother. Jane simply wrote: 'Henry at White's. Oh! what a Henry!'[4]

Perhaps the invitation signalled that Henry's position in society remained stable and elegantly assured.

In a letter of 23 June 1814, Jane wrote to Cassandra: 'I certainly do not wish that Henry should think again of getting me to Town. I would rather return straight from Bookham; but if he really does propose it, I cannot say No, to what will be so kindly intended.'[5]

It is a letter that reveals the affection that Jane felt for Henry, but might there be a tiny hint that Jane felt exploited by him? However, on 23/24 August, in a letter written to Cassandra while staying with Henry in Hans Place (to which he had moved a few months earlier), Jane is in high spirits. She even began to speculate about a possible second marriage for him:

> Henry wants me to see more of his Hanwell favourite and has written to invite her to spend a day or two here with me. His scheme is to fetch her on Saturday. I am more and more convinced

that he will marry again soon, and like the idea of her better than anybody else at hand.[6]

The 'Hanwell favourite' was a woman called Miss Harriet Moore, but there was also another contender, Miss Frances Burdett, the youngest sister of Sir Francis Burdett (1770–1844). He had married Sophia Coutts, daughter of the banker Thomas Coutts. Such a link with the prestigious banking family might have enhanced Henry's banking career, but it was not to be. Jane (like Emma Woodhouse in *Emma*) was completely mistaken in her prognostications; Henry did not remarry until six years later.

He was a restless soul. Sometime before August 1814 he had moved house yet again. This time he kept a small flat for his own use in Henrietta Street but changed his main residence, as has been mentioned above, to a five-storey house, 23, Hans Place in Knightsbridge, where his close neighbour was James Tilson (1773–1838), who lived with his wife and ten children at number 26. Tilson was now a named partner in the Austen Bank. James's oldest brother, John Henry (1768–1836), had been a lieutenant colonel in the Oxfordshire Regiment and had worked closely with Henry in their time together in the military. It had been a close family friendship. The third partner in the bank, Henry Maunde (1761–1816), did not live in such grand circumstances. He was based at York Buildings, on the edge of the Marylebone Road, in a five-storey house that was much smaller than either Henry or James Tilson's houses in Hans Place. Henry Maunde's wife Sophia had died in 1808, leaving him to bring up their two small daughters.

In a letter of 23–24 August 1814, Jane recorded the 'crouded' [*sic*] nature of the stagecoach by which she travelled to see Henry in London and wrote that she was delighted by his new home:

It is a delightful Place – more than answers my expectation. Having got rid of my unreasonable ideas, I find more space and comfort in the rooms than I had supposed, and the Garden is quite a Love.

> I am in the front Attic which is the bedchamber to be preferred. Henry wants you to see it all.[7]

In September, in her letter to Martha Lloyd, Jane wrote of Hans Place:

> I am extremely pleased with this new House of Henry's, it is everything that could be wished for him, and I have only to hope he will continue to like it as well as he does now, and not be looking out for anything better – He is in very comfortable health – he has not been so well, he says, for a twelvemonth.[8]

Jane seems to be hinting that Henry was often looking out for something newer and better than what he already owned. But she does say, by contrast, that the political situation at the time was not cheerful.

Jane was back at Hans Place in November, where, in a letter to her niece, Fanny Knight, she explained that she was negotiating a second edition of *Mansfield Park* with Thomas Egerton: 'We are to see Egerton today, when it will probably be determined – People are more ready to borrow and praise, than to buy – which I cannot wonder at – but tho' I like praise as well as anybody, I like what Edward calls Pewter too.'[9]

The question is, what was happening to Henry's 'pewter'? Was his bank surviving the change in circumstances brought by the peace? The peace would not last long, for in March 1815, Napoleon escaped from Elba, which meant that war was again declared. Perhaps the army agency side of Henry's business would perk up again? The escape of Napoleon coincided with another milestone in Jane's life: she finished *Emma*. But whilst the Hundred Days war with France and Napoleon had to be navigated, there were beginning to be rumblings of concern at Henry's bank. The concerns centred on what were known as Extents.

Clive Caplan explains:

> When tax money was owed to the Crown, a writ of Extent in Chief could be issued, which reserved first call to the Crown on any

assets of the debtor. Debtors to the Crown could in their turn issue writs of Extent in Aid, calling upon the assets of those owing money to them. On 11 April 1815 Austen & Co. issued an Extent in Aid against James Harfield, a maltster and farmer of Candover, Hampshire, for a debt to them of £3,748. Harfield, his wife, and his seven children were then committed to the Fleet Prison for the next two years while he petitioned Parliament for relief.[10]

Henry had lost at least £6,000 over the Lord Moira affair. Now he was owed a further £3,000 by a maltster from Hampshire. In banking terms, the sums were not huge, although £3,000 would be the equivalent of £334,000 today, but for a struggling bank they were significant. Bad debts meant that the viability of the bank could be called in question. There is no mention by Jane in her letters about what she and the family might have thought of the harsh treatment of the Harfield family: all of them in Fleet Prison. It was difficult for Henry, but even more injurious, of course, to the Harfield wife and children.

The economic difficulties faced by Henry were not peculiar to him. The national economy was unstable and difficult following the end of the Napoleonic Wars. After several years of poor harvests, the Corn Laws of 1815 imposed high tariffs on imported corn, which kept prices high, and at the same time, wages declined. It is not entirely surprising, therefore, that the background of a national economic malaise, plus his own bank's particular difficulties, began to take its toll on Henry. In October 1815, he was struck down by a bilious attack and fever. Jane was staying with him as she was wanting to come to an agreement with the publisher John Murray II (1778–1843) about her books. She began her letter to Cassandra with a description of Murray: 'he is a rogue of course, but a civil one. He offers £450 but wants to have the Copyright of Mansfield Park and Sense and Sensibility included ... It will end in my publishing for myself, I dare say. He sends more praise than I expected.'[11]

In fact, *Emma*, which had been drafted at Chawton the previous year, was the subject of her negotiations. Murray offered to publish it, but he insisted that he also required the copyright of her other books. One can assume that Murray was one of Henry's contacts, and as Henry had been so helpful to Jane in getting her earlier books published, the choice of Murray to publish *Emma* must have had something to do with Henry's influence. Murray was the most successful publisher in London and thus to have his imprint on Jane's books would have been good for generating further sales and income.

But Henry was not well, though on the day of her letter, Jane did not recognise it: 'he is calomeling',[12] she wrote, 'and therefore in a way to be better and I hope may be well tomorrow.' It was not to be.

Mr Haden,[13] the 29-year-old 'apothecary' called in to treat Henry, was a physician at the Brompton Dispensary and played an unexpected part in the life of the Austens because Jane developed something of a crush on him, and it was through him that Jane was introduced to the Prince Regent's librarian, James Stanier Clarke. Jane was ten years older than the young physician, and although she had eyes only for him, he did not reciprocate her hopes. On Friday, 24 November 1815, in a letter to Cassandra, Jane wrote: 'Tomorrow Mr Haden is to dine with us.—There's Happiness! We really grow so fond of Mr Haden that I do not know what to expect.—He and Mr Tilson and Mr Philips made up our circle of Wits last night; Fanny played and he sat and listened and suggested improvements.'[14]

The following day, Jane wrote:

> Henry's illness is more serious than I expected. He has been in bed since three o-clock on Monday. It is a fever – Something bilious, but chiefly Inflammatory ... Mr Haydon took twenty ounces of blood last night – and nearly as much more this morning – and expects to have to bleed him again tomorrow but he assures me that he found him quite as much better today as he expected ... Henry is an excellent Patient, lies quietly in bed and is ready to swallow anything. He lives upon Medicine, Tea, and Barley Water.[15]

His illness became so serious that Jane, fearing for his life, summoned the family to Hans Place: James came from Steventon, picking up Cassandra on the way; Edward came from Godmersham, bringing his daughter Fanny with him, and she stayed behind with her Aunt Jane, once the worst was over.

As Henry began slowly to recover, he was taking up the cudgels with John Murray II on Jane's behalf:

> Dear Sir, Severe illness has confined me to my Bed ever since I received Yours of the 15th – I cannot yet hold a pen and employ an Amanuensis – the Politeness and Perspicacity of your Letter equally claim my earliest Exertion – Your Official opinion of the Merits of Emma, is very valuable and satisfactory – Though I venture to differ occasionally from your Critique, yet I assure you the Quantum of your commendation rather exceeds than falls short of the Author's expectation and my own. – The Terms you offer are so very inferior to what we had expected, that I am apprehensive of having made some great Error in my Arithmetical calculations. On the subject of the expence [*sic*] and profit of publishing you must be much better informed than I am – but documents in my possession appear to prove that the Sum offered by you for the Copyright of Sense and Sensibility, Mansfield Park, and Emma, is not equal to the Money which my Sister actually cleared by one very moderate Edition of Mansfield Park.

The letter indicates Henry's courteous approach to negotiation, which, of course, depended for its success on the other party also valuing courtesy. But it also illustrates how committed Henry was on Jane's behalf, that she should have a fair deal. His illness proved to be much graver than had been thought. Amongst other things, it meant that Jane Austen was forced to write to John Murray II on her own behalf twelve days later:

Sir, my Brother's severe Illness has prevented him from replying to Yours of October 15th, on the subject of the Ms of Emma now in your hands – and as he is, though recovering, still in a state which we are fearful of harassing by Business and I am at the same time desirous of coming to some decision on the affair in question, I must request the favour of you to call on me here, on any day after the present that may suit you best ... A short Conversation may perhaps do more than much Writing. My Brother begs his Compliments and best thanks for your polite attention in supplying him with a copy of Waterloo. I am, Sir, Your Obedient, Humble Servant, Jane Austen.

It's a neatly crisp letter. What other authors have ever demanded that their publisher should call on them?

Unfortunately, Henry's illness meant that he himself was unable to travel around Oxfordshire collecting the taxes that were due. It has been suggested that they might have been collected by a deputy,[16] and if that was the case, the payments to the Exchequer would have been delayed. But his illness also coincided with a significant problem at the Alton bank. It was in the process of failing. In common with other small banks, it did not have enough capital to withstand the numbers of people wanting to withdraw their money. But much more significant was the fact that one of the partners, Edward Gray, seeing the way the bank's finances were deteriorating, had withdrawn all the money that he felt belonged to himself, his family and friends, and had left only sixteen shillings behind. It was a simple but awful case of putting self-interest above that of the customers and the other partners. For example, there was a payment he made on 25 November of £1,500 to Michael Rivers, a 'notorious insolvent'. It might have been an attempt by Edward Gray to curry favour with an influential local man, but the result was that the attempt failed.

The extra difficulty with the Alton bank was that Austen, Maunde and Tilson had to spend £6,532 in 'discharging circular notes of the bank or cash balances for which Henry was jointly liable'.[17] In short, Austen, Maunde and Tilson were having to step into the breach as a matter of urgency. If they had not done so, their own bank and the partnership would have been at risk. And at the same time as they were engaged in this frantic salvage operation, they were also due to pay monies to the Exchequer for the taxes that had been collected. The outlook was troubling. Indeed, the rope was in place and the noose was tightening.

Chapter 13

Henry's Illness and his Bank's Demise

While all this high financial drama was going on, Jane received a letter from the Prince Regent's librarian at Carlton House, the Reverend James Stanier Clarke (1766–1834), inviting her to dedicate any future novels to His Royal Highness. Her reply sought further clarification about the processes and etiquette involved. And in his reply to that letter, James Stanier Clarke informed Jane that the Prince Regent had read and admired all her previous works. It was very flattering, but Jane might well have recalled a previous comment she had made about the Prince Regent and his marriage to Caroline of Brunswick. In February 1813, she had written:

> Poor woman, I shall support her as long as I can, because she is a Woman, & because I hate her Husband – but I can hardly forgive her for calling herself 'attached and affectionate' to a Man whom she must detest … But if I must give up the Princess, I am resolved at least always to think she would have been respectable if the Prince had behaved only tolerably to her at first.

But apart from that embarrassing difficulty, she must have been both amused and annoyed when James Stanier Clarke, in his letter to her of 16 November, impertinently and patronisingly asked her to write a novel about clergymen: 'And I also dear Madam wished to be allowed to ask you, to delineate in some future Work the Habits of Life and Character and enthusiasm of a clergyman.'[1]

Unfortunately, we do not have Jane's reply, but we do know that her dedication of *Emma* to the Prince Regent was deft. She wrote:

To His Royal Highness the Prince Regent, this work is, by His Royal Highness's Permission, most Respectfully Dedicated by His Royal Highness's Dutiful and Obedient Humble Servant.

It was honest but her inner circle must have smiled as they read between the lines.

The underlying seriousness of Henry's financial situation was not lost on Jane. It is hinted at in a letter to Cassandra, on 24 November. The letter opens with a delighted Jane saying that the printers of *Emma* had had problems with getting paper for the novel, but the situation had now eased, and she had just received some proofs to correct. She was thrilled: 'I am soothed and complimented into tolerable comfort.'[2]

Her letter went on to say that Edward Knight, her wealthy brother, and Mr Mascall, a lawyer, had visited Henry on the previous day. Clearly, it was a council of war, though Jane does not say as much, but she writes: '[Henry] read me what he wrote to Edward – part of it must have amused him I am sure – one part, alas! cannot be very amusing to anybody – I wonder with such Business to worry him he can be getting better, but he certainly does gain strength.'

It is a strong hint that all was not well, but whether out of sensitivity or confidentiality, she does not specify the problem. Instead, she conveys lots of gossip and details about who is coming to dinner and makes fun of the gift of a brace of pheasants, but then, lightly but ominously, says to Cassandra: 'I send you five one pound notes for fear you should be distressed for little money.'[3]

Two days later, on 26 November, Jane wrote to Cassandra and informed her that Henry was recovering:

Henry gets out in his Garden every day, but at present his inclination for doing more seems over, nor has he now any plans for leaving London before December 18, when he thinks of going to Oxford for a few days – today indeed, his feelings are for continuing where he is, through the next two months. One knows the uncertainty of all of this, but should it be so, we must think the best and hope the best and do the best.[4]

On 27 November, Austen and Co., the London bank, refused to honour payments made by the Alton bank. As a result, the Alton bank collapsed. It was catastrophic for its customers and the local economy – and catastrophic for Henry, still slowly recuperating from his illness. And it was seriously damaging to the bank of Austen, Maunde and Tilson.

On 2 December, Jane wrote another letter to Cassandra saying that Henry had returned to Hans Place, having been away. Her explanation is slightly elliptical, but it is possible that Henry had absented himself from the office to avoid possible conflicts of interest while the Alton Bank failure was being handled by his partners. But there were more difficulties to surmount.

In the meantime, Jane was in regular contact with John Murray II about the publication of *Emma*. On 11 December, she wrote to him about the terms and conditions under which it would appear:

As I find that Emma is advertized for publication as early as Saturday next, I think it best to lose no time in settling all that remains to be settled on the subject ... In the first place, I beg you to understand that I leave the terms on which the Trade should be supplied with the work entirely to your Judgement, entreating you to be guided in every such arrangement by your own experience of what is most likely to clear off the Edition rapidly. I shall be satisfied whatever you feel to be best with the work.[5]

But she then continues in a less placatory mood by asking that a bound copy should be sent to the Prince Regent a couple of days before the date set for publication and also reminds Mr Murray that *Mansfield Park* was ready to go into a second edition. Handling her own negotiations in this way marks a real change in her business confidence; heretofore, Henry had largely dealt with such negotiations, but in his current circumstances she clearly felt that she could manage these things herself and did so with dexterity and panache, though, as a further letter to John Murray II reveals, her instructions about the placing of the dedication to the Prince Regent were incorrect and she expressed herself grateful to Murray for pointing out her error: 'I feel happy in having a friend to save me from the ill effects of my own blunder.'

She was quite a diplomat and continued to exercise her diplomatic skill in letters addressed to James Stanier Clarke. Once again, he had urged her to write a novel about a clergyman. Her response was classic Jane:

> I am quite honoured by you thinking me capable of drawing such a clergyman as you gave your sketch of in your note of November 16th. But I assure you, I am not. The comic part of the Character I might be equal to, but not the Good, the Enthusiastic, the Literary. Such a Man's conversation must at times be on subjects of Science and Philosophy of which I know nothing – or at least be occasionally abundant in quotations and allusions which a Woman, who like me, knows only her own Mother-tongue and has read very little in that, would be totally without the power of giving. – A Classical Education, or at any rate, a very extensive acquaintance with English Literature, Ancient and Modern, appears to me quite Indispensable for the person who would do any justice to your Clergyman – and I think I may boast myself to be, with all possible Vanity, the most unlearned, and uninformed Female who ever dared to be an Authoress.[6]

James Stanier Clarke just did not understand her irony nor her wit, and replied by expressing delight in her previous novels, and then, because Jane had sent *Emma* to him for the attention of the Prince Regent, he had written on 21 December another fulsome letter of thanks: 'You were very good to send me Emma – which I have in no respect deserved. It is gone to the Prince Regent. I have read only a few pages which I very much admired—there is so much nature – and excellent descriptions of Character in everything you describe.'

In his letter, he continued to press her (how could he be so obtuse?) to write a novel about a clergyman. It must have irritated her, but he ended his letter by offering her the opportunity to use his own private library in Golden Square whenever she came to town. It was a generous suggestion, and one wonders if he was a 'fan' who was beginning to fall in love with his literary idol. Jane must have been amused, and perhaps flattered, but above all, she must have been exasperated by his patronising manner and his inability to grasp her subtle way of refusing his tiresome suggestion.

On the very same day that James Stanier Clarke was writing to Jane, it became known that Edward Gray of the Alton bank had been declared a bankrupt, and two days later, on 23 December, Henry had to borrow £10,000 from his own brother, Edward Austen Knight,[7] to help to prop things up. The bank's problems were now impacting upon family members, and the shadow of public failure hung over them. Jane could not fully rejoice in the publication of *Emma* on the same day that Henry must have been extremely anxious. Ruin was creeping closer. The Alton bank, as we have seen, 'owed the London bank £6,500 for notes and cash balances, and £3,200 for other transactions'.[8]

The financial situation was one of increasing urgency, so urgent in fact, that it was on 25 December, Christmas Day, that the Austen bank in London took out an Extent in Aid against Michael Rivers relating to an Alton bank loan, but to no avail. It was the beginning of the end for Henry and his bank.

But why was his bank failing?

As detailed financial records are not available to us, the answer can only be speculative. However, there are two general and underlying principles in banking that need to be observed if a bank is not to fail; first, a bank will fail if it cannot meet its obligations to depositors, and others, including creditors; second, a bank will fail when the value of its assets falls below the value of its liabilities, that is, its obligations to creditors and depositors.[9]

Those are the underlying principles, but the detailed potential causes of bank failures in the eighteenth and early nineteenth centuries can be further analysed by dividing them into two parts. There were internal causes and external causes that could apply to any bank, not just to Henry Austen's bank.

Internal causes of failure include, amongst other things, the bank being undercapitalised and the management/partners being incapable of evaluating risk, and therefore, issuing loans to people or institutions that neither had the capacity nor the willingness to repay the loans. Failure could also be caused by a lack of careful and disciplined oversight of the affairs of the bank by its senior leaders, and by incorrect collection and evaluation of data, i.e. records of transactions being carelessly recorded, and thus the oversight exercised by the managers would be based upon inadequate or inaccurate information. Failure could also be caused by a significant level of fraud being perpetrated by either the owners or one of the employees, and by the inability or unwillingness of the bank's debtors to pay their debts in a proper manner and at an agreed time.

External causes of failure include a sudden and unexpected downturn in the local or national economy, or a severe and sudden loss of confidence leading to a 'run' on the bank, or an unforeseeable event such as a major national disaster, or a catastrophic failure by a large number of indebted borrowers and institutions to repay their loans.

And what is a most significant factor in the case of bank failures in the late eighteenth and early nineteenth centuries is that there was no official Lender of Last Resort. In short, at that point in national history, it was neither the government's nor the Bank of England's legal responsibility to step in and support a failing bank.

So, it is worth asking a question: which were the most decisive factors in the demise of Henry's bank? At a guess, in the long term, it was to do with poor evaluation of risk, inadequate oversight, and undercapitalisation. But there were three other specific and more immediate factors: first, the collapse of the Alton bank coinciding with Henry's illness, against a background of national economic deterioration, made life extremely difficult; second, there was an external factor, and that was the end of the Napoleonic Wars, which meant that income from the agency side of the bank's work was in rapid decline; and third, Henry had been using the money received as Registrar General to pay creditors who were pressing the bank for their money, whereas that money was really owed to the Exchequer. In our contemporary terms, Henry was 'borrowing short and lending long'. It was a juggling act that might have worked if other circumstances had not intervened.

John Avery Jones summarises the situation succinctly: 'The true reason for the collapse was Henry's inability to pay over the tax he had collected at the beginning of the quarter because the Bank had met other liabilities.' He adds, 'Lord Moira had nothing to do with it.'[10]

On balance, it is probably fair to conclude that the collapse was a systemic failure rather than simply the failure of Henry as an individual, though, of course, he bore a major responsibility for what happened.

There was something about Henry's natural, sunny exuberance that suggests that disciplined and detailed attention to problem-solving was not his strongest suit. Nevertheless, it must be acknowledged that the problems of bankruptcy and debt were being felt by many across the country.

In *Persuasion*, which Jane Austen began writing in August 1815, debt is an important theme. Whether or not she had Henry in mind we cannot know but it must have alerted her to the debt problem that was striking various levels of society:

The Kellynch property was good, but not equal to Sir Walter's apprehension of the state required in its possessor. While Lady Elliot lived, there had been method, moderation, and economy, which had just kept him within his income; but with her had died all such right-mindedness, and from that period he had been constantly exceeding it. It had not been possible for him to spend less; he had done nothing but what Sir Walter Elliot was imperiously called on to do, but blameless as he was, he was not only growing dreadfully in debt but was hearing of it so often, that it became vain to attempt concealing it longer, even partially, from his daughter.

Despite Henry's own mounting concerns, as the new year of 1816 arrived, he found time and energy to buy the rights to *Northanger Abbey* from the original potential publisher, Richard Crosby of Ludgate Street. Whether this was typically generous and thoughtful of Henry or whether it was a kind of displacement activity in the financial turmoil can only be guessed at. But there can be no doubt that he was finding his personal financial situation increasingly demanding. He had to let his London house to try to recoup some money with which to repay part of the loan he had been given by his brother, Edward Austen Knight.

However, by January 1816 he had managed to get the Receiver General's books back into a reasonable order. He was now within the £6,500 limit. It must have been a relief, even if it was only temporary. Henry, now recovered from his illness, went to Oxford to collect the quarterly taxes. The amount collected was £51,215. This sum, less the £6,500 that he could keep for three months, was due to be paid to the Exchequer by 5 April. But in March, officers of the Exchequer visited the bank to ascertain the likelihood of Henry being able to meet his obligations. Why this was done is uncertain. Had they heard a rumour that Henry's bank might be heading for trouble? Had the fact that he had paid the sums due in December in daily small packets rather than in the usual lump sum alerted their suspicions that all was not well? The Exchequer officers walked out of the bank's door with only £13,270, which was all that the bank could pay at that precise moment. The bank was left with £22,743 of tax liabilities, which it could not pay. Result: despair.

Where had the tax money that had been collected gone? Henry probably used some of it (almost £5,500) to repay half the personal loan given to him earlier by Edward to tide the bank over; some of it had been used to pay property tax due on the bank; some of it had been used to pay down the old and inherited tax debt. And as for the remainder, who knows? What is clear is that at that point, Henry's bank was seriously under-capitalised. What is more, the collapse of the provincial banks meant that the debts they owed Henry's bank represented almost one-third of the book value of the bank's assets.[11] It was a dangerously unstable situation.

On 15 March 1816, the bank was issued by the Crown with a formal and alarming notice. It was an Extent in Chief, an official and immensely powerful way of demanding that £22,743. 8s. 10d. be paid to His Majesty by the bank. There was a further £21,702 owed by Henry himself.[12] It was a huge sum, which proved to be the final straw.

The following day, 16 March 1816, the bank, Austen, Maunde and Tilson, ceased to trade.

It is almost impossible to imagine the conversations between the three partners as they came to their grim decision. Three days later, Henry was up in front of the Commissioners of Bankruptcy. No doubt, he remained charming, but in his heart of hearts he must have been deeply shaken. He was required by the Committee of Creditors to realise as many of his assets as possible. Everything that he owned in Hans Place and everything he owned in the bank's premises in Henrietta Street had to be sold. The bailiffs moved in, not only to Henry's property but also to the properties of his two partners. The inventories of the three properties, carefully analysed by Deirdre Le Faye, make melancholic reading.[13] It is interesting to note, as an aside, that the bailiffs recorded that the banking hall in Henrietta Street contained, amongst many other things, not only an oval breakfast table on mahogany legs, a japanned coal hod and fire irons, eight pewter inkstands and an eight-day bracket clock, but more surprisingly, a musket. What was the purpose of that? Was it to frighten would-be robbers?

When the bailiffs made their inventories of Henry's Hans Place house, they kept a careful and detailed record, even down to a single butter knife, but, sadly for us, they did not record Henry's books; instead, they simply described them in terms of their quantity: 'about 100 books, bound and unbound on various subjects'; whereas, in the Tilson's house they noted that amongst many others, the books consisted of twelve volumes of Shakespeare, seven volumes of Secker's *Sermons*, six volumes of Pope's works, plus Stackhouse's six-volume history of the Bible.[14] In Maunde's house there were fewer books, but he had five volumes of Paley's *Theology*, five volumes of Pope's Homer's *Iliad*; he too, like Tilson, had *Johnson's Dictionary*, plus Blair's *Sermons*, and copies of *The Rambler* and *The Idler*.

There is a notable difference in the quantity of wines and spirits that were catalogued by the bailiffs: Henry had almost 1,000 bottles of wine, comprised of 576 quart bottles and 240 pint bottles of Claret, 48 bottles of Sauternes, 72 bottles Madeira, and 24 bottles of 'Constantia' (a dessert wine from South Africa) – but no Port; whereas, Tilson had 80 bottles of Port, 44 bottles of white wine and 18 bottles of hock, but Maunde had only 4 bottles of white wine. The impression one gets from Maunde's inventory is that he was less wealthy than either Henry or James Tilson. But might the very large collection of claret that Henry possessed have been related to his dealings in the wine trade, or had he laid them down as an investment?

What is noticeable in the case of all three partners is that no items of clothing were confiscated. So, at least, they were left with something, but the harrowing loss for James Tilson's wife in seeing all the linen and bedclothes confiscated, especially the bedding from the babies' cots, must have been dismal. It was not simply the loss of things; it was the grievous loss of personal and family history that those things represented that must have been very hard to bear.

While Henry was concerned with the poignant and soul-destroying task of seeing the bailiffs taking all his worldly goods, his sister Jane was involved in yet more correspondence with James Stanier Clarke. He had written to tell her that he was moving to a new post[15] as Chaplain and Private English Secretary to Leopold, Prince of Coburg (who had married Princess Charlotte, the Prince Regent's only daughter), and suggested that in future Jane might write an historical romance about the House of Coburg.

She brushed him off, politely and wittily, but firmly: 'I could no more write a Romance than an Epic Poem ... No – I must keep to my own style and go on in my own way.'[16]

And to John Murray II, she wrote about 'the late sad event in Henrietta Street' and asked him in future to address all correspondence to her at Chawton. One can sense the curtains of London quietly closing behind her.

In Henry's world, the bureaucratic wheels were turning slowly. In early April 1816, the creditors appointed two men, Joseph Silver and Richard Taylor, 'army clothiers of Charlotte Street in Bloomsbury',[17] to deal with Henry's assets. On 27 April, Henry was present at meetings with the creditors at the Guildhall who allowed him to keep 3 per cent of his remaining assets up to the value of £200. Henry had estimated his total debts to be £58,000 (over £7 million today) and his assets to be £52,000. On 1 May, it was estimated that his debts to the Crown were £44,000 (just under £5.5 million). But the human cost was greater because those who had stood surety for him, his brother Edward Austen Knight, and James Leigh Perrott, his maternal uncle, stood to pay the Crown £21,000 each as a forfeit – a bitter blow for them and their families. They had trusted Henry but had been badly let down. James Austen and Frank Austen had also stood as guarantors and so they, too, had to pay a price. In addition, it meant that for Jane, her sister and their mother, neither Henry nor Frank could any longer contribute to their domestic needs. Nevertheless, having lost deposits at Henry's bank, they now opened other small accounts at Hoares Bank.

In fact, according to John Avery Jones, those who had stood surety, eventually – within twenty-five years – recovered their money, but in the long delay they had lost income from the investment of that money which they otherwise could have had. It was not a comforting result.

Henry's bankruptcy was like a pebble thrown into a pond where the ripples spread wider and further than anyone could have imagined. In the depths of his soul, what he could have been thinking at this time is unknown. But surely, he could not have just shrugged it off. It was not simply a financial matter; it affected all the relationships in the Austen family and in their various friendship circles. And it deeply affected the lives of his partners.

Henry was officially discharged on 8 June 1816, as were his partners. It seems that Maunde's daughters had been sent back to Herefordshire to live with relatives, whilst Henry Maunde himself, his house and all its contents having been dealt with by the bailiffs, moved into rented accommodation in Thayer Street in Marylebone. E.J. Clery speculates that Maunde might have committed suicide in September that year. His funeral took place at St Mary's, Paddington, on 22 September 1816. The inventory made of his possessions reveals, poignantly, that he had owned a copy of *Mansfield Park*.

James Tilson was more fortunate; he was appointed by his elder brother as Deputy Receiver General of Taxes in Oxfordshire – John Henry Tilson had taken over from Henry Austen as Receiver General of Taxes for the county. But the family, meanwhile, moved to Foley Place, Marylebone. However, after the death of his wife and one of his daughters in 1823, James Tilson moved back to the family estate in Oxfordshire.

The discharge document was difficult for Henry to handle after his fifteen years as a banker. He must have looked at it in numb dismay. He was a widower. He had no children. He had no house. He had few possessions. Relationships with some of his former colleagues were under severe strain. He could no longer mix with the upper echelons of London society. He was officially bankrupt. What was he to do now? It was a depressing and daunting prospect.

Chapter 14

The Empty Future?

It cannot have helped Henry's state of mind that the weather of 1816 was dreadful. The ash cloud from the eruption of Mount Tambora had gradually covered Europe, leading to torrential rain and little sun. On Tuesday, 9 July 1816, Jane wrote to James-Edward Austen, her nephew, the son of her eldest brother, James. Her subject was the atrocious weather: 'It is really too bad, it has been too bad for a long time, much worse than anybody can bear, and I begin to think it will never be fine again.'[1] In Germany, 1816 was known as 'The Year of the Beggar' and in England there was considerable anxiety about the hay and wheat crops.

Henry, meanwhile, was staying with his long-suffering and patient brother, Edward, at Godmersham. Edward suggested that one of the things the unemployed Henry could do would be to introduce his nephews to France. Henry was very willing to do this because he could combine it with a bit of legal detective work. For some time, he had been wondering if he might be able to recoup some of the money owed to Eliza from her expropriated French lands, but despite travelling to France in July (accompanied by his nephews, and presumably financed by Edward), it was a hopeless quest. He returned empty-handed. It was a typical Henry idea: totally impractical but heroically romantic, a knight's quest on behalf of his beloved but deceased Lady, with potential financial gain added on.

But what was still preying on Henry's mind was the large sum of money that Lord Moira owed him. He believed that if he could retrieve this sum, it would enable him to go some way to repay his brother, Edward, and James Leigh-Perrott. He must have felt guilty about having let down two such close relatives. So, he set out his plan of campaign. Although Lord Moira was now in India, Henry would go to law to see if the Court of Exchequer in London's Guildhall might find in his favour in relation to the Moira debt. It must have been with some trepidation that he found himself in such a situation. Was his case strong enough to withstand scrutiny? Would his own naïve (?) mishandling of all the Oxfordshire tax revenues be revealed to a public hungry for scandal? Would he, could he, win? The case was 'The King v Ridge'. Mr Dauncey, counsel for the Crown, according to *The Times* of 16 July 1816, assured the jury that the case would not last long. He stated that the facts were simple: Mr Austen was a partner in the banking-house of Austen and Maunde of Henrietta Street, Covent Garden. He had been the Receiver General of land and income tax for the county of Oxfordshire but was now insolvent and had become indebted to the Crown. The Crown, wishing to recover the debts from Mr Austen himself rather than his sureties,[2] was now seeking to claim the money allegedly owed to Mr Austen by Mr Ridge, Lord Moira's agent, that is, the sum of £3,000 in three bills, each of one thousand pounds, bills that were in the possession of Mr Austen.

The response from Ridge's solicitor was that this request should be resisted because Mr Austen had come into possession of the bills by usury. The bills had nevertheless been signed by Lord Moira and Mr Ridge and were dated 13 April 1813, three years previously, and were to be paid within one year of their being signed and issued. They hadn't been. The solicitor for the defendant claimed that the charge upon the bills was 'treble the legal rate of discount', and whether it was Mr Austen or Mr Maunde who had negotiated this, the effect was the same: the 'amount of them could not be recovered by law', because the rate was usurious. As defence counsel, he went on to say that nothing could have been further from Lord Moira's mind than not to pay the money owed.

But at this stage, the situation became murky. Major James, the shadowy figure in the background of the Austen and Maunde banking house, stated that he was the confidential agent of Lord Moira. He claimed that over recent years, bills with just the signature of Lord

Moira had not been easy to deal with because of Lord Moira's reputation and his debts. Mr Dauncey, for the Crown, concurred: 'Of late years His Lordship's credit in the money market had sunk considerably.' Mr Dauncey stated that Major James had sold the bills to Mr Maunde but that the bills had further depreciated in value in the money market once Lord Moira had departed for India. Major James admitted that the bills in question were not worth near their nominal value when he had negotiated them with Mr Maunde.

It would seem, therefore, that no usury had been involved; quite the opposite. So, the question the jury had to answer was, whether the bills had been obtained by usury, or whether the transaction between Major James and Mr Maunde was a *bona fide* sale of them. If they believed the former, they must find a verdict for the defendant, Mr Ridge; if the latter, they must find for the Crown. It took the jury just thirty minutes to find in favour of the Crown. Sighs of relief from Henry Austen and his colleagues, Henry Maunde and James Tilson, but they still did not have the money they were owed. All that the case had revealed was that they were innocent of usurious practice. The relief was not to last long because in April/May 1817, Ridge appealed and the decision of the original court was overturned. It was all highly complex and technical.

Nevertheless, when the original court's decision had been reached, Henry had penned a letter to Lord Moira seeking the money, which, of course, had no effect.

Despite his dire situation, the evidence seems to be that Henry remained incorrigibly optimistic. He was remembered within the family as being invariably cheerful. And it seems that the family, apart from the Leigh-Perrots, bore him no ill will. It is very difficult to understand. Was Henry blind to all the havoc he had caused? Was he so incurably optimistic that reality was never allowed to impinge? Or might there have been a part of his personality, unrevealed to the family, which, in the small night hours when he lay awake, genuinely struggled towards remorse? The surviving evidence does not allow us to come to any well-founded conclusions.

The year 1816 had been an *annus horribilis* for the Austen family. In February, Charles Austen was carrying out his naval duties in the Eastern Mediterranean on the thirty-six-gun frigate HMS *Phoenix*. The war with France having come to an end, the Commander-in-Chief, Mediterranean, Lord Exmouth (1757–1833), ordered Charles to harry the pirates who were operating in the Adriatic. He successfully captured two pirate ships in Paphos harbour, but his ship was wrecked off Smyrna in February 2016 due to the incompetence of the pilots. He returned to England to care for his motherless children but was very poor. One of his daughters, Cassy, went to live at Chawton with her elderly grandmother, Mrs Austen, and with her Aunts Jane and Cassandra. It took Charles another ten years before another command was given to him.

Frank Austen, having had an outstanding naval career, was on half-pay in retirement. In 1815, he was created a Companion of the Order of the Bath in recognition of his distinguished service to the country and was living at Chawton Great House. Having invested in Henry's bank, he was one of the victims of Henry's bankruptcy.

James Austen, the oldest of the Austen brothers, was the Vicar of Steventon but was beginning to suffer from digestive troubles, which would eventually, in 1819, kill him. He was a sick man.

It was only Edward who had the generosity and wherewithal to be able to help some of the family financially. And Jane was beginning to feel unwell, though her symptoms were unspecific.

In July 1816, Henry had returned from France and now an empty future lay in front of him. He had to earn some money, and so, perhaps naturally (or desperately?), his mind began to move towards ordination. At the very least, it would give him a small and regular income, and perhaps, as a single man he could manage to live modestly on a curate's stipend. It was worth consideration ... and so, in due course, on 5 November 1816, he wrote a letter to Bishop Brownlow North of Winchester. It needs to be quoted in full because it provides a (partial) summary of Henry's thinking:

My Lord

In conformity with Mr Gell[3] whose letter I herewith enclose, I have the honour to lay before your Lordship as circumstantial a detail as possible without trespassing too much on your time, of the causes which make me a Candidate for Holy Orders at a more advanced stage in life than is for the most part usual.

I was originally destined for the Church. I was educated accordingly by my father, the late the Reverend George Austen who was a beneficed clergyman upwards of 40 years in your Lordship's Diocese. I obtained a Fellowship at the age of 17 at St John's College, Oxford, of which your Lordship is Visitor. I proceeded regularly to the degree of Master of Arts retaining my Fellowship for ten years.

Soon after taking my degree of A.B. and not being old enough for ordination and the political circumstances of the time 1793 calling on everyone not otherwise employed to offer his services in the general defence of the country, I accepted a Commission in the Oxfordshire Militia. I remained in it until 1800. I have reason to think that by my conduct I acquired and still preserve the [illegible] approbation of my Colonel, Lord Charles Spencer whose character is as much distinguished by every moral virtue as his name is by the rank attached to it. I think I can depend on his fullest recommendation under every circumstance.

After leaving the Militia I engaged in the business of a Banker in London. I was not unsuccessful till rendered so by the conduct of those Gentlemen who unfortunately for me were my partners in the Bank in Alton. Their mismanagement of that concern obliged me to close all my other concerns and resign the respectable situation which I had held for some years as Receiver General of the County of Oxford.

Conscious of no criminality I state my worldly failures without hesitation. I bow [writing illegible: 'much'?] humbly to the Stroke of Providence and am rendered thereby more desirous than ever of devoting the rest of my life and talents, such as they may be, to the more immediate service of religion.

My connections are creditable. I have one brother who is rector of Steventon in your Lordship's diocese, and another who having changed his name to Knight possesses very large freehold Estates in the neighbourhood of Alton. We have all been educated in the strictest attachment to the tenets of the Established Church. For myself, I respectfully assure your Lordship that I am a Candidate for Ordination on the finest motives [writing illegible] unmixed with anything of a worldly nature. I am known, (though slightly) to the Revd the Chancellor of your diocese, Mr Garnie,[4] who was my contemporary at the University and who probably is not unacquainted with the general facts of my foregoing statement. He probably also is aware the closest intimacy has ever subsisted between myself and the President of St John's College, Dr Maslow [? writing illegible] from whom I could provide a strong testimonial.

I have only to add that the Revd Mr Papillon who is desirous of appointing me his Assistant Curate does reside on his living.

Trusting that your Lordship will be satisfied with the minuteness [? writing illegible] and substance of the foregoing statement as well as with the letter testimonial signed by three beneficed clergymen of your diocese who all know me well and of whom two have known me 40 years.

I leave my cause to your Lordship's goodness and have the honour to remain your Lordship's most obedient servant,

What are we to make of that four-page letter?

It begins by assuring the Bishop that as an ordination candidate Henry has gone through the formal processes; this is followed by his statement that he had always been destined for the Church. (Had he? Was this statement true?) He then resorts, diplomatically, to establishing common ground with the Bishop by reminding him that they both had close connections with St John's College, Oxford. He affirms his patriotism (no eighteenth-century bishop would demur) and makes mention of his connections with the aristocracy. Again, in the eighteenth and early nineteenth-century cultural context, who you knew established your place in the pecking order. He explains why he left banking and hints that it was through no fault of his own – it was due to the underhand behaviour of his Alton bank partners – but he does not mention his own mismanagement, nor does he mention the fact that he was a bankrupt. He refers to a 'stroke of Providence', that is, he implies that things were outside his own control. Interestingly, 'Providence' was a concept much in vogue at that time. Think of William Cowper's (1731–1800) poem 'God moves in a mysterious way', in which the following lines appear: 'Behind a frowning providence, He [God] hides a smiling face'. William Cowper was Jane's favourite poet.

Henry continues by establishing another personal connection with the Bishop. He refers to Canon Garnier and tactfully avoids mentioning that Garnier was the Bishop's son-in-law, but then Henry plays the St John's College card for the second time.

In short, the letter is flattering and coy, filled with subtle references to the aristocracy but not entirely frank about the truth of his banking problems. As long as the Bishop did not ask any probing questions, it might do the trick – which it did. So, perhaps the Bishop took the view that Henry's 'conversion' to the cause of religion was heartfelt and that he should be given a second chance.

The letter paved the way in the late autumn of 1816 for a face-to-face meeting with the Bishop. And so, after preparing himself by revising the Greek he had learnt at Oxford, he travelled to meet the Bishop, who had the responsibility of examining his fitness to be ordained.

Bishop Brownlow North (1741–1820) was extremely well-connected. His paternal half-sibling was Frederick, Lord North (1732–92) the Prime Minister, who had appointed him as Bishop of Lichfield in 1771, when Brownlow North was only 30 years of age. In 1774, he became Bishop of Worcester and then was translated to Winchester in 1781. Lord North famously replied, when challenged about the appointment of his brother as Bishop of Lichfield: 'No doubt my brother is young to be a bishop, but when he is older, he will no longer have a brother for Prime Minister.' It summarises neatly the nepotism that existed in the Church of England in the eighteenth and early nineteenth centuries. In fact, Brownlow North ensured that many members of his extended family received livings. It has been estimated that at least twenty-six individuals received about seventy appointments to fifty churches between 1785 and 1820.[5] And he ensured that his eldest son, Francis, Lord Guilford, became Rector of St Mary's, Southampton, held the combined livings of Old Alresford, New Alresford, and Medstead, was a Canon of Winchester Cathedral and the Master of St Cross – the combined incomes of which would have been considerable.

So, when Henry turned up to meet Bishop Brownlow North (at Farnham Castle?) asking to be ordained, he was in the company of a man who was used to discharging his episcopal functions with largesse. Henry might have been apprehensive about the examination, wondering perhaps which part of the New Testament in Greek Bishop North would require him to translate. He need not have worried. It is said that on meeting him, Brownlow North, who was a keen botanist, placed his hand on a Greek New Testament and declared, 'I dare say it is some years since either you or I looked into it.'[6] We do not know Henry's reply, but his warm personality and optimism seem to have won the day. He was firmly *en route* to his new career.

But first there were a few legal preliminaries to be undertaken. He had to provide a copy of his Certificate of Baptism. James, his brother, the Vicar of Steventon, kindly obliged. In addition, James had to read aloud a document to the congregation of Steventon:

Whereas Henry Thomas Austen of this parish intends to offer himself at the ensuing Ordination of the Lord Bishop of Winchester ... This is to give notice that if any person can show sufficient excuse for its impediment, or notable cause for which the said Henry Thomas Austen ought not to be admitted to that Holy

Order he may now declare the same and give notice thereof to the Lord Bishop of Winchester. Dated October 27th, 1816, signed by James Austen, and countersigned by the churchwarden, W F Digweed.

W.F. Digweed was the resident of the Manor House and a long-time friend of the Austen family.

What the ordinary members of the congregation made of this announcement we cannot know, but it is bound to have been the subject of gossiped conversation as the worshippers made their way back down the hill to their cottages in the valley.

Henry was made a deacon by John Fisher,[7] Bishop of Salisbury, in Salisbury Cathedral on 22 December 1816, after Letters Dimissory by the Bishop of Winchester. And a few months later, on 2 March 1817, he was ordained priest also by Bishop John Fisher at the Quebec Chapel, St Marylebone in London, again after Letters Dimissory from the Bishop of Winchester.

There is a serendipitous moment recorded in the Bishop of Salisbury's Act Book concerning that ordination. Alongside Henry in the Quebec Chapel was a much younger man also being priested. That man was the Reverend Charles Richard Sumner who, ten years later in 1827, would become Bishop of Winchester, and therefore Henry's diocesan bishop. When they met some years afterwards they are bound to have discussed the happy coincidence of their being ordained on the same day.

Meanwhile, following his ordination as a deacon, Henry became the curate to the Reverend Mr Papillon of Chawton, a distant relation of the Knights. The Austen family joked that Mr Papillon was sweet on Jane.

Henry's stipend at Chawton was fifty guineas[8] per annum, which was enough to allow him to keep a horse but was by no means overgenerous. Socially and culturally, it was a very long way from his life in London's West End and from the parties with the Regency set in London that he had so much enjoyed. And a long way from the houses he had inhabited in Sloane Street, Henrietta Street and Hans Place.

The wealthy, high-living and well-connected society banker had become a poorly paid curate. But it was not just the monetary lack that would have impacted on Henry. There were other social markers that would have marked his failure.

The late eighteenth and early nineteenth centuries, as we saw in Chapter 2, were caught up in an almost feverish fashion for 'improvement'. Humphry Repton (1752–1818) was the foremost garden designer of his day and incidentally, the first person to describe himself as a 'landscape gardener'. He drew up plans for the design of gardens of great estates across the country and was employed, for example, at Stoneleigh Abbey, the seat of the Leigh family, a place where the Austens sometimes went to stay. Nearer to home, Edward Austen Knight's Great House at Chawton had had its gardens remodelled into the English Landscape style in 1763–80, including a ha-ha and sweeping lawns. And, of course, in Jane Austen's novels, gardens are frequently featured, including the famous occasion in *Mansfield Park* where Humphry Repton is mentioned:

> Mr Rushworth, who was now making his appearance at Mansfield for the first time since the Crawfords' arrival. He had been visiting a friend in a neighbouring county, and that friend having recently had his grounds laid out by an improver, Mr Rushworth was returned with his head full of the subject, and very eager to be improving his own place in the same way; and though not saying much to the purpose, could talk of nothing else ... 'I must try to do something with [Sotherton],' said Mr Rushworth, 'but I do not know what. I hope I shall have some good friend to help me.'
>
> 'Your best friend upon such an occasion,' said Miss Bertram calmly, 'would be Mr Repton, I imagine.' 'That is what I was thinking of as he has done so well by Smith. I think I had better have him at once. His terms are five guineas a day.'

And a little later in that novel, when the manipulative, wealthy and arrogant Henry Crawford is trying to persuade the young Edmund

Bertram about the potential of his future parsonage at Thornton Lacey, he declares:

> The farmyard must be cleared away entirely and planted up to shut out the blacksmith's shop. The house must be turned to front the east instead of the north – the entrance and principal rooms, I mean, must be on that side, where the view is ... very pretty; I am sure it may be done. And there must be your approach – through what is at present the garden.[9]

Edmund rejects Henry Crawford's advice, but Henry Crawford is determined to win the argument and suggests that the parsonage should be a place that has the air of a gentleman's residence. Interestingly, he compares the potential of the house with the traditional and poorer residences of clergy: 'It is not a scrambling collection of low single rooms, with as many roofs as windows; it is not cramped into the vulgar compactness of a square farmhouse.'[10]

The late eighteenth and early nineteenth centuries saw many vicarages and rectories rebuilt in a much grander and more sophisticated style than clergy houses in previous generations had been.

'Improvement' was the fashion, therefore, not only in the parks and gardens of the wealthy but was also being practised by some clergymen in their vicarages, gardens and glebe. For example, Henry Tilney, the parson of Woodston in *Northanger Abbey*, lived, as his father General Tilney declared, in:

> a mere Parsonage, small and confined, we allow, but decent perhaps and habitable, and altogether not inferior to the generality;– or, in other words, I believe there are few country parsonages in England half so good. It may admit of improvement, however. Far be it from me to say otherwise; and any thing in reason – a bow thrown out, perhaps – though, between ourselves, if there is one thing more than another my aversion, it is a patched-on bow.[11]

But for Henry as a perpetual curate, the lack of a house with fashionable bow windows, the lack of a garden with acres of lawns, the lack of a 'sweep' running up to the main door, and the lack of glebe would have made him extremely conscious of his 'fall' from society. His life had something of Icarus about it. His enviable worldly status had now completely disappeared. He was a bankrupt and instead of confidently walking the streets of fashionable London, he was now walking the muddy lanes of Chawton, entirely dependent on his poor stipend as a Church of England minister. He must have reflected upon his dramatically changed circumstances and have looked back over his life trying to chart the moments of worldly success and crashing worldly failure. It must surely have weighed upon him, even though he might have worked hard to disguise it.

Whilst the family was remarkably supportive, they must occasionally have wondered how Henry could have had his glittering life of wealth and worldly success turned upside down so dramatically.

Chapter 15

Return to Chawton and Jane's Death

In the same year that Henry had become a lowly curate, Jane had gone to fashionable Cheltenham to take the waters, and somehow, despite sharing with her mother and her sister in caring for her young niece, had managed to complete *Persuasion*.

Henry, meanwhile, as Mr Papillon's curate, would have known that his foremost duties involved preaching and taking services according to *The Book of Common Prayer*. Holy Communion was required in law to be celebrated just three times in a year, but in some churches, a celebration of the Eucharist was an added extra after Matins. Even so, it was hardly onerous – Chawton parish only had a population of about 400 people,[1] and thus there could have been just a few times each year when Henry might have been called upon to take baptisms, weddings and funerals.

However, as we can see from *Mansfield Park*, the role of a clergyman in early nineteenth-century England involved more than just taking services. He was supposed to set an example of proper living to all the inhabitants of the parish.

The background to the following dialogue is that Miss Crawford is talking with Edmund Bertram, who is going to take Holy Orders:

'But why are you to be a clergyman? I thought that was always the lot of the youngest, where there were many to choose before him.'

'Do you think the church itself never chosen then?' [replied Edmund]

'Never is a black word. But yes, in the never of conversation which means not very often, I do think it. For what is to be done in the church? Men love to distinguish themselves, and in either of the other lines distinction may be gained, but not in the church. A clergyman is nothing.'

'The nothing of conversation has its gradations, I hope as well as the never. A clergyman cannot be high in state or fashion. He must not head mobs or set the tone in dress. But I cannot call that situation nothing which has the charge of all that is of the first importance to mankind, individually or collectively considered, temporally and eternally – which has the guardianship of religion and morals, and consequently of the manners which result from their influence. No-one here can call the office nothing. If the man that holds it is so, it is by the neglect of his duty, by forgoing its just importance, and stepping out of his place to appear what he ought not to appear.'

'You assign greater consequence to the clergyman than one has been used to hear given, or than I can quite comprehend. One does not see much of this influence and importance in society, and how can it be acquired when they are so seldom seen themselves? How can two sermons a week, even supposing them worth hearing, supposing the preacher to have the sense to prefer Blair's to his own, do all that you speak of – govern the conduct and fashion the manners of a large congregation for the rest of the week? One scarcely sees a clergyman out of his pulpit.'

'You are speaking of London: I am speaking of the nation at large.'

Whilst that dialogue in *Mansfield Park* is obviously part of the novel's storyline, nevertheless, it suggests that the role of the clergyman was being discussed at various levels of society and was a discussion that Jane would have heard not only around the family table but also when she was visiting some of the great houses in Hampshire and East Kent. Indeed, in the eighteenth century there was some degree of pessimism about the clergy. Penelope Corfield describes how a document entitled 'An Enquiry into the Causes of the Infidelity and Scepticism of the Times' was one of several tracts to report upon the readiness of people to scoff at the clergy and the Scriptures.[2]

But that sense of pessimistic criticism is not one that seriously features in Jane Austen's novels. It raises a question: were rural people less likely to scoff than the London literati? Or did they simply keep their views to themselves?

Jane Austen, as someone who lived in the countryside but who through Henry had some insights into the mores and behaviour of London society, was herself something of a connoisseur of clergy and of their sermons. When in London she worshipped with Henry at some of the most fashionable churches, including St Paul's, Covent Garden, and when at home, she had worshipped at Steventon in her early years and then latterly at Chawton. She was outspoken about her dislike of the sermons of her cousin, the Reverend Edmund Cooper, who was the Vicar of Hamstall Ridware, a village parish in Staffordshire.

'We do not much like Mr Cooper's new sermons – they are fuller of Regeneration and Conversion than ever – with the addition of his zeal in the cause of the Bible Society.'[3]

Although Mr Cooper's sermons[4] were published a couple of years after Jane's letter, their tone, content and style, to which she objected, can be seen in his *Practical and Familiar Sermons*, published in 1819. Part of a paragraph from one of his sermons illustrates this:

> Wherever He [Jesus Christ] reigns, there is light, and liberty; but where He reigns not, there is darkness, and slavery. His kingdom is a kingdom of righteousness, peace, and joy in the Holy Ghost: and to every soul, in which it is established, He communicates these blessings, and sheds them abroad in the heart. But does every soul submit to Jesus Christ? Is every heart willing to receive, and obey Him? Alas! far otherwise. When He comes to take possession of the soul, He finds it already occupied. He finds it under the dominion of other lords, even of Sin and Satan, who have fixed their residence, and set up their own kingdom therein. These are Foes, who being

directly opposed to Christ, and anxious to maintain their own usurped authority try every means to exclude Him from the heart. To this end they stir up against Him its secret enmity and unbelief. They fill the mind with prejudices against Christ, and His Religion. They excite against Him the lusts and passions of the natural man. They take advantage of the prevailing habits and evil dispositions of the heart, whether pride, or covetousness, or sensuality, or worldly-mindedness, to arm it against Christ, and to oppose his conquests.

That kind of sermon was certainly not to Jane's taste. But she could jokingly refer to Henry's first preachment at Chawton:

Our own new clergyman is expected here very soon, perhaps in time to assist Mr Papillon on Sunday. I shall be very glad when the first hearing is over. It will be a nervous hour for our Pew, though we hear he acquits himself with as much ease and collectedness, as if he had been used to it all his life.

It might be that the main underlying theme of Henry's sermons was about the connection between knowledge and duty. There is a tiny reference in *Mansfield Park* in which Edmund Bertram is explaining to Fanny Price at great length how he had had a serious and relationship-breaking conversation with Mary Crawford:

She tried to speak carelessly, but she was not so careless as she wanted to appear. I only said in reply that from my heart I wished her well, and earnestly hoped that she might soon learn to think more justly, and not owe the most valuable knowledge any of us could acquire – the knowledge of ourselves and of our duty – to the lessons of affliction.[5]

Does this quotation give us any insight into what Henry Austen might have preached about?

Sermons were the main occupation of a clergyman, but because there were books of sermons in print, a curate could simply read aloud a sermon from such a publication. For example, in 1804, a book was published entitled *Practical Sermons* by the late Reverend Joseph Milner, a Master of the Grammar School and Vicar of Holy Trinity Church, Kingston upon Hull. The book ran into several editions and must, therefore, have been popular. Milner was what had once been called an 'enthusiast' but, despite early opposition to his preaching, he had won over the hearts and minds of the people of Hull. And thus, his sermons, founded upon Evangelical principles, influenced many. Whether or not Henry had a copy of Milner's *Sermons* is not known but the opening sermon of the book will give some idea of the kind of sermons being preached or read at the time.

The sermon is based on the biblical text 'The imagination of man's heart is evil from his youth' (Genesis 8, verse 21):

Such is the character given of man, not by the flattering pencil of man himself, but by him who searches the heart, and who alone knows it thoroughly – the Lord our MAKER.

The doctrine which the words contain is commonly called Original Sin. It is the first doctrine of the Scriptures. The whole religion of the Bible supposes it, requires it, and is built upon it; and it is so much a first principle, that he, who will not learn this, can learn nothing else to make him wise unto salvation.

It must not be expected in one popular discourse, I should do full justice to a subject of so much importance. But I shall throw out a few hints concerning it, for the consideration of those, who either do not believe it, or are not affected with it. And I hope to shew it not only a true, but a most important and most necessary doctrine. The proof of it shall be given from Scripture and from facts. The vanity of objections, and the necessity of a practical learning of the doctrine must be shewn: The Truth of all the rest of the capital doctrines of Scripture must be illustrated on the supposition of the certainty of this: And the great point of instruction in the way of salvation, as the consequence of the whole, must be distinctly stated.

And so, the sermon continues for a further 4,000 words. If it were preached aloud, the sermon would last for at least forty-five minutes.

Sermons of notable preachers in the eighteenth and early nineteenth centuries were not only declaimed from pulpits but were collected and published as books to be read by members of the congregation and by others farther afield. On the bookshelves of gentlemen's libraries could be found multiple volumes of sermons, as was the case, for instance, in the library of James Tilson. Sermons were part of the religious, moral and cultural reading matter of the middle and upper classes.

Henry's life as a curate and as a preacher in Chawton was being carefully observed by Jane, Cassandra, and their mother. In a letter to her nephew James, written on Monday, 16 December 1816, Jane stated, 'Uncle Henry writes very superior sermons,' and then jokingly added, 'You and I must try to get hold of one or two and put them into our Novels – it would be a fine help to a volume; and we could make our Heroine read it aloud of a Sunday evening.'

It is hard to realise that even at this stage in her life, Jane was not at all well. She was glad to have Henry, her favourite brother, as a close neighbour and daily companion.

By April 1817, having completed only a few chapters of her new novel, *Sanditon*, Jane was feeling so ill that she took to her bed. And by 27 April, she had secretly written her will. She knew she was dying. The decision was made that she would receive better medical care if she travelled to Winchester, where she could be placed under the care of a local physician. On 24 May, Jane set off. She said goodbye to her elderly mother and the maids. It must have been a heart-wrenching moment for Mrs Austen, watching her sick daughter climb feebly into a carriage with Cassandra sitting beside her. Henry rode alongside the carriage for the 16-mile journey, accompanied by Edward's son,

William. It was a wet and miserable day. Lodgings had been found at 8, College Street, a quiet road just off the Cathedral Close and near Winchester College. There, Jane and Cassandra made themselves at home, as best they could, on the first floor of the house with a bay window overlooking the street. There were two sitting rooms and two bedrooms.

Jane hoped that Mr Lyford, the physician, might find a cure for her illness. She wrote to her nephew, James Edward, about Mr Lyford and added, 'if he fails, I shall draw up a memorial and lay it before the Dean and Chapter. I have no doubt of redress from that Pious, Learned, and disinterested body.' It was her last surviving letter, and was written, of course, tongue in cheek.

Having seen Jane and Cassandra safely installed in College Street, Henry set off back to Chawton, the grey, wet weather no doubt reflecting his mood.

He travelled back and forth from Chawton to Winchester to see Jane and Cassandra over the next few weeks, but it was clear that Jane was failing quite rapidly. On 17 July at 5.15 pm, Jane had a seizure, but regained consciousness. Mr Lyford was called for and administered something, possibly laudanum, to ease her discomfort.

Cassandra is recorded as asking her sister Jane if there was anything she wanted and received the reply that she wanted nothing now except death. 'God grant me patience, Pray for me, oh Pray for me.'

Cassandra sat next to the bed, with Jane's head resting on a pillow on Cassandra's lap. They stayed like that for the next six hours, until Mary Austen, James's wife, who was helping to care for Jane, suggested that Cassandra should rest and that she would take over the vigil. At 4.15 am on Friday, 18 July, Jane breathed her last. Mary's diary reads: 'Only Cass and I were with her. Henry came.'

Mary's diary entry does not make clear what the time of Henry's arrival might have been. But he will have ridden as rapidly as possible, hoping to be with Jane during her last hours. It was not to be. She had died before he arrived.

It takes little imagination to picture the scene in that upstairs sitting room when he did arrive: Cassandra would have been distraught but resilient. Mary, of whom Jane had not been overly fond, would have ensured that Henry's coat was taken and hung up, and then as they sat before the gentle fire, they would have shared memories of Jane's life. Perhaps Cassandra, even in her own profound loss, was able to write what she so deeply felt. 'She was the sun of my life, the gilder of every pleasure, the soother of every sorrow, I had not a thought concealed from her, and it is as if I had lost part of myself.'

At such a moment, in that upstairs sitting room, as the eastern sun began to slant its early morning light through the windows, Henry's clerical attire might have been valued, for it symbolised his seriousness and his new professional occupation, even though he had been ordained just eight months previously. It is likely that they would have looked to him to talk about, and to decide, what needed to be done next.

Where should the funeral be held? Where should Jane be buried?

Perhaps it was Henry's established contacts with the Bishop of Winchester that helped. Or it might have been the influence of Elizabeth Heathcote, a clergy widow, and an old family friend, who was living in the Close with her sister, Alethea Bigg, that enabled the funeral to be planned so carefully and expeditiously. Jane's brothers Edward and Francis arrived in Winchester on 23 July. James was too unwell to be there, but his son, James-Edward,[6] representing him, rode hard from Steventon to get to the funeral, which took place early in the morning of Thursday, 24 July 1817.

Jane had died in the first-floor bedroom and thus her body had now to be placed in the coffin. It was the final moment for the mourners, including Cassandra, Edward, Francis and Henry, to gaze on Jane and to say their farewells to her in the secret places of their hearts. Once the lid of the coffin had been screwed into place it was carried downstairs and set on a wheeled bier. A purple pall was placed upon the coffin, which was then wheeled from College Street, under the arch of Kingsway and into the close. It was followed, as was the custom, not by Cassandra nor any other female mourners, but by Jane's three brothers and her nephew. At the cathedral the coffin was carried into the nave, where the service probably took place, led by the Precentor, Thomas Watkins.[7]

It followed the pattern ('At The Burial of the Dead') laid down in *The Book of Common Prayer*, with its sonorous opening sentence:

> I am the resurrection and the life, saith the Lord; he that believeth in me, though he were dead, yet shall he live: and whosoever liveth and believeth in me shall never die. (St John 11, 25–26)

Other biblical texts were declaimed, followed by two psalms: Psalm 39 and Psalm 90. And so, the service slowly unfolded.

Part of the way through the service, the coffin was taken to the brick-lined grave in the north aisle, where it was carefully lowered into the vault, while the following words were recited:

> Forasmuch as it hath pleased Almighty God of his great mercy to take unto himself the soul of our dear sister here departed, we therefore commit her body to the ground: earth to earth, ashes to ashes, dust to dust; in sure and certain hope of the resurrection to eternal life through our Lord Jesus Christ; who shall change our vile body that it may be like unto his glorious body, according to the mighty working, whereby he is able to subdue all things to himself.

Towards the end of the service, two long prayers were declaimed, one of which was as follows:

> Almighty God, with whom do live the spirits of them that depart hence in the Lord, and with whom the souls of the faithful, after they are delivered from the burden of the flesh, are in joy and felicity: We give thee hearty thanks, for that it hath pleased thee to deliver this our sister out of the miseries of this sinful world;

beseeching thee, that it may please thee, of thy gracious goodness, shortly to accomplish the number of thine elect. And to hasten thy kingdom; that we, with all those that are departed in the true faith of thy holy name, may have our perfect consummation and bliss, both in body and soul, in thy eternal and everlasting glory; through Jesus Christ our Lord.

It can be safely assumed that Jane would have thoroughly approved of the service, for it encapsulated the doctrine of the Christian faith in which she so firmly believed. And the rhythm of the language, the cadences, and the phrases that she had known since childhood would have meant much to her.

The service concluded, quite simply, with the words of the Grace:

The grace of our Lord, Jesus Christ, and the love of God, and the fellowship of the Holy Ghost, be with us all evermore. Amen.

The three brothers and the nephew would have spent a few moments in silent reflection, before thanking Thomas Watkins, and then they would have made their way slowly back to Cassandra and friends in College Street, where, no doubt, they had breakfast.

There was one major event still to come: the reading of the will. Jane had made Cassandra her chief executor and had left everything to her. But there were two other named legatees: Henry was left £50, perhaps as a way of thanking him for his help in getting her novels published, and £50 was left to Madame Bigeon, the kind Frenchwoman who had been so good to Henry's wife, Eliza. This was a detailed and thoughtful gift to someone for whom Jane had felt great affection and gratitude. Madame Bigeon must have felt deeply touched. And Henry would have been moved by his sister's generosity and kindness.

But there was still one more thing for the family to decide before they went their separate ways: what should be the epitaph carved upon the black marble ledger of Jane's tomb?

Perhaps this too was left to Henry. Whatever the process that preceded the choice, the final wording was as follows:

> In Memory of
> JANE AUSTEN,
> youngest daughter of the late
> Revd GEORGE AUSTEN,
> formerly Rector of Steventon in this County
> she departed this life on the 18th July 1817,
> aged 41, after a long illness supported with
> the patience and hopes of a Christian.
> The benevolence of her heart,
> the sweetness of her temper, and
> the extraordinary endowments of her mind
> obtained the regard of all who knew her and
> the warmest love of her intimate connections.
> Their grief is in proportion to their affection
> they know their loss to be irreparable,
> but in their deepest affliction they are consoled
> by a firm though humble hope that her charity,
> devotion, faith and purity have rendered
> her soul acceptable in the sight of her
> REDEEMER.

It is curiously formal, and almost indifferently impersonal. It might not have been composed by all the brothers putting in their ideas, but it reads like a committee compromise. There is no mention, for example, of her great novels; it is as though they were of little consequence compared with her other virtues, including her undoubted faith.

Jane's wit, her high intelligence, her literary gifts of style, composition and deft characterisation, her understated humour, her insights about her fellow humans and human society – none of these are mentioned. Instead, the epitaph is formulaic. But perhaps she would have been appreciative of the thought that had gone into it and been wryly amused by its pedestrian quality.

Henry returned alone to his curacy in Chawton, and perhaps he spent more time with his mother and Cassandra where, in the privacy of the cottage, he and they were able to share warm and affectionate memories of Jane.

Once August had passed, Henry moved to Sherborne St John for a few weeks, to take services for his brother James, who was unwell.

But on his mind must have been Jane's novels. What might he do to ensure that they reached the audience he believed they deserved?

Chapter 16

Publishing Jane's Books, Chawton and Berlin

Cassandra was the chief executor of Jane's last will and testament, but she had the experienced help of Henry in ensuring that Jane's two unpublished novels, *Catherine* and *The Elliots* were placed in front of the publisher, John Murray. The brother and sister decided that the titles of the novels did not work and suggested that they should be renamed as *Northanger Abbey* and *Persuasion*. It was a wise decision.

It was Henry who not only negotiated the deal with Murray but also appended to the volumes a biographical note:[1]

> The following pages are the production of a pen which has already contributed in no small degree to the entertainment of the public. And when the public, which has not been insensible to the merits of 'Sense and Sensibility', 'Pride and Prejudice', 'Mansfield Park', and 'Emma', shall be informed that the hand which guided that pen is now mouldering in the grave, perhaps a brief account of Jane Austen will be read with a kindlier sentiment than simple curiosity. …
>
> Short and easy will be the task of the mere biographer. A life of usefulness, literature, and religion was not by any means a life of event. To those who lament their irreparable loss it is consolatory to think that, as she never deserved disapprobation, so, in the circle of her family and friends she never met reproof; that her wishes were not only reasonable, but gratified; and that to the little disappointments incidental to human life was never added, even for a moment, an abatement of good will from any who knew her.

In the paragraphs that follow, Henry expatiates on Jane's virtues, and offers some insights about her inspiration in writing:

> Her power of inventing characters seems to have been intuitive, and almost unlimited. She drew from nature; but whatever may have been surmised to the contrary, never from individuals.

Henry also referred to her reading aloud:

> with very great taste and effect. Her own works, probably, were never heard to so much advantage as from her own mouth for she partook largely in all the best gifts of the comic muse.

It is difficult to believe that when the family had gathered around the fire in their Chawton cottage and Jane read the opening line of *Pride and Prejudice* ('It is a truth universally acknowledged') that there wasn't much laughter and warm happiness. Who could not smile and admire and enjoy such a perfectly balanced sentence? And when Mr Collins is described, in the same book, surely the family might have glimpsed not necessarily an individual whom they knew, but at least a 'type' whom they could recognise:

> A fortunate chance had recommended him to Lady Catherine de Bourgh when the living of Hunsford was vacant; and the respect he felt for her high rank, and his veneration for her as his patroness, mingling with a very good opinion of himself, of his authority as a clergyman, and his rights as a rector, made him altogether a mixture of pride and obsequiousness, self-importance and humility.

Perhaps Henry in his biographical eulogy was camouflaging some of the things that went on behind the scenes in the family, recognising that

Jane was not one for self-serving publicity. His brief biography ends on a religious note:

> One trait only remains to be touched upon. It makes all others unimportant. She was thoroughly religious and devout; fearful of giving offence to God, and incapable of feeling it towards any fellow creature. On serious subjects she was well instructed, both by reading and meditation, and her opinions accorded strictly with those of our Established Church.

It is an odd way to end the biography,[2] almost as though Henry were trying to defend Jane against potential criticism and to ensure that she would be seen as a thoroughly orthodox believer; which, of course, she was (you only have to read her prayers to realise that), but perhaps the satirical caricatures of Mr Collins, and some of the humour-filled digs at other members of the clergy in Jane's novels, had resulted in criticism, and Henry, now himself a member of the clergy, wanted not only to ensure that Jane was regarded in the proper ecclesiastical light but that he, as her biographer, should also be seen to be above reproach. Or maybe, more simply, the same kind of formulaic style that was used on the gravestone was thought to be the right way to write a biography. Whatever the reason, it simply does not capture Jane's wit, intelligence, wisdom and occasional acerbic comments. It is bland and hagiographic with little understanding of the importance or joy of literature.

It is difficult to discover Henry's whereabouts after the publication of the two novels, but there is evidence that in addition to his curacy in Chawton he also served temporarily as a chaplain in the office of the British Minister in Berlin in 1818. Certainly, while he was there, he produced and published *Lectures Upon Some Important Passages in the Book of Genesis*. On the cover of that publication, he describes himself as 'Formerly Fellow of St John's College, Oxford; late chaplain to the Embassy at Berlin; domestic chaplain to HRH The Duke of Cumberland and the Right Hon the Earl of Morley'.

The self-description strongly suggests that Henry could not resist the company of a royal duke or an earl. He was like a moth drawn to a candle flame. That had been the case when he was a banker, and it seems that it was also true of his brief time as a chaplain. But who were these people for whom he claimed that he acted as domestic chaplain?

Ernest Augustus, the Duke of Cumberland and Teviotdale (1771–1851), to give him his full title, was the fifth son of King George III. There were some scurrilous and possibly unfounded rumours concerning the Duke put about by the Whigs (he was a very firm, not to say, vehement Tory, as were most Anglican bishops at that time). He survived an assassination attempt by his valet, Joseph Sellis, who subsequently committed suicide, but rumours soon began, suggesting that Sellis had been murdered. The Duke was also involved in a political scandal centred on Weymouth. As a member of the House of Lords, Ernest Augustus was not allowed to be involved in the choice and election of an MP. And yet, at Weymouth, in 1812, it was alleged that that is exactly what had happened. He was sent post-haste to Hanover by the government as an observer of the Hanoverian troops. Rumours, of course, are not firm evidence, but such was the sense of impropriety surrounding him that despatching him to Europe seemed a sensible thing to do. It was to this man and his household that Henry Austen became domestic chaplain. Was it out of the forgiving goodness of his heart that he accepted the position, or was he hoping that close links with the Royal Family might be helpful in his life as a clergyman?

The second family to which Henry became domestic chaplain was that of John Parker (1772–1840), Viscount Boringdon, who later inherited the earldom and became the Earl of Morley. He began his political life as a Tory but gradually moved to a Whiggish position. He was a great supporter of smallpox vaccination, supported Catholic Emancipation, and opposed political action being taken against Queen Caroline. It is possible that Henry had known John Parker at Oxford because they were contemporaries. Two such politically contrasting patrons as the Tory Duke and the Whig-leaning Earl might suggest that Henry was playing his cards deftly, or was it that he was simply appreciative of the support of both, or did he see in his relationship with the Earl of Morley a chance to recoup some of his banking losses?

However, there was a major public scandal attached to the Earl of Morley. As a young post-graduate student, Lord Boringdon – he had inherited the title when he was 16 – had gone on the Grand Tour, and in Rome had met and fallen in love with Lady Elizabeth Monck, a married woman with two children. They soon began an affair. As a result, Elizabeth Monck bore him three illegitimate sons.

After Boringdon returned to the family seat at Saltram in Devon, he was frequently visited by Elizabeth Monck, and her three sons regularly spent the summers in that splendid house with their father. He asked Lady Elizabeth to divorce her husband, but she refused. Boringdon then married Lady Augusta Fane, but, true to form, he subsequently had an affair with a dancer in Bristol. Lady Augusta Fane had not been at all pleased that, in addition to the dancer, he was still sustaining his relationship with Elizabeth Monck. Meanwhile, to add to the marital complexities, Lady Augusta was being pursued by Sir Arthur Paget and eventually she eloped with him. It was a delicious and very public scandal.

In February 1809, Boringdon was granted a divorce on the grounds of his wife's adultery. No mention, of course, of his own dalliances. Within five months, he had met and married Lady Frances Talbot. She was generous enough to look after his five illegitimate children, as well as their own legitimate offspring. Interestingly, Jane Austen had sent a copy of *Emma* to her when it was first published in December 1815. No one is quite certain why that happened or how Jane might have known her. But it is generally assumed that it was Henry Austen who was the common link. It was also in 1815 that Boringdon was created Earl of Morley. Strangely, there was a rumour at the time that *Emma* had been penned by his second wife, Lady Morley, who was herself a novelist. However, as far the marriage between the Earl of Morley and his second wife, Frances, was concerned, it turned out to be a marriage that lasted thirty-one years. Lord Morley died in 1840 with debts of almost £250,000. Frances, Countess Morley, died seventeen years later, in 1857.

It is puzzling that Henry should have been drawn to such a scandal-ridden man as John Parker, the Earl of Morley. Was it an attraction of opposites? Or was it that Henry himself, for whatever reason, found himself fascinated by risk-taking people? Morley, of course, was not the first. The same had been true, for example, of Henry's relationship with Charles Spencer, his Colonel in the Oxfordshire Militia, to whom he had unwisely lent several thousand pounds – a loan that was never repaid. And the relationship with Major James raises more questions than it answers. There is an undercurrent in that business relationship that is murky and troubling. What was the advantage to Henry in working with Charles James, if any? Who had the power? Was it a relationship based on mutual lack of trust?

Whatever Henry's reasons might have been for developing such relationships, he had begun a new chapter in his life, and was now a clergyman of the Church of England. In that capacity, during his time in Berlin, he wrote over twenty lectures about the biblical book of Genesis. Later, he turned those lectures into a small book, and in the preface expressed the hope that having submitted the lectures to the public 'with all the apprehensions of an author', he also anticipated that they might be useful to some of his reverend brethren, 'especially to such as have lately entered on the Holy Office'.

It is a disarming and carefully composed sentence, but nowhere within it does Henry disclose that he himself had been ordained just over one year previously. He gives the impression that he is speaking from long experience as a priest. It is breathtakingly conceited and perhaps reveals the over-confident side of his character; it betrays a singular lack of self-awareness, not to mention an immodest arrogance, but undoubtedly his personality was one that people found very appealing, including his sister, Jane.

His opening lecture on Genesis begins thus:

> He who studies history aright, makes himself wise by the experience of others; and whosoever devotes a due portion of his researches to the authentic history of the creation may make himself thereby wise to everlasting salvation.

It is a finely honed sentence, almost, but not quite, an aphorism. He was saying nothing that an intelligent graduate of the early nineteenth century would not have said. However, it is interesting that he was in Berlin at the same time as a noted radical theologian, Friedrich Schleiermacher, who was lecturing at the university there.

Schleiermacher was exploring new ways of interpreting the New Testament and was trying to understand the relationship between religious thought and feeling. David Jenkins describes Schleiermacher's theology thus:

> the genius of his work lay in his insight that religion need not be one human activity amongst many others, to be accepted like sport or politics; rather, it lies at the heart of all human endeavour ... To be religious, he argued is part of what it is to be human. In his book *'The Christian faith according to the fundamentals of the Evangelical Church systematically set forth'* he set out to explain what he meant by 'feeling'... and shows that this is not a sentimental 'feeling', nor a passing emotion or a sudden experience, but is rather the profound awareness of the existence of the One on whom all existence depends – both ours and that of the world around us. Thus, it is not an undefined or amorphous feeling, for its clear and specific content is our absolute dependence on God. Such feeling is not based on rational faculties nor on moral sentiment, but it does have significant consequences both in rational exposition and in ethical responsibility.[3]

Judging from Henry Austen's lectures on Genesis, there is no evidence that he was aware of Schleiermacher's thought. This is not a criticism. He was not alone amongst English clergy in being almost entirely insular and failing to keep abreast of Continental thinking. But probably, he would have taken issue with Schleiermacher and would have argued, as he does in his lectures on Genesis, that Christian belief does not derive its understanding of truth through human feeling, nor as a result of pure rationality, but upon revelation, that is, God takes the initiative and reveals to humanity through the person of Jesus Christ, who God truly is.

We only have one of Henry Austen's own sermons to be able to judge what his own deepest theological beliefs might have been. And, of course, to draw conclusions from just one sermon is to run the danger of distortion. Perhaps, for the moment, all we can safely assume is that he was an English clergyman typical of his age, and one who was mildly evangelical, that is, he was convinced that in the Bible especially, and in the services and doctrines of *The Book of Common Prayer*, there was sufficient profundity of truth and moral teaching to satisfy and challenge all people.

Chapter 17

What did Henry Believe?

Henry grew up in an isolated country rectory, was taught at home by his father, the Rector, listened to his father's sermons Sunday by Sunday, and went to an Oxford college where attendance at chapel was compulsory. None of this, of course, guarantees belief – there are plenty of examples of individuals who have rebelled against such an upbringing, but Henry seems not to have been a rebel. As a man-about-town and successful banker in London he regularly attended Anglican churches. His faith was part of who he was. Like his sister, Jane, his faith was not worn on his sleeve but was woven into the depths of his personality. So, what can we discover about him from the one sermon of his that is extant?

It was preached at St Andrew's, Clifton, in Bristol on 22 March 1829, when he was a mature man of 58 years old. The sermon was over 7,000 words in length and the date of the sermon is significant, as we shall shortly see. When it was preached, he had been ordained for almost thirteen years and at the time of the preachment was the Perpetual Curate of Bentley, Hampshire.

Like all preachers he would have given attention and thought to the text upon which he would base his sermon. He chose: Luke 9, 55. 'Ye know not what manner of spirit ye are of'.

It is part of a biblical verse in which Jesus rebukes his disciples, James and John, for their narrowness of vision. The context is a brief episode in which Jesus, on his way up to Jerusalem, enters a Samaritan village but is rejected by its inhabitants. The disciples, James and John, are furious that their master should be treated so disdainfully and remonstrate with him. In their anger they say: 'Lord, wilt thou that we command fire to come down from heaven, and consume them, even as Elias did?' Jesus responds to their fiery outburst by rebuking them and saying: 'Ye know not what manner of spirit ye are of.' It is this phrase that forms the basis of Henry's sermon.

Having offered the congregation the raw text, Henry begins to explore it by providing a paraphrase of what he thinks Jesus meant when he rebuked James and John:

> The words of your mouth, and consequently the meditations of your heart, are in direct contradiction to the sentiments which my disciples must cherish towards all men, on all occasions – which they must cherish, or they are none of mine.

And then Henry draws a contemporary, personal comparison:

> if those words were said to his disciples who had been with Jesus from the beginning, is it not likely that we fall under the same condemnation, and deserve to suffer the same rebuke?

So, as a preacher, Henry has set out his stall and has offered the congregation a demanding question. But he does not attempt to answer the question he has set; instead, he places the biblical text in its literary context, explaining the background to Jesus' expostulation. In doing so he echoes, consciously or unconsciously, phrases (underlined below) from *The Book of Common Prayer*'s Communion Service:

> The object of his [Jesus'] present journey was to do the greatest of all good – the only good universal in extent and everlasting in duration – to do the will of his Father, and finish the work which he had been about – to offer himself up for the sins of this world, a full, perfect, and sufficient sacrifice, atonement,[1] and satisfaction.

The congregation would have recognised the allusion.

Having established that connection, Henry then makes another comparison:

> It is good for us, my brethren – nay, it is necessary for us, thus to dwell on the unchangeable features of our Saviour's character, that we may accurately estimate the graces which were so full in him, and profitably lament that they are so faint in us. How little did those who followed Jesus partake his feelings – how slow to apprehend what spirit he was of! It is indeed impossible to conceive a more complete contrast, than that exhibited between the patient, tolerating, comprehensive tenderness of Christ – and the impetuous, inconsiderate, and bigoted resentment of man.

Much of the central part of the sermon is concerned with a series of contrasts: Jesus was not a judge, but men are hasty in their judgements; the disciples offended, and we should be careful not to offend; Jesus was magnanimous, we are prejudiced; the disciples were proud and hypocritical, so are we ... and at one point, Henry pleads with the congregation not to assume that their own beliefs are coterminous with God's will: 'It is a dangerous indulgence to consider ourselves either individually or nationally the selected instruments of God.'

It is this statement that provides the pivotal point in the sermon. Up to this moment, Henry has been addressing his remarks to the individual believer, the man and woman in the pew, and has said nothing that the congregation would not have expected any preacher to say – but now he turns his attention towards national matters.

Sermons, of course, are shaped not only by the preacher, but they also echo consciously or unconsciously the context of the times in which they are preached. In the case of this sermon, Henry alludes to what was a deeply troubling national debate about the nature of Roman Catholicism and its potential role in the state. If the congregation had been paying attention, they would now have sat up in their seats wondering what he would say next. He declares his own committed position as an Anglican:

> we beg and intreat that no one will leave this place under a false impression – under an impression that we are not as warmly, as rationally, as devotedly, as exclusively attached to that branch of Christ's Holy Catholic Church in these realms established, as the most alarmed, most unquiet, and most clamorous. We are firmly persuaded that it does adhere closely to that form of doctrine which the apostles taught, and to that hope of salvation which our Lord died to establish.[2]

But he goes on to say that the persecution of those with different views and beliefs is inherently wrong, whether that be physical persecution or persecution by words:

> Persecution, of any sort, is a tree, whose extremest root is bitterness, whose smallest fruits are poison.

And he argues strongly that in turbulent political times people should be patient and should check what their underlying motives might be before they consider taking any action:

> We do therefore humbly submit to the consideration of every one who handleth or heareth the word, whether it be not the bounden duty of the present period – that he endeavour to know what manner of spirit he is of – that he search the spirit – that he ascertain what spirit actuates him – whether it be the genuine spirit of Protestantism, unmixed, unadulterated, un-debased with any expectation of what he is likely to gain, any fear of what he is liable to lose, of rank and wealth and power, by a change in the religion of the state.

He reminds the congregation that the nature of God is love and that that love should be appropriated in the present time. He believes that by magnanimity towards believers of a different church those believers might be inspired to share the spiritual blessings of the Established Church:

> If we enable them to read the record of their civil equality in the book of our earthly statutes, the time may not be far distant, when they will press forward, to read, mark, and inwardly digest, the testimonies of our common salvation, in the volume of the Lord. God of his infinite mercy grant it! Grant that before this generation pass away, the inhabitants of two islands, so close in position, may become still more closely united in faith, and so far fulfil the prediction of their Lord and Saviour, as to become one fold under one Shepherd.

It was a courageous but eirenic statement to make, especially at a time of high national anxiety. The Catholic Emancipation Bill of 1829 was still being debated in Parliament when Henry preached his sermon. That Bill promised to grant, for the first time since the Reformation, the right of Catholic men to sit in Parliament, to be part of the judiciary, and to vote. Tempers had risen during the debates in Parliament and across the nation. Politicians such as Robert Peel and the Duke of Wellington had changed their positions from arguing against Catholic Emancipation to arguing in favour of it because they were genuinely concerned that if the Bill did not receive Royal Assent there would be civil insurrection in Ireland. One of the problems they faced as politicians was that King George III was vehemently opposed to the Bill because, as he saw it, it would invalidate the oaths he had sworn at his coronation to 'maintain the laws of God, the true profession of the Gospel and the Protestant religion established by law'. Bishops who took part in the debates in the House of Lords were split; some, such as Bishop Van Mildert of Durham opposed the Bill, others, such as Bishop Sumner of Winchester, supported it. At such a tempestuous political time, Henry's sermon calling for a growth in understanding between Anglicans and Roman Catholics and expressing the hope that one day they might become more closely united, was very brave.

Sadly, for us, however, that sermon is missing its last few pages and so we are unable to read Henry's final conclusions. And we need to be wary of assuming that that sermon encapsulates the kernel of Henry's thinking. Sermons are an art form, and every preacher knows that like all art forms, central messages and ideas can change over time. The most we can say is that the sermon gives us some clues about Henry's life as a theologian. He was an eirenic, humane, biblically based, committed Anglican, not afraid to voice opinions with which others might strongly disagree. It is no wonder that his sermon was published at the request of the St Andrew's congregation. They obviously felt the need to ponder all that he had said. What they might have made of the subscript of the printed sermon which stated that Henry was the Perpetual Curate of Bentley and also domestic chaplain to the Right Hon. the Earl of Morley, is anyone's guess. More to the point, was Henry still in sycophantic thrall to an aristocrat?

But let's now turn from that remarkable sermon to Henry's life as a curate in Hampshire.

He was a curate in Chawton from 26 December 1816 until 15 January 1820, and we can assume that he carried out his duties in a seemly manner. How demanding that work was is a matter for debate; for example, Henry took five funerals in 1817, including three that must have been harrowing: on 6 May, he took the funeral of Thomas Ewance, aged 10; on 7 June, he took the funeral of Henry Ewance, aged 6, and on 25 July, the funeral of Ann Ewance, aged 21. In 1818, he took no funerals – he was in Berlin; in 1819 and in 1820, he took no funerals at all. Clearly, it was not a demanding curacy.

Coincidentally, it is noteworthy that at this time in the nation's history, there were discussions about the work and purpose of a clergyman. We met it in the extract from *Mansfield Park* in the previous chapter, but we can also find it in books devoted to the clerical life. For example, one such book, published in 1822, opens as follows:

> Not only in a religious, but in a political point of view the well-being of a state depends greatly upon the due discharge of the

sacerdotal office. If the priest be inattentive to his duty, the religion of the people will grow cool or corrupt, their moral conduct will become depraved, and the civil, as well as the ecclesiastical polity will be in danger ... never was the attention of the clergy to every part of their duty, public and private, more requisite than at the present time.[3]

The reference to 'the present time' is to the situation that everyone had witnessed in France during the Revolution. It had been feared that the overthrow of the monarchy, the aristocracy, and the Church, and the subsequent Terror, might easily have spread to England. It was important therefore, that everything should be done to ensure that the nation remained at peace with itself. In 1818, Parliament created the Church Building Act in which one million pounds (over £90,000,000 in today's money) had been voted for the building of new churches in London and across the country. In London, it resulted in churches such as St Luke's, Chelsea, St Mary's, Bryanston Square, and St John's Waterloo, and in the provinces, churches such as St Lawrence, Pudsey, St Peter's, Wakefield, and St George's, Sheffield. It was a massive building programme designed to reinforce morality, religion and good behaviour. It was against this febrile national background that we need to see Henry's early ministry.

In 1820, Henry left Chawton and moved to Steventon to take over the living following his brother James's death. Edward Austen Knight had agreed that Henry could have the living until such time as one of his own sons could be installed. It meant that James's widow, Mary, and the children, James-Edward and Caroline, had to leave the Rectory. Caroline wrote that Henry 'paid my mother every due attention, but his own spirits he could not repress, and it is not pleasant to witness the elation of your successor in gaining what you have lost'.[4] Henry's ebullience in this delicate situation could be seen by some as insensitivity. Mary and the children left for Bath and Henry moved in. But his cheerfulness might also have had something to do with the fact that he was planning to marry. His choice was a woman called Eleanor Jackson, the niece of the Reverend Mr Papillon of Chawton. They were married at Chelsea Old Church on 11 April 1820. Henry was almost 49; his bride was 24.

So, who was Eleanor Jackson? She had been born in London in 1795, the third daughter of Henry Jackson and Sarah Papillon. Henry Jackson was a merchant who had incurred considerable debts. He had a brother who was a Prebendary of St Paul's and had two nephews who were diplomats. However, Eleanor's father had recovered from his debts and was able to live in stylish Sloane Terrace, Knightsbridge, close to Henry's former house in Hans Place.

We know from one of Jane's comments that as a 17-year-old, Eleanor had visited the Austens at Chawton. It is clear that Cassandra thought fondly of her because she gave her Jane Austen's own turquoise ring as an engagement present, and it seems likely that Mrs Austen gave Henry and Eleanor a wedding gift of £40. Eleanor seems to have been a loving companion to Henry and she too became an author, as we shall see later.

Henry and Eleanor's stay at Steventon was relatively brief. He was there for only two years because Edward required him to vacate the living in 1822 so that his own son, William, could be installed. William was to have a long but personally harrowing ministry there. In 1848, his three daughters by his second wife, Mary, died of scarlet fever within a few days of each other: Cecilia, aged 4, and her sister Augusta, aged 3, died on 9 June, and their older sister Mary, aged 5, died six days later on 15 June.[5] It must have been an unbearable grief for their parents and for the rest of the family.

How far Henry was a good rector of the parish during his two years there, from 1820 to 1822, we have no means of knowing. But the question of what constituted a good parson was explored by Jane in *Mansfield Park*. Her ideas are found in a speech by Sir Thomas Bertram when he discusses the problems of multiple benefices being held by a single minister:

> a parish has wants and claims which can be known only by a clergyman constantly resident, and which no proxy can be capable

of satisfying to the same extent. Edmund might, in the common phrase, do the duty of Thornton – that is, he might read prayers and preach without giving up Mansfield Park; he might ride over every Sunday to a house nominally inhabited, and go through divine service; he might be the clergyman of Thornton Lacey every seventh day, for three or four hours, if that would content him. But it will not. He knows that human nature needs more lessons than a weekly sermon can convey; and that if he does not live among his parishioners, and prove himself by constant attention their well-wisher and friend, he does very little either for their good or his own.[6]

Henry, having had to vacate Steventon, was about to practise what his sister in her novel had so cogently urged should be the parson's proper occupation ...

Chapter 18

Henry's Life as a Clergyman in Farnham

In August 1822, Henry moved to Farnham in Surrey, where he became the Perpetual Curate. He received a stipend of £75 per annum, plus surplice fees of £35 and lived in tied accommodation – the house was in West Street, where the so-called Schola Grammaticalis[1] was also situated.

Why did Henry become the Perpetual Curate? It was because the Rector, the Reverend Henry Warren, had been appointed Rector of Ashington in Sussex in 1797, and in 1799 had been appointed, in addition, Rector of Farnham. Technically, because Ashington was within the 30-mile radius of Farnham, he was not breaking the law by staying in Sussex, hence the need for a perpetual curate. It meant that, for all practical purposes, Henry was the Anglican minister for Farnham. But to put that in context, fifty years earlier, in 1780, only about 38 per cent of parishes had resident incumbents and 36 per cent of Anglican clergy were pluralists.[2] The Reverend Henry Warren, by choosing not to live in Farnham, was following a long but declining tradition.

So, having uprooted from Steventon, and having moved to Farnham, on 18 October 1823, Henry became the Master at Farnham Grammar School.[3] It provided an additional source of income for him. At least, it might have done so if there had been any pupils. The anonymous author of *The History of Farnham Grammar School* states that in 1800 the Reverend Samuel Locke came from London to take over the Grammar School, bringing with him twelve private pupils, but he refused to take any local boys. The author continues, 'By 1809, when his pupils were gone, all appearance of a school ceased, and it remained in abeyance until 1849 when it was reorganised.'[4] It is a puzzling phrase because the same publication includes Henry Austen's name in the List of Headmasters. Is it possible that Henry, living at 25 West Street, might have had a handful of pupils? Unfortunately, no records remain, but we know that he was duly appointed as Master in October 1823 and duly resigned the post in October 1827.[5]

The effect upon Henry and his wife of their move to Farnham should not be underestimated. It was culturally and socially a very different place from Steventon and Chawton. Whilst there might have been dances in Farnham at the Goat's Head (a coaching inn on the corner of Castle Street and The Borough), or in the Bush Hotel, those assembly rooms[6] did not act as nodal points for the landed gentry as happened in Alton and Basingstoke. Why not? Because there were no great landed families living in close proximity to Farnham. The major landowner in Farnham was the Bishop of Winchester. His acres encircled the town, which meant that the landed gentry were on the farthest edges of his estates. By contrast, the Reverend George Austen as Rector of Steventon had been at the centre of a Hampshire network of landed gentry and minor aristocracy. The Austens had been friends with the Digweeds at the Manor House, the Chutes at The Vyne, the Biggs and Bigg Withers of Manydown and the Harwoods at Ashe Park. In addition, of course, Edward Austen Knight's house at Godmersham had enabled the Austens to socialise with many of the landed families of Kent. Nor should we forget that at one stage in his life, Henry had known and fraternised with the landed gentry of Oxfordshire, including the Spencers. Then, when he had moved into banking in London, he had been on the fringe of the Regency set of Carlton House. But Farnham in the early nineteenth century was very different. It was a small workaday market town whose wealth was based on the flourishing hop and brewing industry. Who would Henry and Eleanor Austen's social equals be in this new setting? It did not have a county set; it was 'trade' rather than 'landed acres' that dominated. Might he and Eleanor have struggled to develop a network of friends?

An instance of the social shift experienced by Henry and Eleanor Austen can be deduced from the baptism registers of St Andrew's, the parish church. Taking the year 1824 as an example, we can see that in that year Henry Austen conducted approximately 130 christenings. Eighty-seven of those babies were from families in which the husband's work was described as 'Labourer'; the remainder had jobs that were described as follows: Tanner, Butcher, Collar Maker, Brick-maker, Shoemaker, Patten-maker, Coach-maker, Painter, Sawyer, Cooper, Chaise-driver, Potter, Shopkeeper, Huckster [sic], Cordwainer, Baker, Attorney's clerk, Draper, and Wheelwright. Only two families in the baptism register were given the appellation 'Gent', a title that, as Penelope Corfield says, 'was an unofficial (commoner) title, not awarded by the Crown but at the bar of public opinion ... as a concept the ideal of "gentleman" conveyed not just coveted status but also attributes of probity, respectability, chivalric politeness and independence'.[7] Another family described the husband as 'Yeoman', and there was one Excise-man, and one Surgeon.

In short, Farnham was predominantly a working-class and artisan town. But to add a touch of lightness to these statistics, it is worth mentioning that in that same year, Henry Austen christened George Cable Lake, the son of Robert and Grace Lake: Robert Lake was valet to the Bishop of Winchester. And he also christened the baby of someone described as a soldier/Chelsea Pensioner. But, on a more sombre note, four of the babies were the children of spinsters, and had the initials 'B.B' written in the margin of the register, that is, they were Base Born – who knows what the lives of those children and their mothers might have been like?

Just in case 1824 was an exceptional year, the figures for 1825 are broadly similar: in 1825, Henry Austen christened 106 babies, of whom 73 were from households where the father's occupation was described as 'Labourer'; only one family was described as 'Gent'.[8]

The challenge for Henry and Eleanor in moving to Farnham was not only cultural and social, but it also involved a massively increased workload compared with what he had been used to; for example, in the two years that he was in Steventon as Rector, in 1820 he had conducted only two christenings and two funerals; and in 1821, six christenings and four funerals. And here he was in Farnham, where in 1824, in addition to the 130 christenings, he conducted 33 weddings and took 97 funerals. And, of course, he was required to preach at least one sermon every Sunday. In the early nineteenth century it was expected that a sermon should be, at a minimum, 4,000 words long. And as if that were not enough, he had also been appointed as Perpetual Curate in Bentley, and there, in that same year of 1824, he took one wedding and eight funerals, plus nineteen christenings. In total, therefore, in Farnham and Bentley, in one year, Henry Austen took 149 christenings, 34 weddings and 105 funerals.

It is a pastoral load that is in complete contrast to the clergy in Jane Austen's novels. She relishes delineating their various characteristics – the Reverend Mr Elton in *Emma*, for example, is initially seen by Emma as 'a good humoured, well-meaning, respectable young man, without any deficiency of useful understanding or knowledge of the world'[9] (Emma changes her mind about him a little later), but the clergy's work is barely touched upon. Instead, they always seem to have time to drop in for a game of whist, to take part in hunting, or go for an elegant walk with one of the heroines, and perhaps above all, they are useful to make up numbers at the dining table. Perhaps those clerical and gentlemanly activities might have been true in Steventon or Chawton, but in Farnham there was little time for such relaxing experiences.

The consequences of the pastoral workload that Henry had should not be underestimated. It brought him into contact with a huge number of families at key moments in their lives. He must have shared the joys of christenings and weddings, but also the sorrows of bereavement. In the case of the latter, what might have been the effect upon himself when in Bentley, in 1824, he conducted the funerals of Lucy Croucher, aged 21, and Ann Deverill, aged 22 (what might be the stories behind the deaths of these young women?), and what must he have felt as he rode back to his house in Farnham having taken the funeral of a 1-year-old girl called Lucy Ratford? And when ministering in Farnham in 1824, what might he have thought as he visited the family of a young man called John Nixon who had been killed in a fight 'the consequence of a quarrel [indecipherable] a hammer'? The fact that he wrote a note in the funeral register suggests that the event must have had an effect upon him.

But he not only had pastoral matters to deal with, he also had a civic role. The 1601 Poor Relief Act was still operative. That Act placed the responsibility for the poor firmly on parishes. The Annual Parish Meeting was required to appoint two Overseers of the Poor, who might also have been the churchwardens. The overseers were responsible for collecting the Poor Rate from land and property owners in the parish to implement the terms of the Act. It was an Act that made a distinction between the 'impotent' poor and the 'able-bodied' poor. The former were to be housed in almshouses. In Farnham's case, Andrew Windsor, a wealthy seventeenth-century benefactor had founded an almshouse in Castle Street. Over the doorway of the almshouse are the following words: 'These Alms-houses were erected by Andrew Windsor Esq in 1619 for the habitation and relief of eight poor honest and impotent persons.'[10] There is some evidence that in addition to the Windsor almshouses there was a poor house close to St Andrew's Church.

Under the terms of the 1601 Act, those who were unemployed but capable of work (the 'able-bodied poor') were to be put to work in the workhouse. They received what was called 'indoor relief'. But those who were poor and gainfully employed, but who nevertheless remained in need, could apply for 'outdoor relief', that is, sums of money, or goods in kind, which were administered by the churchwardens.

In 1791, a new workhouse was built in Farnham, on the site of what is now Farnham Hospital. A major report[11] by Sir Frederic Morton Eden was published in 1797 about it. In his report he described the Farnham Workhouse, saying that it was built on a good plan about half a mile from the town. 'The old workhouse stood in the town and was said to have been a most wretched one.' The contractor was allowed the use of a house and furniture and the earnings of the poor, for which he received £1,000 per annum, out of which he had to maintain the 124 inmates. Of those 124, 50 were old and infirm. The others who were capable of work were employed in picking wool. The children attended the carding machines but also received a very basic education: they were taught to read. Food was basic and minimal; for example, on Sundays, Tuesdays, Thursdays and Saturdays, breakfast consisted of onion pottage; on the other days it was bread and broth.

How far Henry Austen was pastorally involved with the workhouse is not known, but as the Perpetual Curate, and in conjunction with the churchwardens, he could not have been unaware of the grim conditions of the workhouse and its capacity to create untold misery. And he must have been aware of the poverty that existed within the town, and surely would have known individuals who were classed as needing 'outdoor relief'. Indeed, it is worth noting that whilst there is no evidence from the Farnham Vestry Minute Book that Henry himself was present during the official meetings of that body, the fact that the churchwardens, G.C. Knight and Robert Earle, were present means that he must have been kept informed about the proceedings. At one meeting, on 5 November 1828, Robert Sampson was also present and was appointed as an overseer (the same man whose wedding Henry had taken just four years earlier). The presence of the overseers and churchwardens strongly suggests that Henry must have been privy to the issue of poverty in the parish.[12] Again, the contrast between the poverty in the parish and his life when he was a high-flying military agent and wealthy banker is remarkable. In any case, his wife, Eleanor, following a long-established custom would also have been involved in visiting the sick and the poor and distributing charitable gifts. The extent and nature of poverty in the town must have featured in conversations between Henry and Elizabeth. It was a subject that could not be avoided.

There was another source of charitable giving in Farnham, however, and that was the Bishop of Winchester at the castle. At Christmas 1828, Bishop Charles Sumner, following his predecessor's tradition, made arrangements for the distribution of clothing and blankets for the poor. The number of people arriving at the castle gates overwhelmed the process. It was chaotic. People were shoving and shouting. Sumner was not amused and promised his wife and staff that such disreputable scenes should never happen again. The following Christmas, he and his wife created a new system in which the recipients were handed a coloured card; that card directed them to a specific table marked by a similarly coloured flag in the Great Hall, where the clothing and blankets had been organised into parcels. It was much more sensible, decorous even, but might the recipients have missed the enjoyable chaos of the previous year?

There were only two other recorded events in Farnham in which Henry must have been involved. The first was the occasion at the castle when Bishop Sumner called together the clergy of the Farnham area to address what he believed to be a weakness in the diocese, namely, the poor support of missionary societies. He pointed out that the Society for the Propagation of the Gospel, for example, only received £70 annually from the entire diocese. It was not good enough. A more zealous commitment was required. Again, we do not know what Henry Austen made of this, but the Bishop was successful. By the end of his episcopate in 1874, that sum had risen to over £6,000.

The second event was the ordination at the castle on the last weekend of July 1828.[13] It was so unlike Henry's own experience.

Bishop Sumner had instructed that the ordinands should be at the castle on the Thursday morning. Having arrived, they were then examined for their theological competence by one of the Bishop's chaplains. They had been asked to prepare a paper that they were required to defend in a viva. Afterwards, each ordinand met the Bishop, who also gave them an examination. Those who were to be ordained priest had been instructed to send to the Bishop three of the sermons they had preached in the previous year. The Bishop then cross-questioned them. It was a daunting experience.

That same evening, a number of local clergy arrived at the castle, having been invited by the Bishop. Presumably, Henry was amongst them. They stayed for dinner and mingled with the ordinands. It was a way of providing some congenial encouragement to them. It is doubtful if Henry would have divulged his experience of his own desultory examination as an ordinand by Bishop Brownlow North ...

Unfortunately, little else is known about Henry's time at St Andrew's, though there is a record of a 'Beating of the Bounds' during his time, getting out of hand:

> At half-past seven commenced walking or perambulating the Bounds of the Parish. Having waited until this time for the Rev. Mr. Austin [*sic*] who then took the lead, supported on the right and left by the Churchwardens and Overseers, the High Constable, Constables, Thos. Pisley the only tithingman present and a numerous train of followers with white wands. The procession was accompanied by drums, bugles and fifes. Boys were 'bumped' to make them remember the boundary marks and 'the painting of faces' was carried to too great an excess to the annoyance, and I am sorry to say disgrace, but the body of young men were so numerous that it was impossible to prevent it and it continued until everyone was disfigured more or less.

There must have been a culture of mischievous rumbustiousness amongst the young in Farnham in the 1820s, because when Charles Sumner had first arrived in the town, having been appointed Bishop of Winchester in December 1827, he and his family found their carriage surrounded by laughing young men who unhitched the horses, got into the shafts themselves, and hauled, pushed and shoved the carriage through the town at great speed, careering up the steep hill to Farnham Castle, where they deposited the Bishop with much enjoyment on their part.[14] It is not recorded how the Bishop or his wife felt.

Henry had served conscientiously as Perpetual Curate of Farnham for eight years. He had christened babies, taken marriages, buried the dead and preached innumerable sermons. Perhaps he was beginning to feel tired. Did he have one more job left in him? His heart began to pull him 5 miles south of Farnham, to Bentley …

Chapter 19

Bentley and Final Days

It was in November 1827, according to Angela Barlow,[1] that Henry and Eleanor moved to the Parsonage in Bentley, and he commuted back to Farnham when necessary to fulfil his curacy duties there. It must have been a propitious beginning. His wife Eleanor celebrated her thirty-second birthday that same month and they had moved to a spacious new rectory with large grounds and a beautiful view.

If they felt entirely happy in their new house, by contrast the times in which Henry Austen ministered in Farnham and Bentley were politically difficult. In 1830, three years after Henry and Eleanor had moved to Bentley, a mob of agricultural workers had stormed up to the castle demanding that the Bishop should hear their grievances.[2] That mob was part of a much wider movement of discontent amongst agricultural workers. In August 1830, an outbreak of violence had occurred in Kent in which a threshing machine had been destroyed. Agricultural workers, fearful of the effect on their jobs caused by the increased mechanisation of farming, deeply worried about rising rents and wanting an increase in wages, were on the march. They were angry, not least because under the Enclosure Acts much of their common land was being enclosed, leaving them with nowhere for their own livestock to feed. Known as the 'Swing Riots', the discontent soon spread from Kent into Surrey and Hampshire. Within days it had spread even further: in thirty-six counties there were 1,475 protests. The riots were not just centred on the problems in agriculture, there was serious unhappiness about the state of society itself and therefore, in some places, people representing the Establishment, for instance, bailiffs, magistrates and Overseers of the Poor, were physically assaulted. William Cobbett even went so far as to suggest that individuals who were aggrieved should keep a gun ready in their house. Letters and bread stained with blood were delivered to the homes of some farmers and landowners. The threat of civic breakdown was very real. As a result, there was a concerted attempt by the Lords Lieutenant and High Sheriffs to contain the riots by enlisting and empowering special constables, and via the magistracy, to punish the ringleaders. In villages and towns, leaders of the riots were brought to trial and were ordered to be hanged, imprisoned or transported.

Henry might have known that the Bishop, being aware of the impending difficulties, had already met with local landowners and had asked them to treat their agricultural workers with sympathy and understanding, and to raise their wages. All seemed settled, but a few days later, a mob rushed up Castle Hill to confront the Bishop. With some of his servants and members of his family, Charles Sumner went out of the castle, closing the gates behind him to protect his wife and family, and listened to the protestors. Gradually, the mob calmed down and dispersed. Peace, of a kind, had been restored.

If only we knew what Henry Austen thought of such disturbances. It is likely, in common with many of his fellow clergy, that he would have been on the side of law and order, but might his own experience of bankruptcy have given him some sympathy with the poverty of the protestors?

In 1830, Henry Austen formally resigned his Farnham duties and became the full-time Perpetual Curate at Bentley in Hampshire.

St Mary's Church in Bentley is a Norman foundation that has undergone several building and restoration projects over the centuries since it was first consecrated. Amongst its features are some incised and painted consecration crosses on the pillars near the chancel. The crosses are thought to be the result of an instruction by William Wykeham (1320–1404), the Bishop of Winchester, to his suffragan bishop 'to dedicate the chancel of the parish church of Bentley and the High Altar which has recently been built and the other altars if necessary'.[3] Also on the same pillars are some incised graffiti saltire crosses whose original purpose is a matter of speculation. Some claim that they were carved by pilgrims walking the nearby 'Pilgrims' Way'[4] from Winchester to Canterbury, others suggest that they might have been created to mark the taking of an important vow.[5]

Whether Henry Austen was interested in such ecclesiastical antiquarian items is unknown, but the consecration crosses cannot have escaped his notice, nor can the Norman font[6] in which he baptised the babies of the village. What might well have also caused him to reflect would have been the ancient yews in the churchyard (they are thought to be over 600 years old), nor can he have failed to make pleasurable comparisons between the similarity of the narrow lanes leading to the isolation of his father's church at Steventon and the deep narrow lanes leading to the similar remoteness of the church of St Mary, from much of the rest of the village of Bentley. He must have felt at home.

He had an income of about £120 per annum and was now 59 years old. Prior to his arrival, the churchwardens in 1819 had petitioned the Bishop saying that despite a population of 600, Bentley did not have a parsonage. An application was made to Queen Anne's Bounty and that produced the sum of £800. A further £400 was raised by subscription and finally, 'a house on the turnpike road with seven acres of land was bought and added to for £1,206 [worth just under £200,000 in today's prices]. This was a spacious Georgian House with large windows looking across garden and meadows towards the forest of Alice Holt and the meandering River Wey.'[7] It must have felt like a peaceful oasis after the great pastoral workload he had undertaken in Farnham. Perhaps he began to think of his ministry in Bentley as a pre-retirement bonus.

If so, was he content just to minister to his flock and ignore the outside world, or was he in any sense aware of stirrings in the Church of England at a national level? In 1833 at Oxford, John Keble had preached his powerful Assize sermon on National Apostasy. It centred on the relationship between the Church of England and the state. He argued that the state was gradually moving away from its Christian founding principles and was encroaching upon the rights and responsibilities of the National Church. He raised two questions. First: 'What are the symptoms, by which one may judge most fairly, whether or no a nation, as such, is becoming alienated from God and Christ?' Second, 'What are the particular duties of sincere Christians, whose lot is cast by Divine Providence in a time of such dire calamity?'

The situation that prompted the sermon was the government's Church Temporalities Act of 1833, which reduced the number of Irish Anglican bishoprics from twenty-two to twelve. From Keble's perspective this was the state interfering in what he believed was essentially a Church matter. It had followed on from the Reform Act of the previous year (1832) in which the Whig government of Lord Grey had radically changed constituency boundaries and had extended the franchise. To the Tories, including many bishops, the reforms were anathema. They were politically turbulent times.

In Bentley, it seems that Henry was concentrating his efforts on parish renewal. He spent a great deal of energy in restoring the church and was assisted in his endeavours by donations of £25 each from Charles Sumner, the Bishop of Winchester, and from the Earl of Durham, and he himself contributed £30. He also sought the help of his family and received £5 each from his brother Charles, from his sister-in-law, Mrs Frank Austen, and from his nephew, J.E. Austen.

Could Henry really afford his own donation? It was one quarter of his stipend.

In a letter to his churchwarden, Mr Thresher, when he had news of significant financial help, he commented: 'We have conquered the invincible. We have got money out of the Treasury.' It was, as Midgley comments, 'a remark which would have delighted Jane'.[8]

But he was also concerned about social questions, and in particular, the amount of drunkenness and misbehaviour that was occurring in the village. He was part of a local campaign to erect a cage in which miscreants could be kept while they recovered from their drunken misbehaviour. The Beer Act had been passed in 1830, which had been the government's attempt to ensure that beer would be cheaper than gin and would deter gin drinkers such as had been satirised in Hogarth's 1751 print *Gin Lane*. The Act was destined to fail. All that happened was that beer became cheaper because any ratepayer having paid a licence fee of two guineas was entitled by the Act to brew beer, and that meant that more of it was drunk by the poor. Public houses mushroomed.

Henry was deputed to write to the Bishop of Winchester, who was Lord of the Manor, to ask if he would allow a cage to be erected in which drunks could be held until they had sobered up. The Bishop replied that the decision was not for him to make. Nothing daunted, the churchwardens contacted the wealthier members of the parish asking for a subscription to pay for the creation of a cage. They argued that the stocks, which were in the middle of a pond, were not the best form of deterrent and in the colder months would not be able to be used; moreover, the suggestion that a local public house should be used as a 'lock-up' was obviously not the wisest of alternatives. By July 1833, sufficient money had been raised (including a £3 donation from the Bishop: roughly worth £408 at today's prices) for a brick-built cage to be created. The cage, which cost £41 (approximately £5,576) and was vested in the churchwardens, presumably achieved its deterrent purpose because it was demolished sometime in the second half of the nineteenth century. A granite obelisk commemorating Queen Victoria's jubilee in 1897 (and the jubilee of Queen Elizabeth II), now marks the spot where it once stood.[9]

But from time to time, even as he was trying to do something about drunken behaviour in the village, Henry could not avoid more personal and demanding pastoral events. The registers reveal, for example, that on 22 August 1830, he recorded in the funerals register the death of a suicide. It was a 61-year-old man called Edward Astlett. Henry wrote the following explanatory note in the register: 'Hung [sic] himself. Coroner's Inquest brought in a verdict of insanity. Had been in St Luke's Hospital and discharged as sane only one day before he "committed"[?] [word illegible] the act.' Was this St Luke's Hospital, Old Street, Islington, an asylum for the insane that had been founded in 1751? If so, it was a long way from Bentley. An asylum nearer St Luke's was in Guildford, but this was not founded until 1856 as a Poor Law Infirmary.

Henry took, on average, about ten funerals per annum in Bentley but sometimes there are gaps when he was away. Might he have been in Bath in 1826, for example, seeking a cure for his wife, Eleanor? There were seventeen funerals in Bentley that year, but Henry conducted only six. The rest were taken by the curate, whose name in the registers is indecipherable but might have been Grosbie/Crosbie Monsell or Morgan. Similarly, during much of 1828, he was also unavailable, for he conducted no funerals that year. Was he in France with his wife, Eleanor, trying to find a cure for her ill health? One year later, in 1829, he was signing the registers with the subscript 'Incumbent', so, presumably, his status had changed.

One of the advantages of Henry having moved to Bentley was that he was nearer to Chawton and could visit Cassandra. He and Cassandra would have talked about the future of Jane's books. John Murray had written to Cassandra in 1831 asking for the copyright of all of them. Cassandra, being shrewd and wanting to preserve Jane's spirit of independence, refused Murray's offer. But one year later, in 1832, Henry was in talks with another publisher, Richard Bentley, about Jane's novels. Richard Bentley drove a hard bargain and agreed to buy the copyrights for £210 but also insisted that the sum of £40, which he had had to pay Egerton's for the copyright of *Pride and Prejudice*, should be deducted from the agreed total. Reluctantly, Henry and Cassandra agreed. Their dismay was partly related to the lack of quality in the printing and binding that Bentley offered, but it was also about the deal that had been brokered. Henry and Cassandra were both agreed about the important literary quality of Jane's works (and they have been proved right), whereas Bentley seemed only interested in making a quick profit.

Authorship and the Austens seems to have been a delightful family activity, even for those who became an Austen by marriage. And so it was, that in 1831, Henry's wife Eleanor published *An Epitome of the Old Testament*. It was dedicated to the Bishop of Winchester and was written for the inhabitants of the parish. It consisted of a series of questions and answers about the Old Testament.

Winifred Midgley describes it in some detail:

> It proceeds by question and answer and occasionally sounds as if addressed rather to children, for example: 'Q. 437. What are the names of the twelve minor Prophets, repeat them in the order in which they are placed in our Bible?'
>
> The Epitome seems a competent piece of work, though to compress so much information into a small book of 135 pages must have been a formidable task and Eleanor was inevitably selective. Genesis and Exodus are dealt with in detail and occupy 57 pages; the Prophets are valued only for their foreshadowings of Christ; and the whole of the Psalms, Proverbs and Ecclesiastes are disposed of in fewer than two pages. As one would expect at this period, she accepts all the biblical statements quite literally.[10]

It was a work designed for parochial consumption, though it would be interesting to know how many of the inhabitants of Bentley were able to read, and if they could read, how many would have been interested in studying and answering detailed questions about the Old Testament.

By contrast, on the national stage, major social reforms were being considered. In 1832, Bishop Blomfield of London had been asked to chair the Poor Law Commission. It was a large and challenging task. The purpose of the commission was to report on the current state of the Poor Laws, which were ramshackle and inefficient. Not only did Blomfield have to analyse what was going on across the country, he and his committee were also required to make suggestions for radical improvement. Questionnaires were sent to parishes and, in addition, over 3,000 parishes were visited. No one could claim that the committee members were being lazy or dilatory, for within two years, Blomfield and his colleagues had completed the task. Their report was presented to Parliament in 1834, and the debates began. The recommendation that

Poor Law administration should be centralised and be placed in the hands of three nationally appointed commissioners was warmly welcomed. The commission had also recommended that the country should be divided into areas capable of supporting one workhouse per area, and that the collection of monies to support the workhouses should be organised not by individual parishes, as had been the system previously, but by unions of parishes presided over by local Boards of Guardians. It was a significant change in the way the poor were to be cared for. And for the Church of England, it represented the moment when power began to slip away from parishes and moved towards a central bureaucratic body overseen by Parliament. This shift in power does not seem to have been recognised by the Church of England at the time, and although several bishops took part in the debates about the Bill in the House of Lords, their collective voice, it could be said, was that of the Establishment. For example, Blomfield argued that 'the best schools were those where the children were taken from their parents and clothed and educated without them. 'These schools', he continued, 'always produced the best servants.'[11]

We cannot know whether Henry Austen was aware of these kinds of arguments, but if he had been, it is likely that he would have supported the thinking of the bishops. He was not, by nature, a rebel.

In 1836, Henry took time out from his duties in Bentley and from his rented house in Duke Street, London, wrote to Mr Thresher, his churchwarden, 'Mrs. Austen continues to gain ground – she does not expect ever again to be a decided walker, but she gets about the house comfortably and will probably be able to move from one floor to another.' This suggests some disabling form of rheumatism or arthritis, but despite her poor health, Mrs Austen outlived her husband.[12]

Meanwhile, Bentley was in the care of the newly appointed curate, Charles Jackson, who was the son of Francis Jackson, Eleanor's cousin.[13]

One year later, in 1837, Henry would have heard, or read, the Visitation Charge[14] of his Diocesan bishop, Charles Sumner. The Poor Law Amendment Act had received the Royal Assent in 1834, and although Bishop Sumner mentioned workhouses briefly in his Charge, his main concern was to encourage the clergy in their ministry and exhort them to greater efforts. Perhaps Henry was stirred by the Bishop's words: 'Where are the absentees from church? Have we taken note of this? Have we gone to search for the stray sheep upon the mountains?' The clergy were urged to 'stand upon the watchtower, and look round the city's walls, and survey well her breaches, to stand in the gap and inquire into the obstacles which impede the progress of religion in our parishes'.

While these episcopal messages were being proclaimed, Henry's mind must also have been on more personal matters: the debts that he had carried over from his banking career. He owed James-Edward, James's son, £400, which James-Edward seems to have been generous enough (or realistic enough) to have written off. And there was another early debt of £800, which Henry on his clerical stipend could see no way of paying. In addition (and this must surely have troubled his conscience), he owed Madame Perigord, the daughter of Madame Bigeon, £100. However, there was some personally sad, but financially comforting, news: In 1837, Mrs Leigh-Perrot died and left much of her husband's capital to James-Edward. She had been living on the interest on the capital and had not been allowed, under the terms of her husband's will, to use the capital itself. But she bequeathed to Henry £1,000, and the other nephews and nieces received the same amount. It must have come as a great relief to Henry, though it must also have been tinged with guilt because of his previous indebtedness to the Leigh-Perrot family. In the circumstances, he was fortunate to receive anything at all.

At the age of 67, in 1839, Henry retired. He left Bentley, where one senses he had been happy, and moved to Colchester, where he and Eleanor lived for the next three years ... but he was now determined to pursue George Rawdon-Hastings, the son of Lord Moira, for the money he had lent to Moira many years previously. Henry believed that the failure of his bank had been caused by the failure of Lord Moira to honour his debts. His angry and self-pitying letter ('I lost everything') had no effect upon Lord Moira's son. Sadly, it was the way the early nineteenth-century world operated. Trust and honesty were sometimes more honoured in the breach than in the observance. However, Henry's moral concerns were not limited to his demand for justice over the money he had lost through the fraudulent behaviour of Lord Moira. In retirement he was also involved in the movement for the international abolition of slavery. In June 1840, a Convention of Abolitionists was held at the Freemasons' Hall, Great Queen Street, London.[15] Delegates came from around the country, of whom Henry, representing Colchester, was one, and there were other delegates from across the world. It was a truly international occasion energised by a powerful moral purpose.

The origin of the convention can be traced back to the work of the 'Society for the Mitigation and Gradual Abolition of Slavery Throughout the British Dominions', which had been founded in 1823. That society had focused its attention on the abolition of slavery in British overseas territories, and through the passing of the Slavery Abolition Act of 1833 had largely achieved its objectives. The convention of 1840, which Henry attended, had a much wider remit. In 1839, a new organisation had been founded by Joseph Sturge, a devout Quaker. He wanted to see slavery abolished not only in British overseas territories but throughout the world. The convention, under the auspices of the newly formed British and Foreign Anti-Slavery Society, was addressed by John H. Treadgold, the Secretary of the Society.[16] In a stirring speech he rehearsed the background to the convention and explained its objectives. He declared that slavery was 'utterly at variance with the spirit and precepts of Christianity'. He told the delegates:

> For the purpose of promoting this great and truly Christian object, the Society had concluded to hold a General Conference in London, to commence on the 12th of June, 1840; in order to deliberate on the best means of promoting the interests of the slave; of obtaining his immediate and unconditional freedom; and by every pacific measure, to hasten the utter extinction of the slave trade. To this Conference they earnestly invite the friends of every nation and of every clime.

Thomas Clarkson (1760–1846), himself an Anglican deacon and the son of an Anglican vicar in Wisbech, a dedicated, hard-working, long-time leader of the abolitionist movement, was welcomed to the convention, though the welcome was quiet because he was in a frail state of health. For everyone present, including Henry, to be in the presence of abolitionist 'heroes' such as Clarkson must have been deeply moving.

Interestingly, one of the other delegates at the convention was Dr Stephen Lushington MP (1782–1873), a combative radical and abolitionist. His father, until he had died in 1807, had been a partner in the Boldero and Lushington bank, which had collapsed in 1812 with serious consequences for Austen, Maunde and Tilson. Might Dr Stephen Lushington and Henry have taken the opportunity during the intervals of the convention to reflect on the perils of the world of banking, or might they have discreetly avoided each other? Perhaps Henry might have felt more at ease with another delegate, the Reverend Joseph Johnson, the minister of the Independent/Congregationalist church in Farnham. Might their conversations have given Henry a twinge of homesickness?

There was a follow-up convention in 1843, but Henry, for whatever reason, was not a delegate.

Two years later, on 22 March 1845, while staying with her brother Frank in Portsmouth, Cassandra, Henry's sister, died of a stroke. She was buried next to her mother in Chawton; only a few mourners were there – just her brothers, Charles and Henry, and some of her nephews. In her will, it became clear that Cassandra had been a much better financial manager than Henry. Her estate was worth about £16,000 (the equivalent today of over £2,000,000). Cassandra left £1,000 each to Henry, Edward, Frank and Anna (she was James's oldest daughter but was now a widow with seven children to care for). The bulk of Cassandra's estate was left to her brother, Charles. But she seems to have given back to Henry some of Jane's jewellery, including a gold watch and chain and a miniature of Eliza de Feuillide.[17] The wheel of fortune had slowly, very slowly, turned and now stuttered towards Henry with a few bits of benevolence. Henry and Eleanor had moved to Tunbridge Wells from Colchester, perhaps to be near Eleanor's spinster sister, Henrietta, or perhaps they moved there because that part of Kent had close associations with the Austens. Henry's father, George, had been educated at nearby Tonbridge School; it had been the home of his great-grandmother, and it was there, on 12 March 1850, that Henry died and was buried in Woodbury Park cemetery – a cemetery that celebrated 175 years of existence in 2024.

And what happened to any monies he might have had? Henry's will is frustratingly unhelpful. He left everything, without stating its value, to his 'beloved wife', Eleanor.

Chapter 20

Conclusion

When David Cecil wrote the prologue to his classic biography of Jane Austen, he said: 'as her would-be biographer, I had to face the fact that information about Jane Austen the woman was limited and fragmentary, she remains for me – as no doubt she would have wished – not an intimate but an acquaintance.'[1]

It has been the same in trying to write a biography of her brother, Henry. He remains an acquaintance but also an enigma: affable, charming, thoughtful, and deeply attached to the Austen family as he was, there are elements of his life that remain wrapped in mystery. It is true that his life as a successful army officer is reasonably clear, but even so, there are parts of that life, for instance, his ability while managing the Militia's accounts to open a private and discreet banking service for fellow officers, which could be suggestive of questionable practice. What would his father, who was committed to the importance of prudence, have said if he had known? And when, on leaving the Militia, Henry opened his military agency, his working relations with Major Charles James are oddly secretive, as though there might have been something to hide. There are similar questions about his work as the Registrar General of taxes for Oxfordshire: it was indeed lawful for him to keep a certain amount of the money collected before handing it to the government, but why did this process become mired in such confusion? Was it simply a result of poor record keeping, or poor management, or was he out of his depth and cheerfully unaware of the limits of his own abilities? And when his bank failed, what were the deeper causes? How far was that failure due to circumstances beyond his control, or did his personal disposition mean that he was unable to face and deal with difficult financial realities?

But then came his Damascus Road experience when, having been declared bankrupt and having thereby jeopardised the finances of his close family and his friends, he decided to leave the glamour and glitter of Regency London, abandoning the hedonism and vibrant street life of Covent Garden, and to become ordained. Was this the result of a sense of genuine calling – a vocation that had always lain beneath the surface but had now come into sharp focus? Was it a way of salving his conscience, or even some kind of acknowledgement of sorrow for his behaviour as a banker? Or was the curacy in the deeply rural quietness of Chawton a soul-cleansing way of turning his back on the tawdry excitements of Covent Garden and of the world of banking?

Whatever his inner motivations might have been (and we can never know what they really were), what cannot be denied is that in his life as a perpetual curate in Farnham, he worked extremely hard for very little financial reward. But still the questions remain: why, just after ordination did he take himself off to Berlin and in his theological publication about the biblical book of Genesis, declare unashamedly that he was the domestic chaplain to two people who had been involved in scandalous behaviour? He seems, like many of his contemporaries, to have been infatuated with people he regarded as important and influential, and yet, time after time, they let him down. Was he naïve, or did he enjoy the adrenaline rush of high-risk behaviour?

James Austen-Leigh, in his biography of Jane, declared that Henry had 'great conversational powers, and inherited from his father an eager and sanguine disposition. He was a very entertaining companion, but had perhaps less steadiness of purpose, certainly less success in life, than his brothers.'[2] It is a cautious description, in which as a member of the wider Austen family, James-Edward seems not to want to reveal too much detail about Henry's character. His phrase about 'less steadiness of purpose' is the kind of statement that conceals more than it reveals. Does it hint at a more wayward, risk-taking disposition than the family would have wished?

There are more questions than answers about Henry Austen, but we should not overlook the fact that he was Jane's favourite brother. She found him amusing, thoroughly enjoyed his company and was deeply fond of him. He was, quite simply, good to be with. And during the tragic episodes of his life, it was Jane to whom he turned. She was his closest soulmate and friend. On both sides, they had an affectionate and loving respect for each other. It was a fruitful relationship on which Jane relied, and from which, despite everything, she drew comfort. And Henry, it is clear, was enormously proud of her.

What can be stated categorically and unequivocally is that without Henry's determined and passionate commitment in getting Jane's novels published, our lives, and the life of the world, would be so much the poorer. And for that alone, notwithstanding the complex mysteries of his life, we are profoundly in his debt. 'Oh! what a Henry!' indeed.

Appendix

The appointment of Henry Austen as Master at Farnham Grammar School.

Whereas the Right Reverend Father in God, George, Lord Bishop of Winchester did duly on or about the 18th day of October 1823 license me the undersigned Henry Thomas Austen A. M [*sic*] to perform the office of master in the Public and Free Grammar School at Farnham in the County of Surrey within the same Lord Bishop's Diocese and jurisdiction, Now know all therein by these presents that I, the said Henry Thomas Austen, Clerk, do by the presents resign the said office, with all the Rights, Members, Advantages, Emoluments and Appurtenances ... wherein I have hereunto set my hand seal [*sic*] this 24th of February 1827.

Peggy Parks Collection: Volume 32, Farnham and District Museum Society. HRO 21 M 65/12/6/8.

Notes

Chapter 1: Enter Henry Austen, Jane's Favourite Brother

1. Robert Sampson had arrived in Farnham from Devon in the 1820s. He prospered and created his business as a maltster in a part of what is now Farnham Maltings. In 1854, he gave five cottages in Mead Lane, Farnham, as almshouses for the poor of the town. These later fell into disrepair, but the trustees commissioned Harold Falkner, a famed local architect, to create new almshouses in West Street, Farnham. The connection with St Andrew's continues: the Rector is a trustee.
2. Mount Tambora in Indonesia had erupted in 1815 and had caused severe disruption to the pattern of the weather across the world in subsequent years. 1816, for example, in England, was known as 'the year without a summer', and in Germany as 'the year of the beggar'. The summers following were wetter than normal. William Cobbett wrote about the weather in August 1822 when, referring to a poor hop harvest, he said that 'the summer has been so cold and now so wet': Arts and Museums Industries, Waverley Borough Council.
3. A perpetual curate in the Church of England in the early nineteenth century was a clergyman who was paid from an endowment fund but had no right to monies from glebe or tithes. In Henry Austen's case, he received an income of £75 per annum, of which £35 came from 'Surplice Fees', that is, monies paid for christenings, weddings and funerals etc. *See* Ellen Moody, *Reveries Under The Sign of Austen*, https://reveriesunderthesignofausten.wordpress.com/2012/10/20/henry-thomas-austen-1771-1850-a-4th-son-the-man-who-published-jane-austens-6-famous-novels-2/.
4. Church of England clergy were required by the 1604 Canons to wear specific robes. *See* Canons 17 and 58.
5. The 1851 census records a population of 185.

6. Amy/Austen-Leigh, 2021 p. 69.
7. Sometimes called 'Cow Parsley' (*Anthriscus sylvestris*).
8. Austen-Leigh, 2002, p. 14.
9. *See* https://janeaustens.house/object/map-of-the-glebe-land-at-steventon-hants-1821/.
10. For more details, ibid., p. 86.
11. Fox and Brazier, 2020.
12. Knodel, N. (1997), 'Reconsidering an Obsolete Rite: The Churching of Women and Feminist Liturgical Theology', *Feminist Theology*, 5(14), 106–125, https://doi.org/10.1177/096673509700001406.
13. Fox, 2020, p. 56.

Chapter 2: Growing up in the Rectory

1. Benjamin Lefroy married Anna Austen, on 8 November 1814, at St Nicholas Church, Steventon. Anna was the daughter of James Austen, and niece of Jane Austen and Henry Austen. His sketch of the house is subtly different from the engraving of the Rectory in the 1870 memoir. It's a matter of debate which image was the closest to reality.
2. Philadelphia Hancock, née Austen, sister of George Austen, was born in Tonbridge in 1730 and married Tysoe Hancock, a surgeon in the East India Company. She was one of Henry's favourite aunts.
3. Austen-Leigh, 1942, p. 28.
4. Fox, 2022, p. 68.
5. Fildes, 1982, p. 225.
6. Wyndham, 2021.
7. *See* Sanborne, Vic, https://janeaustensworld.com/tag/18th-century-children/ (December 2010).
8. Mrs Susannah Walter (1716–1811) was the wife of William Hampson Walter (1721–98), George Austen's half-brother.
9. Edward Austen (7 October 1767–9 November 1852).
10. Austen-Leigh, 1942, p. 31.
11. George Austen (17 August 1766–17 January 1838).
12. Le Faye, 1995, p. 487.
13. *See* https://janeausteninvermont.blog/books/jane-austens-reading-a-list/.
14. Austen-Leigh, 2002, p. 15.

15. Later taken over in 1825 by Longman, Hurst, Rees, Orme, Brown and Green. George Austen also had an account at John Burdon's bookshop, Winchester. *See* Byrne, p. 77.
16. In November 1797, George Austen sent a Ms copy of Jane Austen's novel *First Impressions* to Cadell and Davies. They turned it down by return of post. Jane reworked it and it was later published as *Pride and Prejudice*. *See* Mandal, 2006, p. 510.
17. Edwards, 1891, *Early Hampshire Printers*. Pinnock's book, *The First Catechism for Children*, begins with a series of questions and answers; for example, 'What is the meaning of the word catechism?'. 'Answer: Instruction by question and answer.' 'What is instruction?' 'Answer: The act of teaching and communicating knowledge.' 'Question: What is the most important thing to be learned?' 'Answer: Our duty towards God, for "the fear of God is the beginning of wisdom".'
18. Amy/Mary Austen-Leigh, p. 503.
19. Bickham, 1743, *The Universal Penman*, p. 14, reproduced by Dover Publications, 1954.
20. For a right-handed person, the best quill was the third feather in from the left wing of a goose. *See* Inglis, 2013, p. 23.
21. Amy/Austen-Leigh, 2021, pp. 51–2.
22. Hussain, 2023.
23. Cassandra and Tom Fowle did not marry, because he died of a fever in the West Indies in 1796, but in his will he left Cassandra £1,000. *See* Hussain, p. 12.
24. Collins, 1994, p. 5.
25. Lord Lymington was the young son of Lord Portsmouth, whose family seat was at Hurstbourne Park, Whitchurch, Hampshire.
26. Hampshire County Record Office.
27. Ibid., p. 58.
28. Linda Robinson Walker argues that the girls might have been sent away to school in order to free up space in the Steventon Rectory to take extra pupils.
29. Austen-Leigh, 1870, pp. 11–13.
30. Amy/James Austen-Leigh, 2021, p. 51.
31. Austen, 1816, p. 18.
32. *The Gentleman's Magazine*, Wednesday, 15 September 1784, p. 711.
33. Walker, 2005.

Chapter 3. The Political and Intellectual World of George Austen, Henry and Jane's Father

1. For more details *see* Corfield, 2023, p. 6.
2. Between 1760 and 1870, about 7 million acres (about one sixth the area of England) were changed, by some 4,000 Acts of Parliament, from common land to enclosed land.
3. Phillips, 1988, p. 263.
4. *See* https://www.british-history.ac.uk/vch/oxon/vol3/pp1-38 (a digitised copy of the *Victoria County History of Oxfordshire*, Vol. 3, 1954).
5. Ibid., p. 265.
6. Brockliss, 2019, p. 54.
7. Leedham-Green, p. 120.
8. *See* https://blogs.bodleian.ox.ac.uk/archivesandmanuscripts/category/century/18th/ (2023).
9. John Wesley's journal https://www.ccel.org/ccel/wesley/journal.vi.ii.xvi.html.
10. Cecil, 1980, p. 15.
11. *See* Internet Archive, https://archive.org/details/christianityasol00tind/page/n7/mode/2up.
12. Locke, 1690, p. 218.
13. Ibid., p. 289.
14. Bird, 2014, argues that 'Edmund's chosen vocation ... is an externalization of this own preoccupation with fulfilling his duty' and that the conflicts in the novel result from the clashes between dutiful and selfish behaviour.
15. Monaghan, 1978, p. 221.
16. Austen, 1818, p. 52.
17. For the list of sermon texts *see* Selwyn, 2001.
18. Mary Austen-Leigh in her lively defence of her great-aunt Jane against some early twentieth-century literary critics avers that there is one theme common to all Jane's novels, and that is the theme of repentance. *See* Amy/M.A. Austen-Leigh, p. 517.

Chapter 4: Improvement, Enclosures and Livings

1. Riordan, 2022.
2. Clery, 2017, p. 30.

3. Clark, 2015.
4. Austen, 1814, p. 212.
5. Easton, 2002.
6. Austen, 1811, p. 265.
7. Easton, 2002, p. 73.
8. Collins, 1994, p. 24. Details about the numbers of livings are taken from Collins, 1994, pp. 24–5, and details about clergy earnings are taken from Collins, 1994, p. 28.
9. Details of the tithe system, impropriation and glebe are also taken from Collins, pp. 50–6.
10. Austen, 1818, p. 179.
11. Austen, 1811, pp. 175–6.
12. Clery, 2017, p. 30.
13. Cecil, 1980, p. 16.
14. Le Faye, 1997, p. 193.
15. Amy/Austen-Leigh, 2021, p. 92.

Chapter 5: Henry Austen: Oxford University and *The Loiterer*

1. Cecil, 1980, p. 33.
2. In *Mansfield Park* (p. 161) in a conversation with Fanny Price, Edmund Bertram notices that Fanny has a copy of Crabbe's *Tales* and a copy of *The Idler* close by.
3. Geng, 2000, p. 11.
4. Ibid., p. 14.
5. Ibid., p. 20. It should be noted that all the quotations that follow are from Geng's edition of *The Loiterer*.
6. Claire Tomalin argues that 'Sophie Sentiment' was just a pen name for James and Henry. *See* Tomalin, 1997, p. 63.

Chapter 6: The Oxford Militia

1. 1792, an auspicious year for Henry, was auspicious also for Mary Wollstonecraft because in that year she published her book, *A Vindication of the Rights of Woman*.
2. *See*, for example, Le Faye, *Letters*, p. 4.
3. HMS *Daedalus* was a thirty-two-gun, fifth-rate frigate launched in 1780.

4. HMS *Perseverance* was a thirty-six-gun frigate, which was sent to the East Indies in 1789. The HQ of the East Indies station was Trincomalee, a deep-water port on the north-eastern coast of Sri Lanka.
5. HMS *Crown* was a sixty-four-gun third-rate, launched in 1782.
6. Hampshire County Record Office.
7. Western, 1965, p. 251.
8. Willan, 1900, p. 6.
9. Willan, 1900, pp. 9–10.
10. A ruling in 1769 stated that deputies were required to hold £200 in land value, or to evidence that they were heirs to twice that amount. *See* Western, 1965, p. 278.
11. Western, 1965, pp. 290–302.
12. Western, p. 314.
13. Ibid., p. 341.
14. Willan, p. 16.
15. County regiments were usually stationed outside their own counties to prevent the men from joining in any civil disturbances that might erupt in their home county. *See* Western, 1965, p. 261.

Chapter 7: Henry's Promotion and Marriage

1. Western, pp. 344–5.
2. Ibid., p. 359.
3. Willan, 1900, p. 29.
4. *The Gentleman's Magazine*, Vol. 65, Part 1, p. 519.
5. Willan, 1900, p. 30.
6. Le Faye, 1997, p. 1.
7. Ibid., pp. 5–6.
8. Western, 1965, p. 286.
9. Le Faye, p. 12.
10. Tomalin, 1997, p. 118.
11. Tomalin, 1997, p. 9.
12. Ibid., p. 49.
13. Clery, 2017 p. 46. Note: in the eighteenth century, the average height of a man was 5 feet 5 inches, and for a woman, 5 feet 1 inch.
14. Clery, 2017, p. 14.

15. Phylly was the daughter, b. 1761, of William Hampson Walter, George and Philadelphia (Hancock), Austen's half-brother.
16. Clery, 2017, p. 56.
17. Ibid., p. 58.
18. They were married in what has been called the 3rd parish church (not the current one), a brick-built rectangular box of a building with a small clock/bell tower, which in 1742 replaced an earlier church. The clock/bell tower of the 3rd parish church is happily echoed in the design of the current building.
19. Gunn, 1987, pp. 406–407.
20. Solinger, 2005, pp. 272–90.
21. Le Faye, 1995, p. 21–2.
22. Le Faye, 1995, note 1, p. 362.
23. Clery, 2017, p. 43.
24. Mullen, 2018, p. 536.

Chapter 8: The Lure of Finance

1. Le Faye, 1975, p. 66. The Austens lived initially at 4, Sydney Terrace, and then moved to Green Park Buildings, and finally, Gay Street.
2. *See* Todd (undated and unnumbered web-based document).
3. Austen, 1813, p. 43.
4. Amy/Austen-Leigh, 2021, p. 65.
5. Austen, 1816, p. 250.
6. Caplan, 1992, p. 17. Militias were usually stationed in counties at some distance from the militia's origins.
7. Clery, 2017, p. 57.
8. Clery, 2017, p. 68.
9. The house is now an opulent boutique Hotel called 'Henry's Town House'.
10. For details of horse-drawn vehicles in the days of the Austen family *see* Ewing, 2019.
11. Hampshire County Record Office.
12. The document can be found on 'Internet Archive'.
13. The above paragraph is indebted to the writings of Jacqueline Reiter, who has researched the life of Charles James: *see* https://thelatelord.com/.
14. Source, Hampshire County Record Office.
15. Caplan, 1998, p. 70.

Chapter 9: Henry's Success and Luck

1. Allen, 2005, p. 65.
2. Tomalin, 1997, p. 187.
3. Tomalin, 1997, p. 189.
4. Le Faye, 1997, p. 96.
5. apRoberts, 1975, p. 354.
6. Mrs Austen, Cassandra and Jane moved to Southampton in 1805 and resided at Castle Square.
7. The bank failed just four years later, in 1810. *See* Caplan, 1998, p. 76.
8. Turner, 2015, p. 8.
9. Ibid., p. 9.
10. For more details *see* Turner, 2015, p. 111 and following.
11. In Henrietta Street, Henry employed a chief clerk, Mr Barlowe, and at least six junior clerks. *See* Clery, 2017, p. 204.
12. Murphy, 2023, p. 15.
13. Turner, p. 144.
14. Ibid., p. 157.
15. Ibid., p. 179.
16. Clery, 2017, p. 111.

Chapter 10: More Banking Developments and Publications, 1807–1813

1. 10, Henrietta Street is now (2024) the site of a cocktail bar called 'Mrs Riot'. Jane would have loved the garish absurdity of it.
2. Clery, 2017, p. 113.
3. Caplan, p. 78.
4. Murphy, 2023, p. 5.
5. Le Faye, 1997, p. 146.
6. Clery, 2017, p. 124.
7. Caplan, p. 79 and Le Faye, p. 164.
8. *See* http://general-southerner.blogspot.com/2010/03/jane-austen-at-theatre.html
9. Tomalin, 1997, p. 206.
10. Stephens, 1900, p. 67.

11. The house has been refaced and another storey added since the Austens lived there. *See* https://kleurrijkjaneausten.blogspot.com/2014/09/64-sloave-street-london-house-of-henry.
12. For more details *see* Clery, pp. 132–7.
13. Sutherland, 2013, p. 107.
14. Cecil, 1980, p. 10.
15. Ibid., p. 10.
16. Cox, 2023.
17. Le Faye, 1995, p. 182.
18. Ibid., p. 180.
19. Ibid., p. 183.
20. Clery, 2017, p. 132.
21. Tomalin, 1997, p. 224.
22. Ibid., p. 225.
23. Clery, 2017, p. 133.

Chapter 11: Death, Taxes and New Opportunities

1. Le Faye, 1995, p. 184.
2. Cecil, 1980, p. 36.
3. 'Little Charles' was a poem for children composed by Mrs Anna Laetitia Barbauld.
4. Source: Hampshire County Records Office, Winchester.
5. Tomalin, p. 234.
6. Le Faye, 1997, p. 212.
7. Barchas (undated).
8. Le Faye, 1997, p. 213.
9. Le Faye, 1997, p. 214.
10. Avery Jones, 2022, footnote 148.
11. For a detailed description of the situation *see* Clery, 2015, pp. 95–6.
12. Caplan, 1998.
13. Avery Jones, personal correspondence.
14. Avery Jones, 2022, p. 4.
15. Avery Jones, 2022, p. 3.
16. Avery Jones, 2023, p. 4.

17. James Tilson's father was married to Maria Lushington; Maria Lushington's brother, Dr Stephen Lushington, married Hester Boldero, and became a partner in Boldero and Co., and Hester's brother, Charles, was the senior partner in Boldero and Co., and another of Maria Lushington's brothers, William, and her nephew were partners in Lushington. *See* Avery Jones. 2003.
18. Avery Jones, 2023, to whom I am deeply indebted for the quality and clarity of his research about these complex matters.
19. Avery Jones, 2023, p. 5.
20. Le Faye, 1995, p. 215.
21. Ibid., pp. 215–16.
22. Le Faye, 1997, p. 230.
23. Ibid., p. 231.
24. The coach travelled via Bentley to Farnham, where they changed horses, and thence to Kingston; for confirmation of the route *see* Jane's letter of 23–24 August 1814. Le Faye, 1995, p. 270.
25. Le Faye, 1995, p. 218
26. Ibid., p. 223.
27. Ibid., p. 253.

Chapter 12: Increasing Work and Anxiety, 1814–1816

1. Le Faye, 1997, p. 255.
2. Austen, 2014, pp. 239–40.
3. Caplan, 1998.
4. Le Faye, p. 264.
5. Ibid., 1997, p. 265.
6. Ibid., p. 271.
7. Le Faye, 1995, p. 270.
8. Ibid., p. 273.
9. Ibid., p. 287.
10. Caplan, 1998.
11. Le Faye, 1997, p. 291. £450 would be worth approximately £50,000 today.
12. Perhaps a kind of laxative?
13. He introduced the French invention of the stethoscope to England: *see* Halperin, 1985, p. 734.

14. Le Faye, 1995, p. 298.
15. Ibid., 1995, p. 292.
16. Avery Jones, 2022, p. 5.
17. Ibid., p. 6.

Chapter 13: Henry's Illness and his Bank's Demise

1. Le Faye, 1995, p. 296.
2. Le Faye, 1995, p. 298.
3. Ibid., p. 299.
4. Ibid., p. 301.
5. Ibid., p. 304.
6. Le Faye, 1995, p. 306.
7. Caplan, 1998.
8. Clery 2017 p 266.
9. https://www.investopedia.com/what-happens-if-my-bank-fails.
10. Avery Jones, 2022, p. 43.
11. Avery Jones, 2022, p. 31.
12. Avery Jones, 2002, Table 1.
13. Le Faye, 2017.
14. Ibid., pp. 172–89.
15. He was replaced by the Reverend Charles Sumner (1790–1874), who later became a princely and generous Bishop of Winchester.
16. Le Faye, 1995, p. 312.
17. Clery, 2017, p. 282.

Chapter 14: The Empty Future?

1. Le Faye, p. 315.
2. In fact, Edward Austen Knight and James Leigh Perrot were not approached about forfeiting their sureties until 1818.
3. Mr Gell was the Bishop of Winchester's Steward.
4. The Reverend Canon Garnier was the son-in-law of Bishop Brownlow North.
5. The *Hampshire Chronicle* https://www.hampshirechronicle.co.uk/news/23036174.winchester-bishop-put-family-first/.
6. Tomalin, 1997, p. 256.

7. Bishop John Fisher was a great friend of the artist John Constable and commissioned him to paint a view of Salisbury Cathedral.
8. In *Sense and Sensibility* p. 340, Colonel Brandon offers Edward Ferrars a living worth £200 per annum – four times what Henry could earn.
9. Austen, 1814, p. 271.
10. Ibid., pp. 248–9.
11. Austen, 1818, pp. 220–1.

Chapter 15: Return to Chawton and Jane's Death

1. The average size of household in Georgian England was 4.75: *see* Corfield, 2023, p. 75.
2. Corfield, 2023, p. 51.
3. Le Faye, 1995, p. 322. The Reverend Edward Cooper was the son of the Reverend Dr Edward Cooper who married Jane Leigh, sister of Mrs George Austen. He was Henry's cousin.
4. Cooper, 1819.
5. Austen, 1814, p. 473.
6. James Edward Austen-Leigh was the author of *A Memoir of Jane Austen*, published in 1870.
7. Tomalin, 1997, p. 274.

Chapter 16: Publishing Jane's Books, Chawton, and Berlin

1. Austen/Biographical Note, 1818.
2. *See* Wells, 2017, who argues that the Biographical Notice might have had an input from Cassandra, and that to claim that it was solely the work of Henry 'results from speculation and assumption, rather than resting on documentary evidence'.
3. Jenkins, 2011.

Chapter 17: What did Henry Believe?

1. In *The Book of Common Prayer*, the word 'oblation' is used instead of Henry's word 'atonement'.
2. Austen, 1829, p. 21.
3. Anon 2, pp. 1–3.

4. Tomalin, p. 275.
5. *See* the memorial tablet erected in St Nicholas, Steventon.
6. Austen, 1814, p. 253.

Chapter 18: Henry's Life as a Clergyman in Farnham

1. It is now the Surrey County Council Adult Education Centre.
2. Black, 2001, 2008, p. 137.
3. *See* Appendix.
4. Anon, History of Farnham Grammar School, p. 6.
5. *See* Appendix.
6. In *Emma*, Frank Churchill expatiates on the possibilities of a closed ballroom at the Crown Inn: 'he stopped for several minutes at the two superior sashed windows, which were open, and lament that its original purpose should have ceased', Austen, 1816, p. 199.
7. Corfield, 2023, p. 262.
8. The difference in numbers between 1824 and 1825 is accounted for by the fact that several other clergy were involved in taking christenings. These have not been included in Henry Austen's figures.
9. Austen, 1816, p. 32.
10. Heather, 2008.
11. The report was entitled: 'The state of the poor; or, an history of the labouring classes in England, from the conquests to the present period. In which are particularly considered, their domestic economy, with respect to diet, dress, fuel, and habitation; and the various plans which, from time to time, have been proposed, and adopted, for the relief of the poor: together with parochial reports relative to the administration of workhouses, and houses of industry; the state of friendly societies; and other public institutions ... / With a large appendix containing a comparative and chronological table of the prices of labour, of provisions, and of other commodities ... an account of the poor in Scotland, etc. By Sir Frederic Morton Eden'.
12. *See* Farnham Vestry Minute Book 1828–Onwards: Surrey History Centre.
13. Herbert, 2023, pp. 82–3.
14. Ibid., pp. 74–5.

Chapter 19: Bentley and Final Days

1. Barlow, 2018.
2. For more details about the Swing Riots in Farnham *see* Herbert, 2023, pp. 110–13.
3. Hand-held wooden guide plaque to assist visitors.
4. There is dispute about the origin of the term 'Pilgrims Way'; some regard it as a nineteenth-century invention created by a surveyor, Edward Renouard James, for the Victorian Ordnance Survey map of Surrey.
5. Andrews, 2023, p. 8.
6. Re-mounted in 1890.
7. Eggar, 1974.
8. Midgley, 1978, p. 89.
9. The two paragraphs above about the cage are based upon research and an original article of 2022 by Mrs Brigid Fice of Bentley, to whom I am much indebted.
10. Midgley, 1978, p. 90.
11. *Hansard*, August, 1834.
12. Ibid., p. 90.
13. Charles Jackson had signed the Bentley Funeral Register for the first time in April 1736.
14. Sumner 1837.
15. For more details of the relationship between the Austen family and slavery *see* Devoney Looser, 'Breaking the Silence', *TLS*, May 2021.
16. *Proceedings*, 1840, pp. 5–6.
17. Clery, 2017, p. 321.

Chapter 20: Conclusion

1. Cecil, 1980, p. 10.

Bibliography

Allen, Douglas W., 'Purchase, Patronage, and Professions: Incentives and the Evolution of Public Office in Pre-Modern Britain', *Journal of Institutional and Theoretical Economics*, Vol. 161, No. 1 (March 2005).

Amy, Helen, *The Jane Austen Files*, Amberley (2021).

Andrews, Mark, 'Cult or contract? Cross mark graffiti in Worcestershire churches', *Worcestershire Recorder*, 107 (2023).

Anon, *A History of Farnham Grammar School*, Old Farnhamian's Association (undated publication).

Anon, *A Manual For The Parish Priest Being A Few Hints On The Pastoral Care To The Younger Clergy Of The Church Of England From An Elder Brother*, Rivington (1822).

Anon, *Proceedings of the General Anti-Slavery Convention*, London (1840).

apRoberts, Ruth, 'Sense and Sensibility, or Growing Up Dichotomous', *Nineteenth-Century Fiction*, Vol. 30, No. 3 (1975).

Austen, Jane, *Sense and Sensibility*, originally published 1811, CRW Publishing (Collector's Library) (2003).

Austen, Jane, *Pride and Prejudice*, originally published 1813, CRW Publishing (Collector's Library) (2003).

Austen, Jane, *Mansfield Park*, Nelson Classics (undated publication) (1814).

Austen, Jane, *Emma*, Nelson Classics (undated publication) (1816).

Austen, Jane, *Persuasion*, originally published 1818, reissued, Penguin (1965).

Austen, Jane, *Northanger Abbey*, originally published 1818, reissued, Macdonald (1961).

Austen, Henry Thomas Austen, *Biographical Note to Northanger Abbey and Persuasion*, Murray, London (1818).

Austen, Henry Thomas, 'A sermon preached at the Parish Church of Clifton', Browne (1829).

Austen-Leigh, James Edward, *A Memoir of Jane Austen*, originally published 1870, OUP World's Classics Edition (2002).

Austen-Leigh, R.A., *The Austen Family Papers 1704–1856*, Spottiswoode, Ballantyne and Co. (1942).

Avery Jones, John F., 'Henry Austen's Tax Debt as Receiver-General of Taxes for Oxfordshire', Vol. 3, No. 41, *Persuasions*, JASNA (2022).

Avery Jones, John, F., 'Henry Austen: The Eventful Earlier Years as Receiver-General of Taxes for Oxfordshire', Vol. 44, No. 1, *Persuasions*, JASNA (2023).

Barchas, Janine, 'What Jane saw', www.whatjanesaw.org: University of Texas at Austin (undated).

Barlow, Angela, *Henry and Eleanor Austen: The Road to Bentley*, The Rectory Society (2018).

Bird, Paul, 'A Distracted Seminarian: The Unsuccessful Reformation of Edmund Bertram', Vol. 35, No. 1, *Persuasions*, JASNA (2014).

Black, Jeremy, *Eighteenth-Century Britain 1688–1783*, Palgrave Macmillan (2008).

Brockliss, Laurence, *The University of Oxford: A Brief History*, Bodleian Library (2019).

Butler, Marilyn, *Dictionary of National Biography*, OUP (2008).

Byrne, Paula, *The Real Jane Austen: A Life in Small Things*, Harper Collins (2013).

Caplan, Clive, 'Jane Austen and the Militia', *Persuasions*, No. 14 (1992).

Caplan, Clive, 'Jane Austen's Banker Brother', *Persuasions*, No. 20 (1998).

Cecil, David, *A Portrait of Jane Austen*, Penguin (1980).

Clark, Robert, 'Wilderness and Shrubbery in Austen's Works', *Persuasions*, Vol. 26, No. 1, JASNA (2015).

Collins, Irene, *Jane Austen and the Clergy*, The Hambledon Press (1993).

Cooper, Edward, *Practical and Familiar Sermons*, Cadell and Davies (1819).

Corfield, Penelope, *The Georgians*, Yale University Press (2023).

Cox, Brenda S., 'Jane Austen's publishing journey', https://janeaustensworld.com/2023/06/26/jane-austens-publishing-journey (2023).

Cox, Brenda S., 'Sermons by Jane Austen's Family', https://topazcrossbooks.com/2022/12/01/sermons-by-jane-austens-family (2022).

Duckworth, Alastair M., 'Mansfield Park and Estate Improvements: Jane Austen's Grounds of Being', Vol. 6, No. 1, *Nineteenth-Century Fiction*, University of California Press (1971).

Dunning, Ronald, 'Rebecca Hampson, George Austen's Mother', blog: *Jane Austen's World*, https://janeaustensworld.com/2021/11/21/rebecca-hampson-george-austens-mother-by-ronald-dunning (2021).

Easton, Celia, 'Jane Austen and the Enclosure Movement', *Persuasions*, Vol. 24, JASNA (2002).

Edwards, F.A., *Early Hampshire Printers*, Hampshire Field Club and Archaeological Society (1891).

Eggar, Mary, *The Church and Village of Bentley St Mary*, Bentley PCC (1974).

Ewing, Jennifer S., 'As the Wheel Turns: Horse-Drawn Vehicles in Jane Austen's Novels', *JASNA*, Vol. 40, No. 1 (2019).

Fairlie, Simon, 'A Short History of Enclosure in Britain', *The Land Magazine*, https://www.thelandmagazine.org.uk/articles/short-history-enclosure-britain (2009).

Fildes, Valerie, 'The Age of Weaning in Britain 1500–1800', *Journal of Biosocial Science*, CUP (1982).

Fitzgerald, Cathie, *Surrounded By Hops*, Farnham and District Museum Society (2014).

Fox, Sarah, *Giving Birth in Eighteenth-Century England*, University of London Press (2022).

Fox, Sarah and Brazier, Margaret, 'The regulation of midwives in England, c.1500–1902', *Medical Law International*, 20(4), 308–338 (2020).

Geng, Li-Ping, *The Loiterer, a facsimile reproduction edited and with an introduction by LI-Ping Geng*, Ann Arbor, Scholars' Facsimiles & Reprints (2000).

Gunn, Daniel P., 'In the Vicinity of Winthrop: Ideological Rhetoric in Persuasion', *Nineteenth-Century Literature*, Vol. 41, No. 4 (1987).

Halperin, John, 'Jane Austen's Lovers', *Studies in English Literature, 1500–1900*, Vol. 25, No. 4 (1985).

Heather, Pat, *Andrew Windsor's Almshouses*, Farnham and District Museum Society (2008).

Herbert, Christopher, *Building Jerusalem: The life and times of Charles Sumner, Bishop of Winchester 1790–1874*, Farnham and District Museum Society (2023).

Hussain, Azar, 'The Boys at Steventon: Mr. Austen's Students 1773–1796', *Persuasions*, Vol. 44, No. 1, JASNA (2023).

Inglis, Lucy, *Georgian London*, Penguin Random House (2013).
Jenkins, David, *Friedrich Schleiermacher: Father of Liberal Theology*, https://servantsofgrace.org/friedrich-schleiermacher-father-of-liberal-theology/ (2011).
Jones, John Avery, 'Henry Austen's Tax Debt as Receiver-General of Taxes for Oxfordshire', *Persuasions*, Vol. 43 (2022).
Jones, John Avery, 'Henry Austen: The Eventful Earlier Years as Receiver General of Taxes for Oxfordshire', *Persuasions*, Vol. 44, No. 1 (2023).
Knodel, 'Reconsidering an Obsolete Rite: The Churching of Women and Feminist Liturgical Theology', *Feminist Theology*, 5(14), 106–125 (1997).
Le Faye, Deirdre, 'Jane Austen and her Hancock Relatives', *The Review of English Studies* (1979).
Le Faye, Deirdre, *Jane Austen's Letters*, OUP (1995).
Le Faye, Deirdre, '"The Head of a Flourishing Bank": The Bankruptcy Inventories of Austen, Maunde and Tilson 1816', *Furniture History*, Vol. 53 (2017).
Leedham-Green, Elizabeth, *A Concise History of the University of Cambridge*, CUP (1996).
Litz, 'The Loiterer: A Reflection of Jane Austen's Early Environment', *The Review of English Studies* (1961), Vol. 12, No. 47.
Locke, John, *An Essay Concerning Human Understanding* (1690), Everyman Edition, Dent (1961).
Mandal, A.A., 'Making Austen Mad: Benjamin Crosby and the Non-Publication of "Susan"', *The Review of English Studies*, Vol. 57, No. 231 (2006).
Midgley, Winifred, 'The Revd Henry and Mrs Eleanor Austen' (1978), Jane Austen Society Collected Reports 1976–1985 (1989).
Milner, Joseph, *Practical Sermons*, Matthews and Deighton (1804).
Monaghan, David, 'Evangelicalism and Mansfield Park: A Reassessment', *Nineteenth-Century Fiction*, Vol. 33, No. 2, pp. 215–30 (Sept 1978), University of California Press (1978).
Moody, Ellen, 'Reveries Under The Sign of Austen', https://reveriesunderthesignofausten.wordpress.com/2012/10/20/henry-thomas-austen-1771-1850-a-4th-son-the-man-who-published-jane-austens-6-famous-novels-2/ (2012).

Mullen, Alexandra, 'Associations of Thought', *The Hudson Review*, Vol. 70, No. 4 (2018).

Murphy, Anne L., *Virtuous Bankers*, Princeton University Press (2023).

Osmond, Sam, *Famous Farnham Figures*, Farnham and District Museum Society (2022).

Phillips, David, 'Gibbon Redivivus: Eighteenth-Century Oxford', *Oxford Review of Education*, Vol. 14, No. 2 (1988).

Reiter, Jacqueline, 'The Name's James, Charles James: A Napoleonic Enigma', *The Late Lord*, thelatelord.com (2019).

Riordan, Mike, 'The Austen's Long History at St John's', https://www.sjc.ox.ac.uk/discover/news/the-austens-at-st-johns/ (2022).

Selwyn, David, 'Some Sermons of Mr Austen', Report for 2001 The Jane Austen Society (2001).

Solinger, Jason, 'Jane Austen and the Gentrification of Commerce', *NOVEL: A Forum on Fiction*, Vol. 38, No. 2/3, New Work on Eighteenth-Century Fiction (2005).

Stephens, Henry Morse, 'Clarke, Mary Anne', *Dictionary of National Biography: 1885–1910*, Vol. 10 (1900).

Sumner, Charles Richard, *A Charge Delivered to the Clergy of the Diocese of Winchester by Charles Richard Sumner at his Third Visitation*, Hatchard (1837).

Sutherland, Kathryn, 'Jane Austen's Dealings with John Murray and his Firm', *The Review of English Studies*, New Series, Vol. 64, No. 263 (2013).

Todd, E.E.E., 'Notes on Army Pay', https://rapc-association.org.uk/pay-services-history/notes-on-army-pay-3.html (undated).

Tomson, Richard S., 'The English Grammar School Curriculum in the 18th Century: a reappraisal', *British Journal of Educational Studies*, Vol. 19, No. 1 (1971).

Turner, Gareth David, 'English Banking in the 18th Century', University of Durham M.Litt E-theses online (2015).

Viveash, Chris, 'Lady Morley and the Baron so Bold', *Persuasions*, JASNA (1992).

Walker, Linda Robinson, 'Why Was Jane Austen Sent away to School at Seven? An Empirical Look at a Vexing Question', *Persuasions Online*, Vol. 26, No. 1, (Winter 2005).

Weldon, Fay, *Letters to Alice on First Reading Jane Austen*, Coronet (1984).
Wells, Juliet, 'A Note on Henry Austen's Authorship of the "Biographical Notice"', *Persuasions*, Vol. 38, No. 1, JASNA 20171965 (2017).
Western, J.R., *The English Militia in the Eighteenth Century*, Routledge and Kegan Paul (1965).
Willan, Frank, *History of the Oxfordshire Regiment of Militia 1778–1900*, Horace Hart (1900).
Wyndham, https://thebabyhistorian.com/2021/06/28/jane-austens-birth-pt-1/#childbirth (2021).

Index

Abolitionists, Convention of, 198
Act of Union, 19
Adlestrop, 31–2
Alice Holt (forest), 191
Allen, Douglas, 85
Alton, Hampshire (town and bank), 11, 79, 91, 98, 106, 117, 126, 130, 132–3, 144–6
Andrews, Mr and Mrs (painting), 20
Antraigues, Comte de, 103
apRoberts, Ruth, 88
Austen, Anna Elizabeth, 54–5, 199
Austen, Caroline, 178
Austen, Cassandra, 2–3, 7, 14, 15, 40, 65, 67, 73, 75, 81, 87, 98–9, 103, 105, 110, 117, 120, 123–4, 129–30, 143, 157–9, 161, 164, 179, 194, 199
Austen/Leigh, Cassandra, 3–10, 12–13, 16, 17, 31, 55, 66, 75, 87, 157, 178
Austen, Cassy, 143
Austen, Charles, 3, 56–7, 111, 143, 192, 199
Austen (Knight), Edward, 1, 3, 6, 9–11, 16, 56–7, 87, 98–9, 115, 117, 125, 129, 132, 135, 138, 140, 149, 159, 178, 182, 199
Austen, Francis (Frank), 3, 12, 42, 56–7, 86, 89–90, 106, 111, 115, 120, 138, 143, 159, 192, 199
Austen, Francis (uncle), 55
Austen, The Revd George, 3–5, 10–13, 16, 19, 30, 32, 35–9, 54, 55, 68, 75, 86–7, 93, 182, 200
  earnings, 13, 14, 39
Austen, George (junior), 3, 6, 9
Austen, Henry Thomas:
  banking, 76–139
  biographer, 164
  birth and childhood at Steventon, 3–6, 11, 12, 16
  death, 200
  marriage, 72
  ordination, 143–8
  Oxford Militia, 56–74
  Oxford University, 42–53
  Perpetual Curate of Bentley, 184–97
  Perpetual Curate of Farnham, 1, 37, 181–90
  Receiver General, 113–15, 126
  Rector of Steventon, 178
Austen, James, 3, 6, 11, 14, 15, 43, 54, 57, 65, 69, 76, 87, 138, 143, 147–8, 159, 163, 178

Austen, James Edward, 56, 140, 159, 178, 192, 197, 202

Austen, Jane, 2–3, 10, 14–15, 37, 40, 44, 51, 53, 55, 61, 65, 67, 72–5, 79, 81, 85–6, 97–9, 101–103, 105, 108, 110, 115, 117, 120–1, 123–6, 128–30, 132, 137–8, 140, 143, 148, 152, 154, 155, 164–6, 199, 201, 203

  death, 157–63

  novels:

    Emma, 15, 79, 121, 122, 123–4, 125–6, 128–9, 130–2, 164, 168, 184

    Mansfield Park, 19, 27, 28–9, 33, 119, 122–3, 125, 130, 139, 149–50, 152–3, 155, 164, 177–8, 179–80

    Northanger Abbey, 38, 135, 150, 164

    Persuasion, 27–8, 72, 134–5, 152, 164

    Pride and Prejudice, 49, 78, 85, 109, 110, 117, 119, 165, 194

    Sanditon, 157

    Sense and Sensibility, 34, 38–9, 87–9, 101–102, 116, 119, 123, 125, 164

  prayer, 29

Austen, Leonora, 19

Austen, Mary, 158

Austen, William, 19

Austen Lefroy, Anna, 7

Austen Leigh, James, 4, 10, 41, 79, 202

Austen, Blunt and Louch Bank, Petersfield, 91

Austen, Gray and Vincent Bank, Alton, 91

Austen, Maunde and Austen, 92

Austen, Maunde and Tilson, 110, 120, 126–7, 130, 136, 141, 199

Avery Jones, John, 114, 134, 138

Balloon flight, 16

Bank of England, 92, 97

Barlow, Angela, 189

Basingstoke, 4, 11, 79, 86

Bastille, 56

Bath, 17, 32, 75, 86–7, 178, 194

Bathurst, The Revd Thomas, 3

Beating the Bounds, 188

Beer Act, 192

Belgrave Chapel, 109

Belgrave Square, 109

Bellingham, John, 107

Bengal, India, 68

Bentley, Hampshire, 172, 177, 184, 188–90

Bentley, St Mary's Church, 190

Bentley, the cage, 193

Bentley, Richard, 194

Berlin, 166, 177

Bickham, George, 11–12

Bigeon, Madame, 108, 117, 161, 197

Bigg, Alethea, 159

Blomfield, Charles, Bishop of London, 195–6

Boldero and Co. (bank), 114–15, 199

Boringdon, Lord, 86, 167–9
  see also Morley
Brighton, 61
Brownlow North, Bishop of
    Winchester, 143, 146–7, 187
Buchan, Dr William, 105
Burdett, Frances, 121
Buxton and High Peak Bank, 91

Cadell and Davies (publishers), 10
Caillaud, John, 59
Calcutta, 68
Cambridge, University of, 22
Caplan, Clive, 96, 122–3
Caroline of Brunswick, 128
Catholic Emancipation Bill, 176
Caudle, 8
Cavendish, George, 90
Cawley, Ralph, Master of Brasenose, 14
Cecil, David, 25, 40, 102, 106, 201
Chawton, Hampshire, 1, 79, 106, 108–10, 138, 143, 148, 151, 155, 157, 165, 177, 182, 194, 199, 202
Chawton Great House, 115, 143, 149
Chelmsford Barracks, 66
Cheltenham, 152
Child and Co. (bank), 93
Church Building Act, 178
Church Temporalities Act, 192
Churching, 5
Chute family, 55, 182
Clarence, Duke of, 103
Claret, 110

Clarke, James Stanier, 124, 128, 131–2, 137
Clarke, Mary Anne, 100
Clarke, William (publisher), 10
Clarkson, Thomas, 199
Clery, E.J., 103, 139
Clifton Parish Church, Bristol, 172
Cobbett, William, 33, 101, 189–90
Colchester, 197
Commissioners of Bankruptcy, 136
Commissions, sales to officers, 85
Consecration crosses, Bentley, 190–1
Cooke, Edward, 63–4
Cooper, The Revd Edward, 66, 154
Corfield, Penelope, 153
Corn Laws, 123
Court martial, 63
Coutts, Sophia, 121
Coutts Bank, 93–4
Covent Garden, 97
Cowper, William, 10, 146
Cox, Richard, 93
Cox and Greenwood, 79
Crosby, Richard, 135
Culloden, Battle of, 19
Cumberland, Duke of, 105, 166–7

Deane, 3, 4, 8, 17, 32, 55, 56
Defoe, Daniel, 10
De Feuillide, Eliza, 67–73, 80–1, 86, 93, 102–103, 105, 116, 140, 161, 199
  death of, 108–109

De Feuillide, Hastings, 71, 81
De Feuillide, Jean François Capot, 69, 71
Derbyshire Militia, 90–1
Devonshire, Duke of, 91
Digweed, W.F., 148, 182
Drummonds Bank, 93

Earle, Robert, 186
East India Company, 68, 70
Egerton, Thomas (publisher), 43, 101, 109, 122, 194
Enclosure Act 1773, 33, 35
'Enthusiasm', 25
Execution, 64
Extent-in-Aid, 123, 132
Extent-in-Chief, 122, 136

Farnham, Surrey:
    Grammar School, 181, 182
    St Andrew's Church, 1, 182–3
    Workhouse, 185
Farringdon, Hampshire, 79
Fire risk, 94
Fisher, John, Bishop of Salisbury, 148
Flanders, 68
Fleet Prison, 123
Fowle, Charles, 13
Fowle, Eliza, 13
Fowle, Fulmar Craven, 13
Fowle, Tom, 13
Fowle, William, 13
Fox, Sarah, 8
France, 56, 61, 86

Gainsborough, Thomas, 20
George II, King, 19
George III, King, 56–7, 98, 99, 105, 176
Germany, 68
Gibbon, Edward, 21
Glebe, 37–8, 40, 150–1
Godmersham, Kent, 56, 66, 81, 98–9, 115, 117, 140, 182
Gore-Langton, William, MP, 106–107
Goslings Bank, 93
Gray, Edward, 126, 132
Greenwich, 67
Grenville, Lord, 90
Grey, Lord, 192
Guildhall, London, 138, 141
Guyenne, France, 69

Haden, Mr (apothecary), 124
Hampson, Rebecca, 19
Hancock, Philadelphia, 7, 13, 19, 68–9, 71, 93, 108
Hancock, Tysoe, 68
Harfield, James, 123
Harpsden, Oxfordshire, 31
Hastings, Charles, 90
Hastings, George, 12
Hastings, Warren, 13, 68, 70–2, 90
Hatchards (booksellers), 11
Haywood, Eliza, 10
Heathcote, Elizabeth, 159
Hoares Bank, 79, 93–4, 138
Holland, Lord, 76
Horwood Well Bank, 91, 101
Hundred Days War, 122
Hythe, Kent, 91

'Improvement', 32–3
Incised Crosses, Bentley, 190
Isle of Wight, 75

Jackson, Eleanor, 179, 182, 194, 196, 199–200
James, Charles, 81–3, 86, 106–108, 110, 112, 141–2, 169, 201
Jennings, Hannah, 1, 2
Johnson, The Revd Joseph, 199
Johnson, Dr Samuel, 25, 43
Jordan, Mrs, 103

Keble, The Revd John, 191–2
Knight, Fanny, 122, 125
Knight, G.C., 186
Knight, Thomas, 3, 13
Knight, William, 1, 158, 179

Land Tax Act, 77
Le Faye, Deirdre, 136
Leigh, Theophilus, Master of Balliol, 14, 15, 31
Leigh, Thomas, 31, 66
Leigh Perrot, James, 39, 75, 115, 138, 140
Lilliputian Magazine, 10
Littleworth, Elizabeth, 8, 9
Littleworth, John, 8, 9
Liverpool, Lord, 108
Livings, 1, 3, 36–40, 46, 55–6, 145, 147, 165, 178–9
Lloyd, Martha, 56, 122
Lloyd, Mary, 56
Locke, John, 26, 27

Locke, The Revd Samuel, 181
London residences and properties:
    Albany, 86
    Canon Row, 86
    Cleveland Court, 80
    Hans Place, 120–2, 130, 136, 148, 179
    Henrietta Street, 96–7, 116–17, 136, 141, 148
    Michael's Place, 86
    Orchard Street, 71
    Sloane Street, 102–103, 105, 110, 116, 148
    St James's Square, 80
    Upper Berkeley Street, 81
Loiterer, The, 42–53, 101–102
Lunardi, Victor, 16
Lushington, Dr Stephen, 199
Lushington and Co., 114, 199
Luther, Martin, 24
Lyford, Mr, 158
Lymington, Lord, 13

Madras, India, 68
Marlborough, Duke of, 59
Matthew, Anne, 54
Maunde, Henry, 81–2, 85, 90, 95, 121, 137, 139, 142
Methodists, 24
Midgley, Winifred, 195
Milner, The Revd Joseph, 156
Moira, Lord, 82–3, 89, 108, 110–13, 116, 123, 134, 140–2, 197–8
Moore, Harriet, 121

Morley, Lord, 166, 168–9, 177
  see also Boringdon
Mount Tambora, 140
Mullen, Alexandra, 74
Murphy, Anne, 97
Murray, John (publisher), 123–5, 130–1, 138, 164, 194

Napoleon, 84, 122, 134
Nelson, Lord, 89
Newbery, John (publisher), 10
Newcomen, James, 21
Newhaven, East Sussex, 63
North, Lord, 146–7
Nottinghamshire Militia, 86

Overseers of the Poor, 185
Overton, Hampshire, 4
Oxford, 3, 14, 70, 135
  Bodleian Library, Radcliffe Camera, 22
  St John's College, 14, 21, 30–1, 42, 144–6, 166
Oxfordshire Militia, 57–61, 62–4, 73, 78–80, 99, 121, 144

Pall Mall, London, 80, 109
Pantheon, London (opera house), 99
Papillon, The Revd, 145, 148, 155, 179
Paris, 68, 71
Parish, Henry, 63
Paternoster Row, London, 10
Peace of Amiens, 84, 86
Pearson, Mary, 67

Peel, Robert, 176
Percival, Spencer, 107
Perigord, Madame, 105,108–109, 117, 197
Perrot family, 31
Petersfield, Hampshire, 79, 91
Pilgrims' Way, 191
Pinnock, William (publisher), 11
Pitt, William, 90
Poor Laws, 195–6
Poor Relief Act, 185
Portsmouth, 110, 199
Prince Regent, 89, 108, 128–31, 137
Pupils, boarding, 13

Quebec Chapel, London, 148
Queen Anne's Bounty, 191

Ramsgate, Kent, 105
Reading Ladies' Boarding School, 15
Reform Act, 192
Repton, Humphrey, 149
Reynolds, Sir Joshua, 109
Ridge, Captain John, 110, 112, 141–2
River Wey, 191
Rivers, Michael, 132
Rochester, Bishop of, 21, 30
Rousseau, Jean Jacques, 47
Rowlings, Kent, 66
Roworth, Charles, 101
Royal Naval Academy, Portsmouth, 56
Royal West Middlesex Regiment, 104
'Rule, Britannia!', 19
Russell, Dr Richard, 105

Sadler, John (publisher), 11
Sampson, Robert, 1, 2, 186
Schleiermacher, Friedrich, 170–1
Scott, Sarah, 10
Seven Years War, 30–1
Sheerness, Kent, 66
Silver, Joseph, 138
Slavery, 31
　abolition of, 98, 198
South Devon Militia, 86
Southampton, 90
Spencer, Lord Charles, 90, 101, 104, 112–13, 144, 169
Spencer, George, 57
Spencer, The Hon. John, 104, 113–14, 116
Spouting clubs, 11
Spring Gardens, Piccadilly, London, 109
St John-at-Hampstead, 81, 108
St Luke's Hospital (Islington?), 193–4
St Paul's, Covent Garden, London, 154
St Swithin's, Walcot, Bath, 32, 87
Stagecoach termini, London, 96
Steventon, Hampshire, 1, 3, 32, 55–6, 65, 67, 69–71, 81, 83, 105, 109, 115, 143, 145, 147, 178, 182–3, 191
　St Nicholas Church, 3, 4, 35, 38, 54–5
　The Manor House, 3, 148
　The Rectory, 4, 14, 17
Stoneleigh Abbey, 32, 149

Stuart, Charles, 19
Stuarton, Count, 95
Sturge, Joseph, 198
Sumner, Charles, Bishop of Winchester, 11, 148, 176, 186–90, 192–4, 196–7
Sutherland, Kathryn, 101
Swift, Jonathan, 10
Swing Riots, 189

Taylor, John (publisher), 10
Taylor, Richard, 138
Taylor, William (publisher), 10
The Times, 141
The Vyne, Sherborne, 55, 182
Tilson, James, 99, 114, 121, 124, 136–7, 139, 157
Tindal, Matthew, 26
Tithes, 14, 34, 37, 40, 76
Tomalin, Claire, 67, 69, 108
Tonbridge School, Kent, 20
Treadgold, John H., 198
Tull, Jethro, 20
Tunbridge Wells, Kent, 199

Van Mildert, Bishop of Durham, 176
Vanderstegen, Master, 13

Wales, Prince of, 99
Wardle, Gwyllym Lloyd, MP, 100
Warren, The Revd Henry, 181
Watkins, Thomas, Precentor of Winchester Cathedral, 160–1
Watlington Park, Oxfordshire, 99

Watts, Isaac, 10
Wedgwood pottery, 40–1
Wellington, Duke of, 176
Wesley, Charles, 24
Wesley, John, 23, 24, 26, 31
Western, J.R., 60
White's at Burlington House, 120
Wilberforce, William, 98
Winchester, 10, 157

Winchester, Bishop of, 182–3
Windsor, Andrew, 185
Woodbury Park Cemetery, Tunbridge Wells, 200
Wykeham, William, Bishop of Winchester, 190

Yarmouth (Great), 66
York, Duke of, 100